The Big Marsh

The Big Marsh

The Story of a Lost Landscape

Cheri Register

MINNESOTA
HISTORICAL
SOCIETY PRESS

www.mnhspress.org

The Minnesota Historical Society Press is a member of the
Association of American University Presses.

Manufactured in the United States of America

10 9 8 7 6 5 4 3 2 1

♾ The paper used in this publication meets the minimum requirements
of the American National Standard for Information Sciences—
Permanence for Printed Library Materials, ANSI Z39.48–1984.

International Standard Book Number
ISBN: 978-0-87351-995-3 (paper)
ISBN: 978-0-87351-996-0 (e-book)

Library of Congress Cataloging-in-Publication Data
available upon request.

This and other Minnesota Historical Society Press books are available
from popular e-book vendors.

And yet with all these growing signs of prosperity I realized that something sweet and splendid was dying out of the prairie. The whistling pigeons, the wailing plover, the migrating ducks and geese, the soaring cranes, the shadowy wolves, the wary foxes, all the untamed things were passing, vanishing with the blue-joint grass, the dainty wild rose and the tiger-lily's flaming torch. Settlement was complete.

—Hamlin Garland, *A Son of the Middle Border*, 1917

As conquerors and as gardeners we came to a landscape with serious intentions: not simply to know, but to change; not just to visit, but to possess. Much that was done was good, much was bad. We presumed too much. We imposed on what we found; we could not cherish without embellishing or altering what was simply there.

—Gretel Ehrlich, "Surrender to the Landscape," *Harper's Magazine*, September 1987

Contents

The Big Marsh

Prologue

The grass is wild—not the kind my dad seeds and mows in the yard. It reaches all the way up my short legs, brushes my waist with wispy plumes, and hides me if I squat. It tickles and itches, squeaks between the palms of my hands, and can cut me if I'm not careful. Spiky balls of pinkish purple peek up like polka dots through the grass, come loose in my fingers, and ooze sweetness between my teeth. Down a steep bank near the edge of the highway, mud squishes between my toes. My cheeks tingle with droplets of moist air. I can see across the highway and across a field sometimes covered with bales of hay to the slough, where frogs chirp and cattails rise in clumps. I know the cattails' feel, like the velvety cloth on a chair, and I want to touch them, but I can't go there. The highway is my boundary. I wait and look and listen. The sounds are comforting, the music of spring and summer, of freedom— no coat, no snow pants, no shoes. Two birds call to me: one sings a melody; the other trills the same line again and again. They will forever be the sounds of home. Above me, in a dome of sunlit blue sky, puffy white clouds like mashed potatoes float on a single plane. This is my earliest sensory memory.

$\backsim$

A girl from long ago stands in the uncut grass beside her father's smithy. She has been promised many times that the papa she barely recalls will ride up someday on his new horse when the war is over and the cavalry comes home. It's a hard word to say—"cabalry." She practices touching her lip with her teeth the way big sister Marietta has taught her. Papa

3

will fire up his forge again and teach George and DeWitt the black-smith trade. The dome of Amanda Speer's world is a hazy blue. She tips her face up toward the white and shadowed shapes that float overhead. A breeze flits across the Big Marsh and picks up a pleasant watery chill. Out in the pasture where the animals graze, a bird her mother calls a meadowlark sings its pretty melody. Up the creek where the marsh fans out, birds with red patches on their wings trill their tune from cattail perches.

〜

A few miles and years away, a ten-year-old lopes through fields and meadows, cutting through grass that sometimes reaches boy high. He wants to catch the exact moment when the marsh sounds take over—the quacks and honks, the constant chorus of peepers, the *konkaree* of the red-winged blackbird that sends waves of joy through his chest. The watery world beckons him, and he delights in the moist air, the shimmering sunlight, the pattern of clouds overhead, the gleam of water stretched out before him. The sounds and sensations produce words and rhythms in his mind, the poems that will help him preserve these moments. Each year of his youth, Elbert Ostrander ventures farther, until he reaches the eastern shore of the big lake at the north end of the marsh, where he finds black walnut trees, flowering alder shrubs, shore willows, pigeon cherries, wild lilies, and irises of royal blue. He returns again and again to climb on and lie under the arch of the mysterious oak that bent over and grew back into the ground. In his later years, he will recall Geneva Lake as "the lake of my childhood dreams, the embodiment of an Eden, a Paradise."

〜

Here in our contiguous Edens, we are finding beauty. We have no mountains to teach us grandeur, no roaring ocean surf to fill us with awe. We learn to love subtlety: the iridescence of a dragonfly, the bronze and copper hues of November, the brief blue twilight of a midwinter morning, the swish of a muskrat's tail rippling still water, the crunch of acorn caps underfoot. We are Midwesterners making ourselves at home.

PART I

The Lay of the Land

Hollandale: *An Introduction*

There was a time—an eon of time—when water pooled and ribboned freely among the oak savanna and hardwood copses and in the prairie potholes of southern Minnesota. Crops grow there now, on dry land that might yet hold water in its low spots after a heavy, heavy rain. The absence of the old wetlands is to some a tale of triumph: agriculture's conquest over waste and wild to feed a hungry humanity. To others it is a doomsday story of irreversible damage to the natural environment. We Minnesotans like to think of our state as "natural," and it is often colored a lovely deep green on the US map. Yet the original landscape has been radically altered in less than two centuries of European settlement, not least by the miles of drainage ditches that crisscross the farmland and the even lengthier grid of hollow clay and concrete tiles and plastic piping buried beneath its soil. Freeborn County alone, now with 340 miles of ditches, had lost 98.5 percent of its wetlands by 1981.

Many people don't know this subterranean network of field drains exists until, for example, a flood brings to light the risks of draining a heavy spring thaw or torrential rains into an already overburdened river. Alarms are sounding about the polluting effect of farm runoff—soil, fertilizers, and pesticides—on lakes and rivers, especially the Minnesota, which empties into the Mississippi, clogging Lake Pepin with sediment and nitrates and contributing to the "dead zone" in the Gulf of Mexico. Yet the state's farmers face continuing economic pressure to drain and cultivate more land.

The story that follows recounts one obscure but vital piece of Minnesota's agricultural history: the drainage of an eighteen-thousand-acre

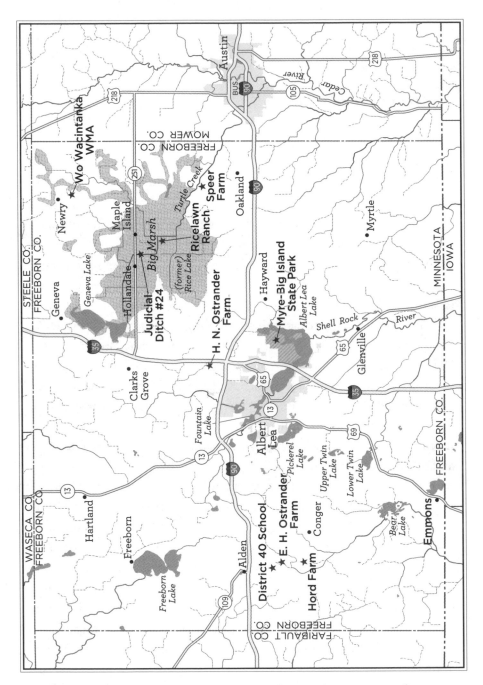

Map of Freeborn County, Minnesota, 2015, showing locations significant to the Big Marsh story

wetland between Albert Lea and Austin. For generations, Dakota, Sac and Fox, and Ho-Chunk people, as well as family farmers of Anglo-European heritage, lived with this Big Marsh, gathering wild rice, hunting, fishing, trapping, and haying, until nonresident investors appeared on the scene in 1890, determined to turn it into a showcase of industrial-scale agriculture. For not yet a century, the drained bed and environs of Rice Lake, the deepest portion of the Big Marsh, have gone by the name of Hollandale. The upbeat public story of how Hollandale came to be verges on myth and miracle, and it ignores the first three decades of the drainage effort. This new account of the Big Marsh's fate is a more complicated story of hope and loss, of conflicting values, of political intrigue, of family and home.

∽

As a child in Albert Lea in the 1950s and 1960s, I thought of Hollandale, fifteen miles to the northeast, as "different," an expression of skepticism in rural Minnesota. It was flat like Holland—flat and Dutch—with canal-like ditches. The rest of Freeborn County was rolling savanna or prairie, covered in corn and hay or grazing dairy and beef cattle. Hollandale farmers grew onions and potatoes, carrots and celery, asparagus and sugar beets, which were weeded and harvested by hand, by Mexican hands—Mexican Americans, actually, who spent the growing season in abandoned farmhouses or migrant shacks and left in the fall in pickup trucks and beat-up cars, headed back home to Crystal City, Texas. Hollandale seemed a distant place except to city teenagers who spent the summer in the scorching onion fields in years when migrant labor ran short. Albert Lea saw more of the migrant workers than of the Hollandale farmers. Saturdays treated us to snatches of Spanish and strains of Tex-Mex accordion music that hung on as the soundtrack of childhood summer evenings. Dutch diphthongs and the fricative "g" were seldom heard in Albert Lea, and Dutch music, whatever it might be, stayed confined in Hollandale's two Reformed churches, one theologically and socially conservative and the other a little less so. We dominant Lutherans and Catholics counted the Dutch Reformed—if we thought about them at all—as a more pious form of Methodist or Presbyterian.

The Hollandale kids were bused to Albert Lea for junior high and high school. Blond and broad cheeked, they filled the De- seats toward the front of the classroom and the Van- and Ver- seats in the back. They stuck together at first, likely out of shyness and familiarity, which the rest of us easily misread as arrogance. Eventually, a few of the girls joined the popular clique while the boys retained a tinge of rural awkwardness. By graduation, we had probably driven some Hollandale friends home, dropping them at farmhouses along narrow roads or in the circle of houses on Maple Island, a grove of trees on a slight rise in the flatness. Some of us knew, if our families told stories, that Maple Island was once a real island and that Hollandale sat in the bed of an old lake. We heard that the Dutch were brought in specially to farm the

Swampland converted into fertile celery field, Hollandale, 1926

wet, spongy soil, a job they were suited for because their ancestors had wrested Holland from the sea. They were newcomers, newer at least than the Danes in Clarks Grove and Alden, the Irish in Newry and Twin Lakes, the Germans in Conger, the Bohemians in Myrtle, and the Norwegians everywhere. Rumors flew that they had gotten rich, so rich they relied on Mexicans to do their work.

The Hollandale kids knew a different story, a proud history of how their grandparents had turned a swampy wasteland into one of the most important vegetable-producing regions in the country. A few of the first settlers in the 1920s were fresh immigrants, but most of Hollandale's 150 families had come from Dutch settlements in Iowa and Michigan, recruited with the promise of a decent family living on just twenty acres of fertile peat soil. The Hollandale kids heard tales of economic hardship and the physical challenges of farming easily flooded land, and how so many had failed and left their plots indebted. Those who survived were the strong, devout, and hardworking.

The local museum, the Hollandale Heritage Huis, tells how George Payne of the Payne Investment Company in Omaha, Nebraska, discovered reedy Rice Lake in 1918 and saw its potential for farming if it could be drained. He had helped develop sugar plantations in soggy Louisiana and would go on to build vegetable-farming communities in central California. Payne masterminded not only a successful drainage but also the colonization of "Hollandale the Wonderland," the name he gave his "dream," according to a promotional booklet put out by Albert Lea Farms Company, the holding company he formed to buy and sell the reclaimed wetland. Payne dreamed big, envisioning Hollandale's products shipped to markets in the Twin Cities, Omaha, Milwaukee, Chicago, St. Louis, and Kansas City. And his dream was precisely executed. "Nothing was left to chance," the booklet boasts. Payne oversaw the layout of drainage ditches and roads, the choice of seeds, the branding and marketing of the crops, the selection of farmers, the bungalow design of the farmhouses, the Hollandale village plat, even the placement and design of schools and churches. The Dutch settlers began arriving in 1922, and Payne's dream was realized on September 4, 1926, when two railroads—the Chicago, Rock Island and Pacific, and the Chicago, Milwaukee and St. Paul—met at a union depot in Hollandale, from which the area's bounty would be sent to market.

The Albert Lea Farms booklet called Payne's vision "monumental":

By the expenditure of much money and hard work, a large tract of land, which for uncounted centuries was unfit for human habitation and which added nothing to the food supply or to the wealth of the world, has been completely transformed. For untold centuries yet to come, that tract of land will do its full share towards furnishing food for the world. It affords today and will continue for all time to afford comfortable homes for hundreds of families. And the children of those families, under the influence of church and school, will grow up, generation after generation, to be good citizens of the republic, citizens who by their intelligence and their industry will bring prosperity to themselves and make Hollandale a credit to the nation.

Of course, the dream was overblown. Heavy rainfall could be devastating, and drought and the Depression took their toll on Hollandale farmers as well as others in the county. Despite serving on the board of the American Peat Society, Payne evidently didn't foresee that peat soil deprived of its water source and the annual cycle of plant decay would dry up and lose its fertility. Thirty years later, a small vegetable plot could no longer support a family a third the size of the original settlers'. Some farmers sold out and others bought up until farms grew too large for a single family to manage and required migrant labor, in violation of the Dutch ethic that a respectable farm family does its own work. Soon these larger farms required expensive machinery as well, and fertilizer to replenish the depleted soil. Like so many of their rural cohort, Hollandale's third generation took "their intelligence and their industry" off to towns and cities and more dependable, less rigorous work. Corn and soybeans reign in Hollandale now, as in the rest of the county, and its farms are few, large, chemically fertilized, and expensively mechanized. Trains no longer run there, and even the tracks are gone.

The half century in which Hollandale enjoyed its unusual reputation is a brief, colorful blip in the landscape's history. Ethnic and economic unity made for shared values, habits, and pastimes that generated treasured memories. Age-old theological differences and the competing needs of "upland" and "lowland" farmers—in a landscape that looks flat to outsiders—complicated and spiced those communal memories. Yet, among other county residents, the miraculous Hollandale story carried a shadowy undertone. When my dad, born in neighboring Moscow Township, talked about how Hollandale had once been a lake, he didn't share in the awe of George Payne's creation story. I sensed that something had been lost. Rice Lake seemed to stand for something regrettable: a faulty decision, a mistake in judgment, some obscure, localized fall from paradise. "My granddad always said God put the sloughs there for a reason," Dad told me in his later years.

Hollandale natives I have talked with about this rueful tone sense it themselves and read it as being "looked down upon" or as outright hostility. Certainly the lens through which I saw Hollandale was marred with distorting scratches. I wondered what might account for this mutual wariness but had no inkling of the contentious effort to alter the landscape that predated George Payne's vision of a garden paradise. In fact, I stumbled upon the inglorious earlier story of the draining of the Big Marsh quite by accident.

One day while at work on another project, I sat down in the Minnesota History Center's microfilm room and began scrolling through issues of the *Freeborn Patriot*, a Depression-era newspaper sympathetic to Minnesota's Farmer-Labor Party. A headline on the front page of the July 19, 1935, issue caught my attention: "Connivings of Dishonest Men/Cheat Nature As Well As/Fellow Beings, Writer Avers." The article opened with a nostalgic description of Geneva Lake, Hollandale's northwest boundary, in its natural state, back when it was the author's "boyhood 'Mecca.'" It went on to rail against a drainage project completed years before the creation of Hollandale that had been "conceived in iniquity" and "taken up by foreign interests who employed local mercenaries." The drainage had emptied Rice Lake and threatened the existence of Geneva Lake. The essay didn't name the culprits, but "the Spoiler who with wanton malice laid the hand of greed and avarice with dire devastation on the beautiful scene" had obviously arrived well before George Payne. The author also charged malfeasance in the construction of the ditches and a conspiracy to cover it up. The hyperbolic tone of the essay made his point of view clear: "We, the lifelong residents of the county, massed together in solid array against the Spoilers, who, intent only on furthering their own material interests at the expense of the natural resources that are the common property of all people, and we demanded that the hand of greed and guilt be stayed in regard at least to this one beautiful lake."

The accusation of conniving and misdeeds in my placid home territory piqued my interest, but it was the byline that aroused my passion to pursue this hidden history. The author of the essay was Elbert H. Ostrander, my great-grandfather, my dad's beloved maternal granddad. We who know anything at all about our ancestry likely have one forebear around whom legends spin. In my family's case, it's Elbert

Elbert Ostrander, his pet bear, and his daughter Marvyl, about 1915

Ostrander, the man who kept a pet bear, befriended felons out on parole, and was personally acquainted with Minnesota's radical governor Floyd B. Olson, to whom he dedicated a poem commemorating a state moratorium on farm foreclosures. Grandpa Ostrander's appeal to me was tangible: the brown folder in our basement rec room desk that held samples of his poetry and essays. Someone in my family *wrote*. I could feel, in the urgency of his words and in the ghostly presence hovering about me as I walked from the history center to the parking lot, that my great-grandfather would like me to expose those dishonest connivers and tell the people's story. I, however, set out to look for the truth of the matter.

I immersed myself in the area's earlier history, before Payne brought in his Buckeye ditching machine and his fleet of tilers to finish the job. I focused on the first two attempts at drainage, in the 1890s and the first decade of the twentieth century. I wanted to know how this massive transformation had been accomplished and whether others in the community were as strongly opposed as Elbert Ostrander. If they were, how was their opposition overcome? Was it really a case of conniving? It began to look as though the drainage marked the arrival of agribusiness in Freeborn County, which threatened the family farm culture established by Yorker and European farmers who made no secret of their disdain for land speculators. Yet those Yorkers and Europeans had already altered the landscape by plowing up the prairie forbs and grasses and planting foreign trees among the bur oaks and scattered swatches of hardwood forest.

I often found my fascination drifting from legal wrangling and the mechanics of ditching to imagining what eighteen thousand acres of wetland might look like. I wanted to know how people lived with this wetland, how it served them, and how it inhibited their daily efforts to live well. Did they enjoy its bounty of fowl, fish, and furs, or did they curse it as a worthless eyesore and obstacle? I tried to see the landscape layered with the memory of all who have passed over it. I thought about the landscape's own memory and how it relives its past when heavy rains leave water standing in the fields or send it cascading down the

Turtle Creek ditch and into the Cedar River to flood farms and cities along its banks in Iowa. All along, I thought about how landscape shapes our sense of comfort and beauty and security. What happens to us when our familiar home landscapes—be they marshes or deserts or forests or seacoasts or even ditches and vegetable fields—are transformed over and over by changing human needs and attitudes?

The greatest fascination that writing holds for me is learning how personal stories intersect with public history. So it felt like a benefit that the history of the drainage is to some degree my family's story. Just what role did Elbert Ostrander play in this drama? What about the Speers and Registers, my ancestors who farmed along Turtle Creek, the path of the main ditch? How much of my curiosity is due to a family heritage of opposition and loss, a six-generation claim on the landscape of Freeborn County? The deeper we probe the personal, the more likely we are to achieve universal resonance.

What writers and readers both long for are stories. Woven together, stories make history. "History—what is history?" Elbert Ostrander asks in his *Freeborn Patriot* article, then answers, "A record of the past from which we may better shape the events of the future. It is a harbinger of civilization, a record of the rise and fall of nations, an established marker of the pitfalls that have engulfed the multitudes along the trodden pathway of Time." Maybe a close look at just one pitfall will offer stories enough.

Freeborn County: *Home, but No Biome*

As a biologist, I find all natural ecosystems brimming with intricacy and beauty. However, only the savanna fills me with emotion that I seem unable to plumb. I return to it again and again, to see what else the savanna has to say to me. I am passionate about its restoration.

—Sue Leaf, "One Seed at a Time," *Minnesota Conservation Volunteer*

I lived at the edge of the world, on the border between an enclosed, secure environment and a wide-open, intimidating mystery. The change was subtle, but I could detect it on my family's ten-mile Sunday drives west from Albert Lea to visit grandparents in Alden. I knew the route along US Highway 16 by heart. I could trace the curve along the Remakel farm's white rail fence and catch the last glimpse of wooded, rolling hills south of the highway, where Pickerel Lake glistened in the distance. We passed two low spots in the fields where bushes (probably hazel) and spindly trees (probably willow and young cottonwood) marked the lines of drainage ditches. I knew where to look for a stile over a fence and for little boxlike houses arranged in a field on a mink farm. Shortly before Alden, the vistas began to widen in a way that made me uneasy, and I was relieved to see the row of metal corncribs, beams of reflected sunlight along the western horizon, that marked the turn into Alden. Beyond Alden, the land grew flatter, the trees fewer, the sky more imposing.

I kept that larger landscape in mind when I walked along my favorite country road toward Pickerel Lake. Between the gravel of the road and the barbed wire enclosing the farmland, milkweed puffed and wild roses bloomed pink among the more standard clover. I listened and watched for frogs in the low spot where cattails overtook the farmer's attempt at corn. Even though the road wasn't elevated, I felt as if I were balancing on the spine of the earth. To the east, I'd tumble gently into tree-sheltered, rolling land. To the west, I'd be blown onto open prairie.

I was less familiar with the landscape of northeastern Freeborn County, where the Big Marsh once thrived. We skirted it on the west when we drove to the Twin Cities and on the south when we went to Austin, twenty miles to the east. Sometimes going to or from Austin, we would turn north and follow a roller-coaster road to Moscow and "the old homeplace" where my dad was born. Tiny Moscow village sat in a pretty little glen, and the old homeplace stood nearby alongside Turtle Creek, which Dad remembered fondly, although it looked like a barren ditch to me. If we drove back to Albert Lea on country roads, I would see the flatness that was Hollandale. Occasionally we "went for a ride" through Hollandale—our family's term for a habit of socio-logical tourism. We gawked at "Mexican shacks" and tsk-tsked at the farmers who would house their help in such decrepit conditions. Sto-ries of the land's aquatic past would emerge here, too.

Geological maps of Minnesota divide the state neatly into three original environments, or biomes: northern pine forest, eastern hard-wood forest, and western tallgrass prairie. The line between forest and prairie bifurcates Freeborn County, giving some credence to my sense of living on the edge. Yet I knew of no single spot where you could step out of a hardwood forest and marvel at the prairie's distant horizon. It was easier to see the delineation between Minnesota and Iowa nine miles south of my house: the highway suddenly narrowed, the land flat-tened, and signs advertised colored oleomargarine just ahead. I had no language then to sum up all that I was observing about my home county and to fit its character into the biome schema. I have learned since that Freeborn County is mostly oak savanna, a transitional zone of glacial drift between forest and prairie, a place where water collects in marshes, lakes, and sloughs. It is a landscape of moraines, eskers, drumlins, swells, and swales dotted with oak openings, or small groves of bur oak and thickets of hazel and willow.

Knowing the names for things lodges them in our memories and draws them into our affections. I want to shout those names to travelers driving along Interstate 35 following the Owatonna end moraine, the tongue of the glacier that created this landscape. To travelers crossing the county quickly on Interstate 90 in their rush between the bluff country of southeastern Minnesota and southwestern Minnesota's prairie, I say, slow down. Take in the craggy profile of a bur oak against a vast blue sky. Watch for a narrow ridge that might be a gravel-laden esker. Check that line of cattails and reeds winding along a swale between planted fields. It's the remnant of an old slough. Look, and remember you have been here.

Looking for the Big Marsh

Heading south through Minnesota on Interstate 35, you can tell you've crossed into Freeborn County by the glint of water to your left, where Geneva Lake stretches narrow and shallow at the foot of a glacial moraine. You might not notice, except when they flock to migrate, the white pelicans that began returning to Freeborn County in the 1960s after their extermination eighty years earlier by farmers and fishermen who judged them pests, nor will you see from this distance the egrets

The bent tree on Geneva Lake, 2015

and great blue herons that fish Geneva. You won't see the grill-like barrier that keeps the lake free of carp, a species introduced in Minnesota in 1883, or the cleverly constructed dam that allows the lake to be raised and lowered to optimum level. Neither will you see the oak tree that arches over and grows back into the ground on the east side of the lake. Legend has it that Indians, most likely Dakota, bent and tied a sapling to mark a sandbar where they crossed the lake on foot. The matching tree on the west shore washed away long ago.

You will certainly not see the miles of wetland stretching eastward from Geneva Lake into four townships, nor the lake's southeasterly marsh-ringed sister, Rice Lake. The lake and marsh have been gone for a century, ditched and tiled away by developers for agricultural use, and gone with them flocks of wildfowl so thick you would see them as dark clouds from this distance. Greatly diminished are the numbers of mink and muskrats that flourished there.

The first exit south of Geneva Lake offers a choice of two landscapes, distinct to locals but probably not to visitors, who think all of the area flat. Turn west into Clarks Grove, a Danish Baptist settlement, and country roads take you through glacially formed rolling farmland, past gravel pits where eskers used to rise, past patches of oak savanna not yet bulldozed for more efficient farming or home construction, and into Albert Lea. An 1860 visitor described this route as "somewhat undulating, well watered with running streams, which among the oaks that shade our pathway make the appearance rather picturesque than otherwise." Anyone expecting "picturesque" 150 years later may be disappointed, but it is still a pleasant rural landscape.

Turn east instead, toward Hollandale, and State Highway 251 runs straight and flat like a causeway. Although farm fields, not water, line this road, you may feel that a false turn could be your undoing. The vanishing point ahead urges you on as you hope for a rise in the landscape or the shelter of trees. Several generations of Dutch Americans claim this span of fields as home and find comfort in a level horizon. The village of Hollandale, founded in 1922 as a shipping center for vegetables and sugar beets, lines both sides of the highway for four blocks.

A mile and a half beyond Hollandale sits Maple Island, a ring of houses on a wooded hummock, an island in a waterless sea. A clump of trees to the south locates Hickory Island, where Putnam Dana McMillan, a Minneapolis real estate developer who set out in the 1890s to drain the water that covered this land, claimed his own hummock in the marsh and built Ricelawn Ranch, a large industrial farm.

County Road 30 (850th Avenue) runs south from 251 to Hickory Island. Turn right into the trees and follow a gravel road past a line of ramblers built after McMillan's time. A ramshackle remnant of a workers' barracks sits back in the woods. The road emerges from the trees, narrows in a cornfield, and makes a ninety-degree turn to the right alongside a drainage ditch. When I drove that way for the first time in the new millennium, I was startled to see a bone-dry field, drier than I imagined soil could be in Freeborn County, where, my body remembers, the ground was once soft and moist enough to burrow your toes.

A ditch in Moscow Township, seen from County Highway 25

Once Rice Lake, this dry spot used to be, after its third drainage in the 1920s, a fertile peat bed. Just ahead, an east–west ditch marks the site of the original headwaters of Turtle Creek, which ran a natural winding course from Rice Lake to the Cedar River in Austin. If you come here in the right season, tall, reedy vegetation grows along the banks of the ditch, a spare reminder of the land's aquatic past. I have visited this place in rainier seasons, too, when the lowest fields lay underwater as if Rice Lake were attempting a resurrection.

The first written record of this vast wetland dates to a federal mapping expedition conducted by Lieutenant Albert Miller Lea of Company I of the First US Dragoons, sent out from Fort Des Moines in the summer of 1835 under the command of Stephen W. Kearney. (Mapmaker Joseph Nicollet inscribed "Albert Lea" on the area's largest lake, and the county seat that grew up alongside the lake after 1855 took its name.) The company's log from July 29, 1835, reads,

> This morning to all appearances we should have had a good day's march, but made but five or six miles when we perceived before us a lake stretching as far as the eye could reach, from north to south, and from one half to three miles in width. We bore to the north to try to get around it. But at this time, 12 M., we have come to an outlet on one side and on the other a marsh which is impassable. What course we shall now take is uncertain. The officers are now assembled to concert measures to get out of this difficulty. In the meantime the men are taking their rest in the shade, their horses grazing beside them. No name is mentioned by geographers for this lake.

About seventy-five years after Lea's expedition, local historian Martin V. Kellar studied the documents and traced the Dragoons' route in relation to subsequent township and section lines. He calculated that they entered what became Freeborn County in section 12 of Moscow Township and headed west. The long lake they encountered was, he surmised, Rice and Geneva lakes and the surrounding marsh filled out in a season that history records as especially wet. Later surveyors questioned Lea's report of a lake of such size, but Kellar figured they had come in drier seasons.

It's not easy to picture the 164 Dragoons, who marched military style in a double column, slogging through marshes, skirting lakes, and fording creeks while keeping account of their five wagons and twenty mules, their packhorses, and a small herd of cattle—the company's beef transported on the hoof. Lieutenant Lea's baggage alone included a camp bedstead, a table, two chairs, a "mattras," two blankets, a bed-cover, a pillow, two pairs of sheets and pillowcases, one "musquito" bar, a washbowl, a tin pitcher, brushes and blacking, soda powders, rice, matches, and a tin cup. Somehow they made it past their watery obstacle; the same day's log told of coming upon other landscapes they found more pleasing.

The expedition's log summarizes Lea's impression of the area in this way: "The land about here is good. Grass and herbage of all kinds in the highest natural state. Grass eight feet high. One of our Indians killed a gray eagle on the lake shore. In the afternoon passed the outlet and marched seven miles. Signs of beaver, muskrat and otter. Saw several handsome lakes and some of the most beautiful small prairies I have ever seen since I have been in the West. I have seen some roman-tic and handsome landscapes, but this far surpasses any country I have ever seen both in beauty and fertility." The word "beauty" sur-prises when you think that the Dragoons had come from Dakota Chief Wabasha's village on the awe-inspiring Upper Mississippi and climbed the limestone bluffs and threaded the wooded river valleys of the Drift-less Area.

Lieutenant Lea called the Freeborn County landscape "table land." It is one of the newest landscapes in the Midwest—a ten-thousand-year-old end moraine left where a flow of ice from the Wisconsin gla-ciation stopped and began to recede. Rain that falls there runs in all directions: via the Big Cobb and Le Sueur rivers to the Minnesota, via Lime Creek to the Winnebago River, via Turtle Creek to the Cedar, and south via the Shell Rock River. All of the flowing water eventually reaches the Mississippi, but some water just sits and seeps. Glacial deposits formed a gently rolling upland pocked with basins that trapped water, some of them deep enough to be lakes while others became reed-grown wetlands. Freeborn County is estimated to have had 154,000 acres of "swamp, wet, and overflowed" lands at the time of European settlement, more than its neighboring counties by a factor of ten. Poorly drained soil is rich in organic matter and makes exceptionally fertile farmland, as those who sought to drain the wetlands knew.

The Big Marsh, an unusually large wetland, varied from deeper, water-filled depressions where duck broods matured and black terns nested on floating mats of vegetation to saturated, spongy soil that drew yellow rails, godwits, and sandpipers. It offered habitat suitable also to trumpeter swans, grebes, and sandhill and whooping cranes. Imagining a wetland as a pattern of concentric circles can help us envision the predrainage landscape of the four townships into which the Big Marsh extended: Riceland, Geneva, Moscow, and Newry. At its deepest point in the western section of the marsh sat Rice Lake, open water with patches of free-floating algae and duckweed on its surface. The lake was rimmed by deep marsh, where pondweed, coontail, bladderwort, and yellow water crowfoot thrived. Bulrushes and clusters of common cat-tails indicated the next ring, a shallow marsh where bur-reeds, sedges, and water hemlock grew three to six feet tall. The outer rim was wet meadow, home to bluejoint, prairie cordgrass, thin-stemmed sedges, spike rush, and aster. As the slope rose and the likelihood of standing water diminished, switchgrass, mints, and sunflowers marked the beginning of low tallgrass prairie.

The name given to the lake suggests that wild rice grew in the deep marsh, where water levels varied from one to four feet. The original US Public Land Survey, done in 1854, measured three feet of water on the eastern end of the Riceland–Geneva township boundary, now High-way 251 between Hollandale and Maple Island. Another moment might have yielded a different measure. A wetland is a dynamic landscape that varies by season and by snow accumulation and rainfall from year to year. It's hard to imagine humans controlling this natural volatility, but such is history.

Rice Lake and the Big Marsh have been gone for a century, time enough for them to be rediscovered and reclaimed, if not in actuality then at least in public memory. That's reason enough to turn off the interstate.

PART II

Life on the Big Marsh

No Empty Landscape

I remember being told in school that no Indians ever lived in Freeborn County. Local history began with the arrival of white settlers, not eons back when ancient hunters stalked the woolly mammoth. Declaring the land empty may have helped us descendants of pioneers feel more entitled to it, but I was skeptical. There was too much evidence to the contrary: Boys came to school with arrowheads they had pocketed in newly plowed fields or on construction sites. Rumors persisted of burial mounds on the shores of Albert Lea Lake near the outlet of the Shell Rock River. My family passed on stories of our ancestors' encounters with Indians. The most compelling evidence: Indians *still* lived in Freeborn County—people named Armell, Blackhawk, Decora (also spelled De Cora as though it were Dutch), McKee, Poupart, and Rave.

Even now, as I look for scholarly studies of indigenous people in my home territory, Freeborn County remains an unmarked swath of white on maps of presettlement Minnesota. Dakota villages are noted along the Mississippi and Minnesota rivers, and up the Cannon River toward Faribault fifty miles away, but not along the Cedar or Shell Rock or Turtle Creek. When Dakota moved into bark houses for the growing season and planted corn and squash and beans, they apparently *lived* in those mapped villages. In other seasons, they took their rolled buffalo hides and tepee poles on excursions away from the rivers across the savannas and prairies to their hunting and trapping lands. Surely they set up the tepees and lived along the creeks, marshes, and lakeshores of present-day Freeborn County, where fish, fowl, and fur-bearing mammals were plentiful. Native people inhabited the land in their own way, not on Anglo-European terms of ownership and permanence.

One self-defined scholar did set out to look for material signs of early habitation. Owen Johnson (1899–1987), an Albert Lea mail carrier, spent his free time scouring shorelines within fifty miles of home for artifacts. He carefully noted the location where he found each one. By 1975, when he donated them all to the Department of Natural Resources, he had collected twenty-eight thousand objects, some dating back thousands of years. Although archaeologists quibble about the interpretive value of an amateur surface collection as opposed to a supervised dig, Johnson's oldest projectile point may be twelve thousand years old. His artifacts indicate that human beings witnessed the evolution of this glaciated land from tundra to forest to savanna and wetlands. Other local collectors have found evidence of living along the Big Marsh: a possible village site on the south bank of Turtle Creek in Moscow Township and a seasonal encampment northwest of Maple Island.

The Dakota who frequented the area around the Big Marsh were most likely Wahpekute, the smallest of Minnesota's four Santee Sioux, or Eastern Dakota, tribes, numbering about one thousand in the 1830s. Scholars attribute their lower numbers to frequent wars with the Iowa, Sauk (Sac), and Fox (Mesquakie) tribes over hunting lands, including the area from the Cannon River to the Blue Earth River. The Wahpekute did not usually live in fixed villages but moved throughout present-day southern Minnesota in search of food and other resources. The Big Marsh may also have drawn Mdewakanton Dakota from the village of Chief Wabasha, whose territory extended to the Cedar River, and from Black Dog's village on the Minnesota River, which sometimes sent hunters south among the Wahpekute.

The Big Marsh, like other large wetlands, offered a year-round supply of food and of furs and hides for use or trade. The wild rice in the deepest portion, Rice Lake, was ready for harvesting in September or October and was likely gathered in lightweight two-person canoes.

It was not the only edible plant in the marsh. Dakota women waded into the water to feel for roots with their feet. They dug water-lily roots and a spherical root about an inch in diameter called *psincha*, which they lifted on their feet just high enough to reach with their hands. An oval root about half the size of a hen's egg, the *psinchincha* conveniently floated to the surface after being dislodged. Rice Lake and the creek offered turtles and fish, caught with hook or spear. In winter, the Dakota cut holes in the ice and speared fish as they appeared. The spring and fall migrations brought great flocks of waterfowl, sometimes enough to trade with nonnatives at the forts and Indian agencies. The spring thaw divided the men and women into different food-gathering pursuits. The running of sap in maple trees brought the women to the sugar bush. Maple Island may have been a suitable place for sugaring. The men found success hunting muskrats as the snow melted away and revealed their dark houses. Muskrat fur was in demand for trading, and the meat was tolerable in early spring. It spoiled quickly in warm weather. The preferred source of meat was deer, and both deer and elk were plentiful around the Big Marsh and its adjacent woods. Large-animal hunting followed the ricing season and lasted through much of the winter. Sometimes bison ranged into the area as well.

The Sac and Fox also hunted in the Big Marsh. They are depicted as enemies of the Dakota, but enmity could be held in check and warfare restrained in places where both groups chose to conserve rich game habitat. The Big Marsh may have worked as such a buffer zone, especially in wet seasons when it was difficult to cross. When the US government called representatives of regional Indian tribes to Prairie du Chien in August 1825 to establish firm boundaries between them, spokesmen from several tribes testified that hunting lands were shared space. Nevertheless, the government drew the lines, assigned tribal territories, and got treaties signed. Although the ostensible goal was peaceful coexistence, the division would make it easier to negotiate land cessions and open the area to European settlement. The southern boundary of the Dakota (Sioux) lands, "the Suland," extended westward along the Upper Iowa River, then angled southwest, proclaiming the Big Marsh exclusively Dakota.

Nonnative people soon encroached on this territory, including the prime hunting grounds of the Big Marsh. Senator Henry Rice, a trader and Indian agent historians now regard as deceptive in his dealings with Native people, told a *St. Paul Pioneer Press* reporter in 1877 that he had brought a party of hunters down from Fort Snelling in 1841. Rice "encamped on the shores of one of the numerous beautiful lakes in this vicinity, spending here a part of four consecutive years in daring bravery, startling adventures and rude associations." He called the area a "paradise of sportsmen" and claimed to have seen three hundred elk in one day and killed two of them before breakfast.

The establishment of Minnesota Territory in 1849 signaled plans to annex the Suland to the United States and open it to settlement. In June 1851, Alexander Ramsey, the territorial governor, and Luke Lea, the US commissioner of Indian affairs, set in motion the bargaining, cajoling, lying, and manipulating that wrested the land from its Native inhabitants. Two treaties, one signed at Traverse des Sioux with the Wahpeton and Sisseton, and the other at Mendota with the Mdewakanton and the Wahpekute, transferred southern Minnesota to the United States. The Dakota were left with only a narrow strip of reservation land along the Upper Minnesota River. The Wahpekute were relocated to the Lower Sioux Agency near the mouth of the Redwood River, 125 miles from the Big Marsh.

Despite the treaties, Dakota showed up in greater numbers in Freeborn County in the 1850s as increasing white settlement along the Minnesota drove them to look farther away for open hunting grounds. Some members of Wabasha's band had hidden along the Cedar River to avoid relocation and may have remained in the area. Reminiscences by Freeborn County pioneers report encounters with Native people, usually with a characteristic mix of sentiments: fear of the Indians, distaste for their unfamiliar customs such as "begging"—expecting food— and sitting for long visits without speaking, but also surprise and relief at their nonviolent behavior:

A few days after arrival in Minnesota, Mrs. Rayman, being left alone, Joseph having started for Mitchell, for some supplies, was surprised and startled by the sudden appearance of a large band of Indians in the small clearing of their home. Two of these appeared at the door and demanded by gestures something to eat. Turning to her larder she handed them two loaves of bread, the last she had, and a large pan of milk, being only too willing to sacrifice the pan if only they would leave. The band, though, seemed peaceably inclined and after disposing of their gift, they returned the pan and proceeded on their way.

My elderly great-great-aunt Marietta Speer Whaley recalled her childhood in Moscow Township. She was seven when her family arrived:

During the first six weeks in our new home the only people we saw, with the exception of surveyors, were the Indians. But we saw plenty of them. One night, while father was at Albert Lea, 15 of them stayed at our house. Being a blacksmith, father used to fix their traps for them too—without charging them anything for it. An old [woman] came to our house one day and wanted to bake some bread. She borrowed some salt from mother, stirred it up and baked it. But we all declined when she offered us a taste. Mother was never afraid of the Indians, for they were always pretty friendly. Besides, she had a big dog that disclosed long, white fangs everytime [sic] one got very near.

The Native people Marietta saw around the Big Marsh were not only Dakota. As the Speers were traveling by covered wagon from Wisconsin in May 1855, a caravan of three hundred canoes carried Winnebago families down the Mississippi and up the Minnesota from their reservation near Long Prairie to a new one on the Blue Earth River, with an eastern boundary only twenty miles from the Big Marsh. Once the largest group of Indians in what is now Wisconsin, the Winnebago, or Ho-Chunk, had been moved by the US military across the Mississippi in 1840 and relocated, first in northeastern Iowa. This and subsequent relocations were never complete. The Winnebago lived in scattered

autonomous villages without a central tribal decision-making authority, so treaties signed by some were not binding on all. A few had stayed
in Iowa after removal to Long Prairie in 1848 while others established
villages on the Root River in Minnesota Territory. These people came
through Freeborn County on their way to the Blue Earth Reservation,
and one group spent the entire winter camped in Geneva Township.

Long in the habit of planting crops, the Winnebago farmed and
built schools on the new reservation and adapted in other ways to
European culture. Nevertheless, they were not welcomed as long-term
neighbors. Mankato, just three miles from the reservation, seethed with
anti-Winnebago sentiment, and its newspapers fed fears of drunken
debauchery and violence. Mankato businessmen had expected an in-
flux of white settlers nearby and a flourishing economy. A new treaty
reduced the reservation by two-thirds, leaving only the eastern section
in Waseca County. Settlers began moving onto the western part of the
reservation, and the Winnebago were prohibited from hunting or fishing or trapping there. The nearby Big Marsh, owned by railroad companies and the state but not closely monitored, was an inviting source
of fish and game. But there, too, competition from white settlers began
limiting the Winnebago's and Dakota's access to food and resources.
The settlers not only claimed and cultivated the land around the marsh,
but they also hunted its game and trapped muskrats and mink to supply the fur trade.

By August 1862, greatly diminished opportunities to hunt, growing
debt to dishonest traders, and delays in annuity payments promised by
treaty had left the Dakota starving. An act of youthful violence grew
into all-out war, and the US military prevailed. The Dakota warriors'
vengeance against neighboring settlers shocked white Minnesotans,
even in places such as Freeborn County that saw no hostilities firsthand. With their fears aroused, they demanded action, and the government's retaliation was merciless: a public hanging of thirty-eight men—
the largest mass execution in US history—imprisonment, internment,
and, finally, the forced exile of the Dakota people from Minnesota.
Mankato, the site of the hanging, may have been chosen to intimidate

the Winnebago. In May 1863, they too were rounded up and shipped down the Mississippi by steamboat and up the Missouri to the dreary dust bowl of Crow Creek in Dakota Territory.

Even after such a brutal exile, a few "friendly" Dakota remained in Minnesota. The closest group to the Big Marsh lived under protection of fur trader Alexander Faribault and Bishop Henry Whipple near the Cannon River on the edge of former Wahpekute territory. A "considerable number" of Ho-Chunk returned on their own to Minnesota, Iowa, and Wisconsin. By the end of the century, the sight of an Indian in Freeborn County was an anomaly to be reported—and interpreted in antiquated terms: "A family of Winnebago Indians are encamped on the shore of Twin lakes, and as in times long gone by, are engaged in the peaceful pursuit of game, and trapping muskrats and other fur-bearing animals. They are dressed in white man's costume, the man and his [wife] speak our language and they are altogether inoffensive and harmless."

Many Winnebago had fled Crow Creek for the Omaha Reservation down the Missouri. By 1865, they had acquired their own lands and formed their own reservation in eastern Nebraska. The Freeborn County families I recall from my youth—except for the Ojibwe Pouparts—were living on the Winnebago Reservation in 1940. Calls for labor in Hollandale's vegetable and sugar beet fields brought regional Native people as well as Texan migrants of Mexican ethnicity. Between 1942 and 1955, Ho-Chunk families found their way back to the Big Marsh, which their ancestors had known briefly in its natural state. Some found steadier work and stayed on while others eventually returned to the reservation. Many of the children, like their non-native classmates, joined the migration to urban centers such as the Twin Cities.

It is fair to say now that, except for the years of enforced exile, Indians have always lived in Freeborn County—or at least for as long as the landscape has been habitable for humans.

The Grid That Turned Land
to a Commodity

In the afternoon of August 4, 1854, Deputy Surveyor Edward Fitzpatrick and his crew encountered the wettest obstacle of their first workday laying out section lines in Township 103N, Range 20W, later to be named Riceland. All morning they had "entered" and "exited" marshes, filed through prairie grasses up and down slopes crowned with bur oak trees, and hacked through thickets of hazel, willow, and aspen. They had already traveled a dozen or so miles—depending on the distance from their base camp, where they had pitched their tents and stored their provisions—to the day's starting point. Ahead of them lay a "sluggish stream" 150 links (nearly 100 feet) wide and running eastward between low banks. The half-mile point they needed to mark to delineate sections 11 and 12 lay just across the stream. To the west lay a lake that would obstruct their route up the next south-to-north line, one mile over.

Fitzpatrick's logbook doesn't reveal how they crossed the stream, but he recorded the measures taken beyond it in level, marshy land. I imagine them slogging through the water and the muck underneath in vulcanized rubber waders, an improvement over the brittle hip boots the experienced crew members had likely worn a decade earlier. I listen for the slup and squeak of their boots as they lift them out of the muck and seek dry footing on the marshy land. It had to be a wet and tiring, hot and buggy day's work for Fitzpatrick, his two chainmen and his axman, and any other workers who went unmentioned in the records of the public land survey of Minnesota Territory. Much of this township and the next one to the north would prove wet and marshy. Just to the east, Deputy Surveyor William J. Anderson would find similar conditions in Township 103N, Range 19W, later called Moscow, when he entered it one week later.

Somewhere near this spot nineteen years earlier, Lieutenant Albert Lea and his Dragoons had been stopped on their mapping expedition by an impassable marsh. Lea's party showed up during an unusually wet July; Fitzpatrick's team came through in August, typically the driest, hottest month of an ordinary summer. Both bore witness to the presence of a lake, a stream of measurable size flowing southeastward, and a vast surrounding marsh. Lea's location notes are imprecise, and his drawings, in pencil on tablet pages, hardly resemble the actual outlines of the lakes he sighted. He extolled the beauty of the landscape and assigned fanciful names to certain features of it: Paradise Prairie, Lake Chapeau. Edward Fitzpatrick was a numbers man. Charged with grading the soil he observed as first, second, or third rate, he allowed himself one expression of disapproval: the marshy muck that covered the northeast portion of the township he denoted "worthleß."

Fitzpatrick and crew had been dispatched from the US General Land Office in Dubuque, Iowa, to conduct a cadastral survey of the Suland in Minnesota Territory, ceded to the government by treaty just three years earlier. They were to divide the hunting lands that Native people had used in common into precise square-mile "sections," which would be diced up and sold, the land's use forever after governed by legal title and its value expressed in dollars. Their work was intended to open Indian lands to yeoman farmers of Anglo-European origin, the heroes of Thomas Jefferson's vision for the westward expansion of the United States. Some land would fall into the hands of speculators after the example of the Father of Our Country, George Washington, who began his career as a surveyor but amassed property along the way.

Fitzpatrick's survey team had worked its way north from the Iowa border along Range 20 W beyond the Fifth Principal Meridian, taking a week to measure each township grid. The townships' outer boundaries had been drawn in the late spring by a different survey team led by J. B. Reyman. The marsh appears to have been fully wet at that time.

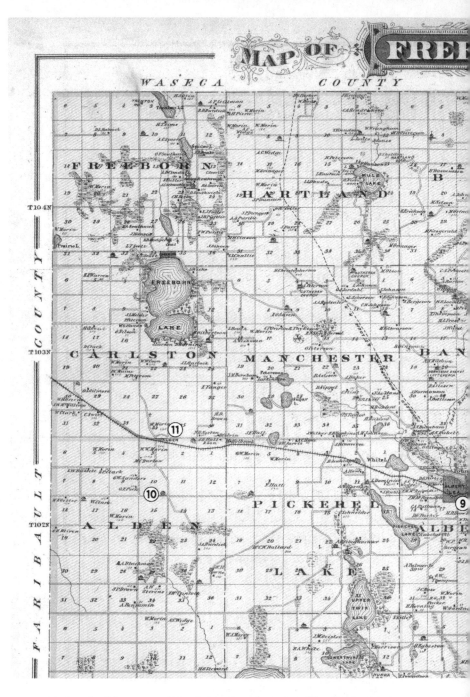

A detail of the map of Freeborn County printed in the Andreas Atlas, 1874. Significant sites include (1) Geneva Lake; (2) the Big Marsh; (3) Maple Island; (4) Hickory Island; (5) Rice Lake;

(6) Moscow woods; (7) the Speer farm; (8) the Ostrander farm; (9) Albert Lea; (10) the District 40 school; (11) Alden. For detail, see page 50.

Of his attempt to trace the northern boundary of Township 103, Reyman wrote, "No possible means of extending the line by triangulation on account of the height of the Marsh Cane and Willows. Can only be extended when frozen—in the Winter." It takes a leap of the imagination to envision the marsh cane and willows from the twenty-first century. The line between Riceland and Geneva townships is Minnesota Highway 251.

Fitzpatrick took his first bearings where Reyman had marked the southeast corner of the township. The crew paced a mile westward along its southern boundary, then moved due north, establishing a section line that they marked with a stake at one-half mile before continuing on to locate the point exactly one mile north of the southern boundary and one mile west of the eastern boundary. There, Fitzpatrick recorded in his logbook, he drove a charred stake into the ground and erected a mound with trenches around it "as per instructions," then planted a locust seed at each corner. No matter the soil's quality, the seeds were meant to grow into a living "monument" of "witness trees" marking the section corner. It seems futile to expect a new species of tree to root itself from seed in a landscape dominated by bur oaks— hardy, gnarly trees that can withstand fire and brutal cold. We know that bur oaks dominated because the survey marked the type and location of trees along the section lines and measured their diameters. William J. Anderson found woodlands along the stream in the township to the east and identified white and bur oak, elm, linden, ash, and hickory, but on most pages of their logbooks, bur oak is the sole tree.

After completing a mile-long section line, the crew turned east and walked back randomly to the preceding south–north line. They located the exact northeast corner of the section, then traced a new line westward, staying true to their bearings. North and east, west and north again, they blazed the bark of trees that stood on the line, drove their stakes, made their mounds, dug their trenches, planted their locust seeds. When they reached the northern boundary, they headed all the way south again, six miles away, to begin the next south–north line; or, if the sun was low in the sky, they hefted their equipment onto their weary bodies and angled back to camp. Curiously, the public land survey did not follow the sections' numbering from 1 to 36. Those numbers move east to west, then west to east, in a pattern called fancifully, from Greek roots, "boustrophedonic," the way an ox would pull a plow.

As head of the crew, Fitzpatrick wielded its most sophisticated tool, a brass compass, the emblem of his status, skill, and responsibility. Another surveyor in Minnesota Territory, Frederick Leavenworth, left behind a collection of letters that provides a rare glimpse into the work of "running lines" in "the desolate country I have traversed on foot for more than four hundred miles." While Leavenworth didn't stint on noting the obstacles—swarming mosquitoes, numbing winter cold, the surprise of thin ice—he also aimed to ennoble his hardy profession. Describing a group of Indians he met near New Ulm, he gloated, "They reverenced my old brass compass, saluted me with a wild but good natured 'Owgh,' gave me kinnick-kinnick to smoke, and passed on in grand procession. . . . The whole band passed me with that deference which Indians always show to a surveyor."

Any deference shown a deputy surveyor by his crew probably depended on his mathematical knowledge and precision, as well as the authority he held over them. With his compass balanced on a Jacob's staff, Fitzpatrick would sight on a distant landmark, then triangulate, measuring angles and calculating distance geometrically to locate the true directional line. Another sign of his leadership was the logbook he carried in his pocket, in which he recorded the measurements, the lay of the land, and its vegetation. When I first untied the laces and folded back the protective paper wrapped around the crumbling little survey book in the archives of the Minnesota secretary of state, I imagined that it had traveled through the Big Marsh 150 years before, that the penmanship—with its Germanic ß—was Fitzpatrick's, that the fading brown ink came from a bottle he carried with him in the field. Yet the book was free of splashes and smears. I learned later that he turned his logbook in at the Dubuque Land Office, where clerks made handwritten copies to distribute to agencies needing reference to the survey. The copies' digitized pages can now be called up online at the Bureau of Land Management's website, but they don't catch the breath the way that little archived volume does.

Fitzpatrick had served as a chainman on a survey team in Wisconsin in 1843, so he had worked his way up in the profession over the previous eleven years. The chainman's job earns my greatest admiration. William Rendall and Henry H. Smith shared the duties in the Range 20 townships. They used a Gunter's chain, a contraption of links and rings sixty-six feet—one hundred links—long that folded accordion style for ease of carrying. Ten chains equaled a furlong, eighty chains a mile, and a square of ten chains on either side made an acre. One man held an end of the chain still at the starting point while the second carried it forward, unfolding it along the way and stretching it toward the compass bearing the surveyor had marked. The man in the rear sighted along the chain to make sure its trajectory stayed true. The axman, R. P. Hammon, walked ahead to clear the path of brush and turned back as requested to blaze the bark of trees close to the line. When the chain reached its full length, Rendall, say, set a tally peg and waited while Smith brought the chain forward and stretched it out again. From the south boundary of the township to the north, they made 480 passes. Stringing the chain through the marsh meant bending and stooping, pulling tally pegs out of the mud, maybe fumbling and dropping the chain in water, a dirty, joint-taxing job. While the work sounds tedious, it was yet more exacting: The chainmen had to follow the curvature of the earth, not the land surface. They could not simply lay the chain on the ground but had to keep it on a horizontal plane. In the end, a farmer in a hilly section would have more land surface to plow and seed than a farmer in a level section.

So far, we have seen four men alone on the landscape, except for any hunters or trappers, Native or white, who knew the marsh's reputation for bountiful game. These four men traipsed northward on their assigned square of land while four other men—William J. Anderson, James Haggard, J. C. Haggard, and Silas Dutcher—covered the township to the east. But is that the whole picture? I would like to provide them with a cook to fry their tiresome provisions of salt pork, throw a line into Rice Lake for some fish, and fire a few shots at ducks and geese flying overhead. Some venison, too, would be welcome after a long day's labor in the August sun. Given that they lined out all thirty-six sections in one week, how quickly and efficiently did they shovel those trenches and mound up those heaps of dirt, whether compact, root-filled prairie sod or squishy peat? Could some unnamed laborer have performed that job? The chainmen and axman signed the logbook to certify that the survey team had completed the work, but the logbook doesn't say there were no others.

In her book *Order Upon the Land*, Hildegard Binder Johnson details the party of forty-three men who accompanied Captain Andrew Talcott on his survey of the northern border of Iowa—also the southern border of Freeborn County—in spring 1852: "fourteen surveyors, a hunter, a doctor, an interpreter, four cooks, chainmen, flagmen, monument builders, teamsters, sod choppers, and general handymen." A township surveyor would want sufficient help, but the finances of the operation limited the size of his crew. A deputy surveyor such as Fitzpatrick or Anderson contracted with the General Land Office for a set salary, out of which he paid his crew and bought supplies. He would want to reserve enough cash for himself and his family, who were minding their own lives without him.

On August 11, after spending most of the day on rolling prairie scattered with bur oak, Fitzpatrick traced his last section, the northwest corner of the township, back in the marsh on nearly level third-rate land, rather wet and among bur oaks that were nearly all dead. It was not a fitting site for a utopian vision. William J. Anderson's summary comments on August 22, 1854, were no rosier: "T 103N R 19W Surface is very level marshy soil 2nd and 3rd rate Timber very poor Scattering Br Oak." His last eight miles of lines had been run through marsh, with one small oasis of "Timber: oak, elm, linden of good quality." His spare notations include "too marshy to build mound," "impassable marsh," "all marsh." On the northwest corner of the map he sketched, he wrote "floating marsh." That final wet, grueling day had apparently flooded Anderson's memory, causing him to forget the mixed hardwoods he had noted along the seventy-five-link (fifty-foot) stream in the southern half of the township, the first- and second-rate soil, the rolling and level land, the drier landscape four generations of my family would call home.

Homing on the Marsh: *The Speers*

Father hunted a good deal in the Moscow woods. One day he took the dog and an ax, and came back with four large raccoons. They were so heavy he could carry only two at a time, and he had to go back for the other two. The second winter we were there, he shot 18 ducks one day in the creek, and the dog brought them in. We also picked and ate a lot of wild strawberries and other berries and fruits. Crab apples grew plentiful, and there were a lot of hazel and hickory nuts in the woods.

—"Mrs. Marrietta Whaley Came to Freeborn Co. In 1855;
Writes Memoirs," *Evening Tribune*, February 14, 1938

The tall farmhouse where my dad, Gordon Register, was born on January 16, 1912, still stands atop a slope on the south bank of the drainage ditch Turtle Creek has become, within sight of the Moscow town hall and the empty creamery, about all that remains of Moscow village. His grandmother Amanda and his father, Leslie, were born on this land as well, in the log house where his great-grandparents Robert and Mary Speer, the first European settlers in Moscow Township, lived out their lives. I, too, might have lived here except for a farm recession and a family grudge.

The vista from the homesite is pleasing but not remarkable: typical southern Minnesota farmland—corn and soybean fields and stands of trees that mark other farmsteads. The land undulates a bit, as you would expect of a glacial end moraine, but flattens dramatically along the northern horizon as you drive west on County Highway 25. When the Speers lived here and in Leslie Register's childhood, the landscape north of the creek was the Big Marsh and the Moscow Woods.

Robert Speer, a blacksmith from Rutland, Wisconsin, chose this site in the southwest quarter of Moscow section 22 as his new home the

Robert Speer

Mary Speer

first week of June 1855, one year before the future railroad magnate
James J. Hill and the future lumber baron Frederick Weyerhaeuser
arrived in Minnesota Territory. Hill would crisscross the prairie with
iron rails and drain the Red River floodplain. Weyerhaeuser would cut
bare the northern white pine forest. The Speers, too, would transform
their land. The oxen that drew the family's wagon along the military
road to Prairie du Chien, then rested on the ferry across the Mississippi
before the long slog through northeastern Iowa and up along the Cedar
River, were hitched to the plow. Age-old roots of bluestem, grama, and
other prairie grasses and flowering forbs, cut and turned, left a fertile
black loam to nurture the corn and potatoes the Speers planted that first
year. Other "pioneers" followed in a line of prairie schooners that wound
along creeks or followed the Blue Earth Road, a Dakota trail that
skirted wetlands from the Cedar to the Blue Earth River. In a remark-
ably brief time, these transplanted Easterners and European immigrants "civilized" the savanna and the prairie beyond with pastures and
cultivated fields. Yet the Speers and their neighbors left the Big Marsh
in place, cutting its grasses for hay and shooting and trapping its wildlife to supplement the food produced on their farms.

Why did the Speers choose precisely *this* place, in a still unnamed
township only recently surveyed? The answer draws on both testimony and conjecture. The Speer family's migration, in communal and
multigenerational moves and stops, is so typical that telling the story
veers close to cliché. They did not come to Minnesota alone but in
a group of neighbors in the prime of life who left parents and siblings
behind, at least temporarily. The Speers were Robert, twenty-eight;
Mary, thirty-three; and their children, Marietta, seven; DeWitt, five; and
George, four. Their companions were Welsh-born Thomas and Mary
Ellis, thirty-one and thirty, with children Mary, eight, and William,
three; and Thomas and David Morgan, Welsh brothers aged twenty
and twelve. Robert Speer's lineage traced back to the Dutch who
claimed the Hudson River Valley in the seventeenth century. Mary,
formerly Hutchinson, was born in Canada. Family legend identifies her

as half-Indian, but no evidence has been found to prove that claim other than the physiognomy of some of her descendants.

Two scant recollections of the journey exist: one, an account of the early years by Thomas Morgan in the 1911 *History of Freeborn County* that dwells mostly on his later near-fatal encounter with a blizzard; the other, a newspaper interview with Marietta Speer Whaley, still sharp in her nineties but as subject as any of us to the vagaries of memory. Morgan had the group leaving on May 8 "to seek a new home in the wilderness." He drove the loose cattle on foot while Speer and Ellis drove wagons pulled by two yoke of oxen and three yoke of "wild steers." Marietta recalled that her mother and Mrs. Ellis insisted that they rest on Sundays. Rest would be welcome judging from contemporary accounts of wagons mired in Wisconsin sand and in Minnesota and Iowa sloughs. Even in the drier months, someone might have to walk ahead with a scythe and cut a path through tall marsh reeds or prairie grasses.

"After various adventures," sadly not described, the party reached Otranto, Iowa, along the Cedar River just south of the Minnesota Territory border. There, Morgan recalled, they met two men who told them that if they followed the Cedar north to Austin, then headed west, they would come to a timberland as yet unclaimed. In Austin, they secured three days' lodging for the women and children. Hotels were popping up all along the westward routes "for the accommodation of the Traveling Public," as an ad for Austin's Lacy House put it in the 1858 *Mower County Mirror*.

The men and cattle headed west, presumably along Turtle Creek. As promised, they came upon segments of eastern hardwood forest standing in among the wetlands and along the creek, protected from prairie fires by the surrounding water. Here Robert would have wood to fuel his forge and water to harden molten iron. Gently rolling oak savanna offered sufficient tillable land and home sites safe from flooding. The Morgans, Ellises, and Speers would be neighbors here while the "Moscow woods," as the timberland came to be called, steadily diminished, felled for lumber and fuel.

The law of preemption, which made land available at $1.25 an acre, required that one signal a claim to the property by erecting a dwelling. First Robert Speer pitched a tent, which sheltered the family while he built a log cabin with an elm bark roof. To practice his vocation, he needed a smithy. He put up a small shanty, and that first fall and winter, he "did considerable blacksmithing." The following year he built "a substantial log building," and "the pioneers came all the way from Blue Earth county for plow-sharpening." It didn't hurt that Isaac Botsford, editor of the new *Freeborn County Eagle*, reported that "R. G. Speer can make anything from a table fork to a ship anchor—yes, and make the tools to make it with."

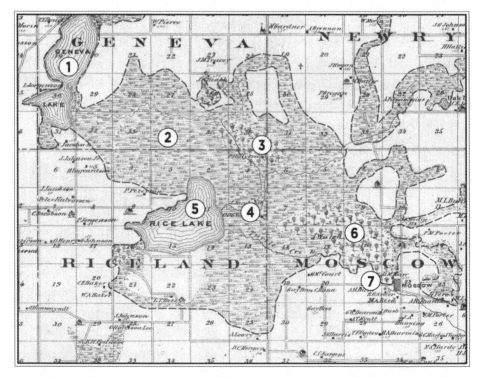

A detail of the map of Freeborn County printed in the Andreas Atlas, 1874 (see p. 38–39) showing Rice Lake, Turtle Creek, the Moscow woods, and the Speer farm (the name appears at the southwest corner of the rectangle designating the village of Moscow)

By the time of the 1860 US Agricultural Census, the Speers had, in the language of the day, "improved" thirty-eight acres of land, meaning they had "broken" the thickly matted sod and planted crops. The harvest that year yielded forty bushels of corn, two bushels of peas and beans, eighty-seven bushels of potatoes, and forty tons of hay to feed the livestock. They owned two swine, two oxen, and two cows that produced 150 pounds of butter. They practiced subsistence farming for a growing family. Market farming—in those days growing wheat for milling—was a more demanding enterprise that meant hauling loads back across the soggy migratory route to McGregor, Iowa, 125 miles away.

Those first five years were hardly untroubled. Legal notices of pending farm foreclosures peppered the late-summer editions of the 1860 *Freeborn County Standard.* One of them announced that the property of Robert Speer and his wife, Mary Speer, would be sold at public auction September 3, 1860, for default on a mortgage debt of $115.28. The land itself was a bargain purchase from the US government, but to buy livestock, seed, and equipment, farmers borrowed against that land. The economic recession we know now as the Panic of 1857, followed by two years of poor harvests, known in pioneer lore as "the year eighteen and johnny-cake" because there was little else to eat, had left many of the county's first white residents in debt. Two days before the scheduled auction, a "large number" of county citizens gathered in Albert Lea "for the purpose of consulting together and agreeing on a plan of action in relation to the land sales." They drew up a resolution to send to Senator Henry Rice and President James Buchanan in which they first described how these worthy settlers had headed west expecting to till the virgin lands and thrive in their new homes. It continued, "Whereas we have failed unqualifiedly to enjoy our expectations, and our Chief Executive has proclaimed our homes for public sale under the most trying auspices, and at a period the most unfortunate for us to save them from the mercenary grasp of the speculative capitalists, or avaricious mania of defunct railroad companies, at a period when we are endeavoring to recuperate our prostrated energies from the critical ordeal of a two years famine and financial privation." The resolution was circulated throughout the county for signatures, and Theophilus Lowry, a member of the county board, brought it to Moscow Township, where twenty-one properties faced foreclosure. I imagine Lowry stepping up to the smithy, waiting while the lean, dark-haired Speer lifted a newly tempered hoe blade from the water of the slack tub and shoved a log of dry hardwood into the forge fire. I have never seen the original resolution, but I feel certain that Robert Speer signed it with a mix of anxiety and hope.

Colonel G. W. Skinner, a county resident said to have influence with the president, carried the resolution to Washington. The newspaper accounts don't say *how* he traveled—overland to begin with, then likely by both steamboat and rail—but he returned in three weeks with a year's credit for the mortgagees and a ban on sales of inhabited land to speculators. The Speers must have paid off their mortgage within the grace period. During these difficult years, they doubled the size of their brood with three more daughters, the final one my great-grandmother Amanda, born August 30, 1860.

Had the Speers forfeited their land, they could have returned to Wisconsin, where Robert's parents, John Dorsey and Maria Speer, lived until their deaths at eighty-five and ninety-three. But Wisconsin had been only a way station for Robert and Mary. They had lived there no more than three years, having met, married, and borne and lost children in their previous home in Michigan. Robert had probably worked with his father, a blacksmith himself, but the demand in an area by then well settled may not have supported them both. Cheaply priced virgin land and a new market for farm tools and cooking utensils likely lured them west yet again.

Born in Tyre in the Finger Lakes region of upstate New York on April 12, 1827, two years after the Erie Canal came through, Robert Speer had begun his westward migration at six or seven. Three generations of Speers packed up and headed west, presumably via the canal and a Great Lakes steamer, to Washtenaw County, Michigan. About eighteen years later, nearly the whole clan, including Robert's aging parents and most of his nine siblings, moved on to Wisconsin. Why leave a place that had served so long as a multigenerational family home? Where was "home," anyway, and how did this constant drive westward affect a person's sense of belonging in a place? Feelings of home—the home we long for later in life—take hold, I suspect, early on as our senses become familiar with certain sights and sounds, smells and tactile sensations. As I picture Robert stretching his five-foot-eleven body to walk from his Moscow smithy to his house at mealtime, I see him gaze across the creek and turn his head to take in the expanse of woods and marsh. This view became his vision of home in the forty-eight years he stayed put in southern Minnesota. It probably reminded him of another view, an acute experience of the world lodged in memory since his earliest years at his first home in upstate New York.

Here is how a Seneca County historian, writing in 1876, described the place:

> The town of Tyre, having a large portion of its surface a waste of swamp, and the remainder a jungle of forest, presented few attractions to those who early sought homes for life in this part of the . . . County. They were met by sufficient obstacles apart from the depressing and unhealthy influence engendered by the immediate presence of an extended tract of stagnant water. Even at this late day, when the appliances of art are so numerous, and land has grown so valuable, the Montezuma Marshes remain unredeemed. How then, save by the trap and rifle, could a living be gained in such a locality?

A blacksmith could earn some income making and maintaining traps and repairing rifles, so "a waste of swamp" would not have deterred Robert Speer. I suspect that a visceral attraction, too, led him to settle just where he did. From the Montezuma Marsh to the Moscow Marsh, I daresay that he found comfort in the sight of a V of geese gliding in for a landing; the gulping call of the American bittern, or "sloughpumper"; the fading sunlight refracted into pinks and golds by the moist air; the rustle of reeds stirred by wind or a muskrat bound for its lodge; even the pungent odor of stagnant water. The Montezuma Marsh remains, despite the sentiment of the county historian, a 9,809-acre national wildlife refuge. The Big Marsh in Moscow succumbed long ago to "the appliances of art." I doubt that Robert Speer welcomed its demise.

The Trip from Otranto Revisited

In the still warm light of a late afternoon near the end of May, Robert Speer eases his oxen out of the yoke and leads them cautiously down a grassy slope to wade and drink where the waters of the Cedar River pool along a gravel shore. The children already splash and squeal at water's edge, the little boys with pants rolled, the two girls gathering up their skirts in their fists. Back at the wagons, parked in the shade of oak and walnut trees, the two Marys rummage for their cooking utensils and enough food to concoct an evening meal. They can stock up in Otranto, just upriver from their campsite, but their hopes are set on only a few more days of travel. They have been on the move for three weeks, and the adventure is wearing thin. Thomas Morgan devises a makeshift pen for the pigs and milk cows while his brother, young David, gathers deadwood for the evening's fire. Thomas Ellis checks the supply of corn feed, then walks out into the triangle of open grassland to see if it's suitable for grazing. Other traveling parties have obviously let their cattle roam here. Mary Speer grabs the water pail and heads down the slope, calling to the children to keep to the shoreline, safely away from the river's current.

This placid grove of trees alongside a natural beach that allows easy access to the river is clearly a popular stopping point for westward travelers. It seems so even 150 years later as I imagine the Speers and their companions camped here, in the place where they learned of the timberland that would become their lasting home. It is easy to be transported to the past here in Otranto Park, across the river from the declining town of Otranto, Iowa. The oaks and walnuts look long lived, and an old, abandoned bridge that crosses the river kitty-corner from the present road adds to the impression of time warp. Of course I can't say for certain that this is where the party stopped. Around the bend in the river to the north is the likely site of Merry's Ford, where wagon trains typically crossed. Otranto's original townsite, where it stood in 1855, lies about two miles north, shunned by the railroad, only crumbled foundations remaining where a hotel, a post office, several stores, and a mill once flourished. The site is on private property, inaccessible without prior permission, so I let my imagination run here in the park, a fine place to linger on a glorious June afternoon. The park fills up with laughing children, snorting animals, squeaky-wheeled wagons as a friend and I stand alone under the trees in a bucolic quiet.

A casual conversation weeks earlier with a friend who recognized the town's name spawned the trip. Daughters of Hamlin Garland's Middle Border, we grew up on opposite sides of the Minnesota–Iowa border: I on the outskirts of Albert Lea, she on a farm in Mitchell County, Iowa. We drove south from Minneapolis that morning, intending to show each other familiar sites and explore new ones. We followed Minnesota Highway 56 southeast through Rose Creek to Adams, where we ate lunch across the street from the noted Prairie School bank, then found one of my friend's ancestral names on tombstones in the Sacred Heart Cemetery. It couldn't have been a finer day. As we continued down county roads to Johnsburg, where we stopped at another cemetery, we kept the car windows open to hear the birds sing and smell the verdant fields. Marsh grasses stood tall along the creeks and drainage ditches as we crossed into Iowa and passed through Stacyville and Toeterville. We remarked on how much more beautiful the rural landscape seemed than either of us could remember. We had entered a different dimension of time, seeing what used to be—woods and prairie grasses and free-flowing streams—as an overlay on the cultivated landscape.

Our plan as we crossed the Cedar after our stop in Otranto Park was to hew as close to the river as possible, letting it guide us to Austin, as I imagine it guided the Speers. From Austin, we would follow Turtle Creek to Moscow. We found a gravel road that took us north between the river and a railroad spur, but it dead-ended all too soon at a hog barn. A paved county road was our only northward option, but it curved away from the river. We kept our eyes on the line of trees that marked the course of the Cedar, hoping the road would veer that way again. So focused were we on that elusive river that we barely noticed the sky to the north.

A border is an arbitrary line drawn on a map to demarcate one jurisdiction from another, but on this day, the state line separated summer splendor from an ominous darkness. Just as we crossed back into Minnesota, a blue-black wall of cloud loomed ahead of us, stretching all across the northern horizon. We both knew, having grown up in this storm-prone region, how localized and bounded the weather can be. I flashed on a memory of running home from a friend's house ahead of the rain, hearing it fall behind me yet staying dry the whole way. We could hurry to the Speer farm and then wait out the passage of the storm in a restaurant somewhere. At lunch in Adams, we had filled up on sandwiches despite the menu's tantalizing list of freshly baked pies. We had counted on making up for that error later in the afternoon.

In our hurry to get to Austin, we ignored the river views from Minnesota's Highway 105. We turned west on the highway I remember as old US 16, and I watched for the Oakland elevator that marked our turn toward Moscow. Raindrops were already striking the windshield, enough to put the wipers on intermittent. We both pushed away our lifelong knowledge about clouds as dark and solid as the ones that faced us when we made the turn. As we crested the hill where the road dips down into old Moscow village, a wind gust broadsided the car and blew over a lawn swing at the house we were passing.

I barely remember turning the car around, but we were quickly heading south again, driving away from the wind on a perpendicular line, our childhoods' tornado instincts in full gear. With the rain falling heavily, I followed the pavement's white edging back into Austin. It was time for pie. We scouted storefronts along our way but saw nothing that promised food and respite. In the center of town, we parked across the street from a coffee shop, ducked under an umbrella, and ran inside.

The shop was closing in fifteen minutes, just enough time to down a cup of coffee and wish for the storm to pass quickly. It didn't.

Just as we shut ourselves inside the car again, a deafening downpour began. The rain fell so thick that we could no longer see the storefronts just a sidewalk's width away. The words "flash flood" came to mind, and we were in the worst possible place for one. Downtown Austin is prone to flooding as the rain overwhelms the storm sewers and the Cedar spills over its banks.

Many long and anxious minutes later, with the rain abating, we wound our way through town, avoiding flooded streets and skirting a new lake in the parking lot of a shopping mall until we were safe and dry on Highway 218 headed back to the Twin Cities. Our reveries had given way to a somber discussion about the damage done to our Midwestern landscape over a century and a half. I mourned the loss of the Big Marsh, which held rainwater in place so that it did not flood the Cedar and inundate towns downstream as it would do three years later with devastating effect to Cedar Rapids. My friend rued the continued tiling and ditching, the dwindling of underground aquifers, and the practice of plowing fields bare in the fall with no stubble to hold the soil in place. We found what solace we could in the land's own memory, its tendency to collect heavy rains in dips and swales in its own effort at wetland restoration. But even the land's memory fades as the soil goes dry and hard and loses its absorbency.

Later I read an account of the weather across Minnesota Territory in 1855. While May was predominantly warm and dry enough to elicit questions about when some respite might come, two thunderstorms, on May 27 and 30, deposited a full inch of rain. I had imagined May 30 as the day the Speers spent driving their oxen along the banks of the Cedar from Otranto to Austin. Now I want to erase that midnight blue wall cloud from their first view of their new home's horizon. Maybe they were wise and weather conscious enough to make their move in the sunny lull between storms. Maybe they spent May 30 huddled in Austin, waiting for the sky to clear before the men headed west to scout the timberland. Austin's dirt streets were surely muddy, but I do not see them flooded.

Claiming the High Ground:
The Ostranders

The gradual rise in elevation that trapped the water within the footprint of the Big Marsh is barely discernible to any but the most practiced eye—say that of a Hollandale farmer. But any Midwesterner should be able to see the soft undulations along the western horizon that mark the Bancroft moraines, once the shoreline of a large prehistoric lake of glacial melt. Up on this higher land, eleven miles almost due west of the Speers' place in Moscow, the Big Marsh's most persistent defender was born and raised. Henry N. and Sarah Ostrander, my dad's maternal great-grandparents, staked their claim on June 12, 1859, to the northwest quadrant of section 26 of Bancroft Township. The public land survey describes the land they chose as "rolling 2nd rate" with bur oak timber.

The Ostranders' move from eastern Wisconsin entailed "many difficulties" left unnamed. They brought along Cornelius, nine; Eva, five; and Ella, two. Sarah was eight months pregnant with Armetta upon arrival, surely a "difficulty" on such a journey. Three more children followed, including Elbert Henry, born on October 28, 1862, amid fear and hatred engendered by reports of war with the Dakota seventy miles to the northwest. Elbert eased into a society that crossed cultures in its own limited way. Nearly all the Ostranders' neighbors were Norwegian, some of them secondary migrants from Wisconsin and others fresh from mountains and fjords. Elbert learned enough vocabulary from his playmates for conversation.

The Bancroft savanna proved to be a fine departure point for independent boyhood adventures. Elbert enjoyed easy access to the natural

Henry N. Ostrander

world and was drawn to the wild and watery. To the west, marsh-lined Bancroft Creek led him into—or away from—the town of Albert Lea. To the east, Rice Lake, Geneva Lake, and the Big Marsh lay open to endless exploration. Elbert's attention to marsh flora and his special fondness for migratory waterfowl filled his mind with images well suited to a favorite family pursuit: writing poems to be shared. Another family value left as indelible an imprint on his character. His father's participation in local governance and the community's welfare aroused in him a commitment to active citizenship that he passed on to his children. I, too, inherited this sense of obligation, and I have long wondered about its origin.

Like Robert Speer, the Ostranders were Yorkers of both Dutch and English ancestry. They had left Plattsburgh, on Lake Champlain, in 1849, along with baby Cornelius and Henry's father and stepmother and their children, including her adult son and his family. Their destination was Fond du Lac, Wisconsin, on another long lake, minus the mountains. Both father and son acquired land in Metomen Township

The Ostranders' log cabin, built in 1860

just south of a new town that came to be called Ripon. First settled as a utopian cooperative community named Ceresco by the Wisconsin Phalanx, followers of the French social philosopher Charles Fourier, Ripon is regarded as the 1854 birthplace of the Republican Party as an antislavery party. Among the town's first establishments was a college, founded "to draw around us a class of inhabitants that would have pride to educate their children and they would be good for every good work." I can't help but wonder whether the Ostranders' proximity to Ripon infused them with concern for the common good and inspired them to educate their children. Despite my dreams of a long heritage of civic engagement, however, I find no evidence in the histories of Clinton County, New York, and Fond du Lac County, Wisconsin, that the Ostranders left any mark there other than the furrows their plows made.

Henry did merit a paragraph but no portrait in the 1882 and 1911 histories of Freeborn County. Among his first acts of citizenship was the construction of the District 22 log schoolhouse known as the Ostrander School. He chaired the Bancroft Township Board of Supervisors and served on the school board and the county board, a fact my dad cited proudly when he was elected a county commissioner himself a century later. His name appears from time to time in the local newspapers: as president of the Freeborn County Cane Growers Association promoting cultivation of amber cane, treasurer of the Farmers' Association, a judge of horse harnesses at the county fair, and the planter of ten thousand tree cuttings at the county poor farm in Bancroft.

One of Henry's appearances in the news illustrates a difficulty of living in a landscape of water-filled swales:

> A few days ago, Mr. H. N. Ostrander, of Bancroft, came into our office, completely daubed with mud. An inquiry into the cause of his sad plight, revealed the fact that he attempted to get into town with a load of wheat, that when he reached a point near the Manley place, where the road is said to be fearfully bad in a wet time, his team and

wagon sank nearly out of sight; and that his two hour's effort to extricate them had placed him in the deplorable condition in which we saw him. He and everyone else who passes over that road, says it ought to be fixed.

I found no follow-up story saying that Henry Ostrander had seen to repairing the road, but I have to assume he tried.

Hazards

"Grandma Speer was pret' near blind, you know. She was milking, and a cow that had gotten into the smartweed switched its tail across her eyes. She and the boys were running the farm while Grandpa Speer was away in the Civil War." My dad dropped snippets of family history like this one into conversation from time to time. We might be driving along a country road or watching a TV western when some detail tripped the switch in his brain that unlocked stories heard long before. They were seldom whole stories, just bits of data, and they needed unpacking to make much sense.

What is "smartweed"? A Google search leads to many varieties of Polygonum, a pink or lavender flower on a jointed stem that grows in shallow water and moist soil in northern temperate climates. It would no doubt thrive along the edges of the Big Marsh. I don't remember it growing in the sloughs of my childhood, but then I was more given to daydreaming than to identifying flora. Nowhere do I read about Polygonum causing blindness, although the term "smartweed" itself offers a clue. Some leaves are irritating to the skin, and chewing them burns the mouth worse than chili peppers. Chunks of leaf tangled in a cow's tail and switched across the eyes might well inflame them.

I imagine it happened one evening in July. The boys had gone to the meadow to urge the family's two cows back to their shed. Maybe the big dog their sister Marietta recalled in her old age ran alongside the boys as they called, "Come, boss!" Who were "the boys"? DeWitt was almost fourteen and George eleven when Robert Speer enlisted in the war effort in November 1863. Marietta, at sixteen, was probably as much help as anyone. I see her now, grabbing clean pails while her mother pulls the milking stool up and squats down on it. They are both tired from a long day of washing—hauling water from the creek, heating it over the firewood the boys helped carry, scrubbing and bleaching and boiling and rinsing and squeezing, then hanging the clothes to dry. A good day for washing, a day with no rain to soak the clothes and no clouds to inhibit the sun's drying rays, is also a hot, prickly day abundant with flies.

Mary hasn't thought to check the cows' tails and brush them clean of clingy debris. Buttercup swings hers vigorously, swatting away the flies. Just as Mary leans in to rest her forehead against the cow's flank, that tail slaps her across the eyes. Marietta runs to fetch cold water, but a scratch across the cornea has done its damage.

Polygonum—also known as arsesmart, water pepper, and knotweed—has many medicinal uses. Another of Dad's family history tidbits credited Grandma Speer with "doctoring" neighbors through illness and injury. I wonder if she used smartweed to clean wounds or clot blood or ease dysentery or bring on a delayed menstrual period. She might even have packed it into her children's ears to kill the worms once believed to crawl in and cause earaches.

To say that Grandpa Speer was away in the Civil War evokes the deadly charge of the First Minnesota Regiment at Gettysburg and the battles at Shiloh and Vicksburg, but in fact he never saw duty in the War Between the States. As a blacksmith in Company C of the Second Regiment of the Minnesota Cavalry, Private Speer spent two years in Dakota Territory shoeing the horses of the soldiers who pursued the Native population in a genocidal campaign that followed Minnesota's own civil war, the US–Dakota War of 1862. I wonder how that assignment sat with a man who had repaired traps for the Indians near his home. Granite tombstones installed by the Moscow Township Board a century later to honor Civil War veterans make no distinction between those sent to fight the Confederacy and those sent to fight the region's indigenous people. Robert Speer's stands mauve and shiny next to the tilting marble stone that marks the grave of "Blacksmith R. G. Spear." The family either didn't bother or didn't succeed in getting the monument maker to correct the spelling. Maybe they reasoned, "Grandma won't know. She's pret' near blind anyway."

What Counts as a Lake?

Our lakes cannot be surpassed in beauty—our climate is as pure and clear as our crystal waters, which bear on their surface acres of goose, ducks, swan and water fowl of every description, and in their depths the very best variety of fish.

　　—*Freeborn County Eagle*, September 25, 1858

As soon as it opened to European settlement, Minnesota Territory began touting its many lakes as a prime natural amenity. Civic boosters and land dealers showed a decided preference for clear lakes over reedy ones. An advertisement in the first issue of the *Freeborn County Standard*, May 26, 1860, invited "farmers, mechanics, professionals and capitalists" to settle in the village of Freeborn: "Our country *Cannot be Surpassed for Health*, beauty or fertility. Our town is situated on one of those lovely sheets of water with which Minnesota is well supplied, and Freeborn Lake *is the fairest of the fair*. The lake is surrounded with EXCELLENT TIMBER! while the banks are hard and very bold, giving us an admirable road bed close to the Lake, the whole length of the town." The mention of "hard and very bold" banks offered assurance that this lake would not spread out willy-nilly into a reedy swamp in a spring thaw or summer cloudburst. The promise of pure, healthy "sheets" of water—"no stagnant pools to send forth poisonous exhalations"—appeared with the frequency of cliché in railroad and realty brochures luring readers to Minnesota. One such singled out Albert Lea, because of its lakes and its "bracing atmosphere," as "a very desirable place for invalids."

A story passed down in my family preserves the hype about lovely sheets of water. My dad's great-uncle Cornelius Ostrander earned renown for "cleaning up" and thus practically creating Alden's Gem Lake. Hired in 1883 by William Morin, its owner, Uncle Corneal sliced up the "sod" of the floating bog and hauled it out, first with a horse team and then in two boats he built for the purpose. The "beautiful sheet of water some twenty-five acres in extent" his work produced was lauded as a fitting centerpiece for a town with ambitions to grow. Albert Lea, too, boasted of its crystalline focal point, Fountain Lake, achieved when a dam constructed at its outlet inundated its wire grass and wild rice. Lakes once marshy have been known to seek their natural state, however. Barely a decade after Uncle Corneal's achievement, the *Freeborn County Times* reported that "the council of wisemen at Alden" was "desperate over the bilious condition of Gem Lake," which had become a "turgid abode of the tadpole and bullhead," no longer worthy of its name. Fountain Lake, too, has required frequent maintenance.

Freeborn County's glacial history left many shallow pockets of water that burgeoned with vegetable and animal life. Many of these were large and wet enough to be called lakes outright. Others were "meandered lakes," bodies of water with shifting shorelines, their boundaries legally defined and drawn on a plat map to indicate property rights. These lakes, too, had their attractions. Although Rice Lake was never "clear" and "crystalline," marshy Riceland Township saw no dearth of eager settlers. Its first federal census, in 1860, listed 125 people, mainly Norwegians, Midland migrants, and Yorkers. The names of Riceland's first arrivals were, fittingly, Ole C. Olson and Ole Hanson. The 1880 census counted 783 people, many of them Danish immigrants. Riceland's arable land must have been fully occupied because the number of residents was not surpassed until 1930, well after the drainage of Rice Lake.

Moscow Township was also thriving despite its lack of a lovely sheet of water. Its geographical reference point was the creek that ran from Rice Lake through woods and wetlands to the Cedar River in neighboring Mower County. "Our river," the Moscow reporter to the *Standard* called Turtle Creek, and what he (or she?) chose to report shows that it contained sufficiently deep swimming holes and abundant fish. Low catches were reported like aberrations. "Our river" was also known simply as "the Turtle."

Turtle Creek swimming hole at the Register farm, 1916

References to the Big Marsh, or the Moscow Marsh, or just "the marsh" also abound in the news from the townships in local papers. Much of the marsh had been deeded to the Southern Minnesota Railroad to support its westward expansion, and some sections, marked "College," were set aside to fund education. No one on site oversaw the use of these lands, so area residents treated them as community property, cutting the tall grasses that grew in soil that was wet in spring and dry by midsummer for hay.

The Moscow correspondent told of neighbors' sightings of wild animals, including a panther and an "American lion" (probably cougars) and a pack of wolves chasing deer out of the "Moscow timber," where local residents cut wood. Reports advised about the sponginess of the path across the marsh and the muddiness of adjacent roads. When the spring thaw slowed mail delivery, citizens were urged to show patience and offer assistance to the mail carrier. In one instance, observations of the beaten path across the marsh seemed to hint at the intensity of a courtship.

The people who settled this area didn't live exclusively off their crops and livestock. They supplemented their diets with hunting and fishing and their livelihoods with trapping. The marsh made that possible. Residents looked forward to the semiannual migration of waterfowl and reported their plenitude in the newspapers. Fishing yielded pickerel (northern pike), perch, bass, sunfish, and bullheads. Muskrats built their lodges in the marsh, and mink and raccoons fed on voles in the wet meadow. Fur buyers traveling through announced their presence in the newspaper or simply knocked on farmhouse doors. It was a decidedly rural way of life, with little need for the picturesque beauty or classy water recreation offered by a lovely sheet of water and enjoyed by the wealthy citizens of Albert Lea.

Surprisingly absent from newspaper commentary on the marsh are complaints about its presence or allusions to acrid smells, biting insects, or outbreaks of illness. The idea that wetlands were wasteland didn't seem to govern the Big Marsh's neighbors, who lived on land they or their parents had chosen through the preemption system.

Wildlife on reedy lakes drew more visitors to the county than the beauty of the crystalline gems. The area's reputation as a "paradise of sportsmen," as Henry Rice called it, must have held because out-of-town hunters continued to camp on Rice and Geneva lakes. One party from Owatonna captured my attention because of the tone of the announcement and the distinctive names, likely to produce results in a search of the census: "Messrs. E. M. Twiford, C. E. Luce, J. C. Ault, Geo. Norton and Holland are out on a week's hunting excursion near Geneva and Rice Lake in Freeborn County. The party took with them tent, camp stove, and a large supply of provisions. Essex Liddington accompanied them as cook, so they expect to feast royally, ducks or no ducks, without subsisting off the county." Eri Twiford, a hardware dealer, and Charles Luce, a harness maker, were both in their thirties and on their way to becoming livery stable proprietors. Jesse Ault, in his early forties, is identified as "street commissioner" in the census. Essex Liddington brought the biggest surprise. Born in Arkansas and a barber in his thirties, Liddington was Black. The separate mention of his name and his function on the trip bring dimensions of race and class to sport hunting, as do other reports that identify the hunters as "gentlemen" or by professional titles and occupations.

The numbers associated with sport hunting confound me. If two men named Frank could bag 103 ducks in one afternoon during the October migration, how many ducks in total flew over their heads? I try to imagine a thick cloud of waterfowl hovering above Rice Lake and its surrounding wetlands, prime habitat for the colorful variety of birds identified as generic "ducks" and "geese." Mallards, teal, pintails, redheads, goldeneye, canvasbacks. Canada geese, cackling geese, snow geese. Ducks and geese weren't the only birds present: "Mr. C. D. Marlett, of this place, brought down three large-sized sandhill cranes at one shot." Some accounts didn't bother to specify the genus of waterfowl. Two men from Alden "bagged a large number of the long necked birds that are to be found in every slough." Herons? Egrets? Cormorants? "Found in every slough" translates easily to "a dime a dozen."

Before the 1890s, when commercial hunting for markets in Chicago and eastward threatened to decimate the waterfowl population, state and local authorities did little to limit the numbers taken. The first game laws established seasons, mainly to protect nesting birds. In the early 1870s, Albert Lea sport hunters banded together purportedly to help enforce these laws. The Sportsmen's Club held its annual hunt in early August at the opening of the prairie chicken season, and it was an unabashedly competitive affair. The headline in the *Standard* of August 20, 1874, aims for drama:

"SPORTING!
The Annual Hunt
THE WHOLE CLUB IN THE FIELD!"

The thirty-six men present—including distinguished citizens, among them the young wheat buyer W. W. Cargill—divided into two sides, each consisting of several detachments. Most headed out onto dry land for prairie chickens, the familiar name for pinnated grouse. The four groups who hunted near Bear Lake were especially successful. One "brought in 125 chickens," another "quieted 110 chickens and one woodcock," another "returned with 62 chickens," and the fourth "took 51 chickens and 7 ducks." In those days, too, a sports reporter felt challenged to vary his verbs. Two sportsmen "visited" Rice Lake and returned with 105 ducks. The report doesn't say how many shots they fired.

At the end of the day, a committee counted the slain birds to determine the winning side. The grand total: 979 birds, the ratio of chickens to ducks about three to two. The newspaper even calculated the average take per hunter at twenty-seven and a half. Although the hunt was termed "a good day's work," its reward was pleasure: "A sumptuous supper was served to the company last evening, at the Webber House, and the bill settled by the defeated party." The article doesn't say whether the supper consisted of their kill.

Not everyone found such stories entertaining. A critic in La Crosse, Wisconsin, lodged "a scathing rebuke": "In this wholesale slaughter of chickens we fail to see where the real sportsmen come in unless it is desirable to exterminate that game entirely, and leave no sport for the future."

While I believe that subsistence-hunting farmers were more likely to shoot in moderation since they had no use for rotting meat, I can't say that they worried about extinction. While they noted fluctuations in the numbers of wildfowl, a wet, green spring of abundance might follow a parched autumn of scarcity. The semiannual migration renewed belief that the wildlife population could be replenished. Few gave much thought to the difference that marshy habitat made. Ducks landed on and decorated the prim town lakes as well.

It has taken us most of another century to realize that the standard ideal of beauty—a lovely, crystalline sheet of water, clear and transparent to the lake bottom and ringed by sand-fill beaches—may be a dead lake. Its glistening surface pleases the refined eye, much as an evenly mowed green lawn does or a weedless flowerbed with squared borders. A cattail slough, a floating bog, and a marsh well populated with frogs seem to await the civilizing use of a dredge just as a child with messy hair awaits the taming stroke of the comb. But some of us find beauty in the random and wild. We treasure the hatchlings cheeping in a light-fixture nest, the raccoon lumbering across a city street after dark, the seed blown in from the prairie on the west wind, the acorn buried by a squirrel and left to germinate in an apple orchard, the rhizome creeping under the loam, all the vagaries of pollination and seed-embedded bird droppings. Our ideal landscape needs water, abundant water teeming with life.

The Evolution of the Drainage Ditch

Anyone reading the early drainage acts will be impressed with the fact that not only were these laws intended to permit drainage but to encourage and promote it as well.

—E. V. Willard, Minnesota Drainage Commissioner, "Northern Minnesota Drainage," paper delivered January 30, 1945

Even lawyers who earn their living in this specialty tell me there is no deadlier reading than ditch law. Minnesota has produced volumes of it as well as a long succession of court rulings that interpret and apply the law. Routing water from one place to another on land divided into gridlike chunks of private property is contentious. A snatch of my dad's voice recorded in memory calls out to remind me of that fact. Watching C-SPAN on television long after his ten-year service on the Freeborn County Board, he shook his head at the bickering on the floor of Congress and muttered, "They're just like a bunch of damn farmers at a ditch hearing."

The impulse to redirect water is primal. Watch kids on a beach with tiny pails and shovels, and you will see ditches and dams and deltas form where once the water had lapped calmly at the shore. Watch long enough and you may see sand fly and hear yelling and crying. A disclaimer here: I was rarely one of those shovel-wielding kids. I was the daydreamer sitting apart, mesmerized by the rhythmic lapping of the waves. I could watch tadpoles dart back and forth in a pond with no lust whatsoever to trap them in a jar and grow frogs on top of my dresser. I knew enough to come in out of a downpour and to crouch in the basement during a tornado because I could never best nature in a fight. So I come to this subject predisposed to let nature alone. Yet when the crop yield and the season's income depend on where the water flows or collects, predispositions get tested.

For as long as human beings have felt the impulse to move water, they have done so. They have dug ditches and underground channels to remove excess rainwater from the land and to keep its surface sanitary. Ancient drainage systems can be found in locations as distant as Ganzhou, China; the Indus Valley; and Machu Picchu. Agricultural drainage that permanently alters landscapes and challenges property claims is of more recent European origin. It dawned on me one day that all of my ancestors came from drained landscapes. The Danes interpret their history through bog mummies and ancient artifacts found in drained peat soil. The Dutch are masters of drainage, having turned a delta subject to the changing whims of the North Sea into a managed system of canals, dikes, and water-pumping windmills. Even my namesake English ancestors saw their lives transformed by Dutch engineering. Natives of England's Norfolk fens, they likely lived on fishing and eeling in earlier times. A massive project begun in the 1630s and developed over two centuries turned this vast area of mudflats, salt marshes, fens, moors, and meres into peatlands interlaced with rivers and drainage canals. My ancestors became agricultural laborers, probably sugar beet pickers. I used to have a recurring nightmare in which I was walking along a causeway as water rose on both sides, threatening to sweep me away. Hard as I tried to rush to the other end, I couldn't make my legs move fast enough, but I always woke up before I lost my footing. Recently I have learned about my great-great-grandmother Harriet Laws Register, who left England for the United States with five children in 1853, after the drained fens were beset by floods. Harriet's address in the village of Southery was "the Causeway." With a family heritage like this, I am bound to find some degree of fascination in the dreary subject of drainage.

Minnesota's drainage laws are as old as statehood. The first allowed individuals who associate for the purpose of digging a ditch to be regarded as a corporate body. The standing water they sought to drain away must be "conveyed to a running stream, lake, river, or other absorbing conduit," yet not "deplete, empty, or overflow" any existing body of water without consent of everyone affected. That same year,

1858, migrants traveling between Austin and Albert Lea with four pair of oxen, two wagons, and a breaking plow reported that they had crossed "over rather a wet and sloughy country—prairie interspersed here and there with [oak] openings—but proceeded without difficulty. . . . This whole country has been condemned as 'sloughy, and good-for-nothing,' but it is excellent grazing country, and our Albert Lea friends, (we consider them such because they make good roads,) are fixing their sloughs to natural meadows, so that travelers for the West have no cause for complaint."

Drainage became a political issue when the Swamp Land Acts, passed by Congress in 1850 and 1860, ceded federally owned "overflowed lands" to the states within which they lay. Minnesota received 4,706,503 acres in 1860, the fifth largest acreage after Florida, Louisiana, Arkansas, and Michigan. That amounted to nearly 274 acres of wetland per Minnesota resident at the time, forty-six acres short of a half section. Most were peatlands scattered across the northern third of the state. The Swamp Land Acts encouraged drainage by specifying that proceeds from the sale of the land finance the levees and drains required to turn it to agricultural use. Nevertheless, Governor Alexander Ramsey asked the legislature to dedicate the proceeds to "great eleemosynary institutions," meaning schools, prisons, insane asylums, roads, and institutions for the care of the blind and deaf. The legislature, however, granted about one-third of the swamplands to railroad companies to help them finance a statewide rail network and spent a small portion of the rest on Governor Ramsey's request. Swamplands already under state jurisdiction were not subject to the rules of the Swamp Lands Act. In 1865, for example, the Southern Minnesota Railroad received four sections to finance every one mile of a railroad to be constructed across the state's southern tier.

Laws governing ditches aimed to settle disputes that arose when the drainage of one person's land affected the lay of another's. Early legislators did not think an offer of compensation was enough to warrant a ditch. The drainage must be "of general utility, or conducive to the public health or welfare" and not simply serve a private purpose. Strict interpreters of the law looked for health benefits, but others saw public welfare in the cumulative "reclamation" of wetlands for agricultural use. A state law passed in 1866 allowed a person who asked to ditch a neighbor's land in order to drain his own to appeal to a justice of the peace if the neighbor refused. In his 1915 legislative history, *Swamp Land Drainage with Special Reference to Minnesota*, Benjamin Whipple Palmer argued that "without such laws less progressive landowners, by refusing to allow their more progressive neighbors to build ditches across their lands, could prevent the reclamation of swamps and marshes, and retard the development of the country." Terminology like Palmer's helped secure a preference for drainage and override objections from those who would leave the wetlands alone. "Reclaim" suggested the land had been created for agricultural use. Left lying "undeveloped" underwater, it was "worthless" and "wasted."

The legislature frequently discussed which level of government should be responsible for decisions about drainage. In 1877, it authorized township supervisors to hold hearings on drainage proposals. Water collected, of course, in naturally formed low spots and didn't respect the township grid, so authority over drainage was passed to county boards in 1879, although water didn't respect county boundaries, either. That year also marks the first proposal to drain a massive watery landscape in Minnesota. It involved federal swamplands that the legislature had given to the St. Paul and Manitoba Railway Company, a predecessor of the Great Northern Railway, on the central stretch of the Red River's wide floodplain. James J. Hill, the railroad's owner, sought this project, which eventually dug fifteen ditches in an area 10 miles by 225 miles.

No large-scale drainage was yet contemplated in Freeborn County. Sentiment in favor of moderate drainage on individual property was growing, however: "The next important branch of improvement after the indispensable breaking of the dry land, will be the ditching of the low, wet land. Probably there is no other one thing that will so materially add to the convenience and value of any particular farm, or to the general prosperity of the whole country, and we are glad to know that parties in this vicinity are fully aware of its importance." Those parties did their own ditching as they saw fit while the areas marked "Southern Minnesota Railway" or "College" on the county plat maps continued to hold water.

A Watershed Year: *1877*

Robert Speer was barely fifty when he retired from blacksmithing. The demands of forge and anvil had no doubt taken their toll on his body, so it seemed time to pass the shop to his sons. George and DeWitt, however, had left home, and their whereabouts still elude the public record. After daughter Jane's wedding on Christmas Eve, only Amanda, seventeen, remained with her parents on the Moscow farm.

The year was 1877, and industrial progress offered other incentives for a blacksmith to close up shop. Iron foundries, where metalwork was done on a larger, more efficient scale, had opened in Albert Lea and Austin. Local implement dealers, termed "happy fellows" in the *Standard*, carried the latest in mowers, reapers, binders, and harvesters. Advertisements disguised as letters to the editor praised the power and durability of McCormick products. The fanciful name Meadowlark Mower sounds like an omen of the havoc the new horse-drawn machinery might wreak on the natural world. Meadowlarks nest in the grass. A farmer with a scythe was a less formidable foe.

It was a tumultuous year for the nation. President Hayes's election was in dispute due to lingering hostilities over Reconstruction. Five years of economic depression had created a new class of homeless poor in large cities. A massive strike shut down railroads in the East and spread west to Chicago and St. Louis. Businesses dependent on the railroads laid off workers. Yet the pages of Freeborn and Mower County newspapers signaled a new prosperity. In addition to farm machinery, their ads offered oil cookstoves, sewing machines, hair dye, cures for intemperance and opium addiction, canned and bottled foods, and the biggest novelty, pianos and organs. A piano merchant in New Jersey peppered the *Standard* with ads and notices touting his honesty. An Albert Lea merchant countered the hype with this modest ad: "LOOK HERE—If you wish to buy a good organ or piano cheaper than any-where this side of New York city, call on A. H. Street. Remember the place, two doors south of post office, up stairs." I like to imagine farm-women's fingers, relieved of hand sewing's tight grip on the needle, dancing over piano or organ keys just for fun.

Freeborn County's leading news of the year shows what turned these frontier farmers into consumers of imported goods: Albert Lea became a railroad hub in 1877. The Southern Minnesota Railroad Company, which had begun running trains through town in 1869, had gradually expanded westward across the state. A new iron railroad bridge across the Mississippi at La Crosse, Wisconsin, linked the SMRR depots in villages such as Alden and Oakland with Milwaukee and Chicago. Short trips between those depots had been a mainstay of the railroad's business. In February 1877, the SMRR advertised tickets at sixty percent of cost for regional passengers traveling to Austin for the Reverend Henry Ward Beecher's speech on "The Ministry of Wealth." Since Beecher was famously unsympathetic to striking railroad workers, a railroad company could benefit from bringing listeners to his nation-wide speaking tour.

The local newspapers rarely covered the strikes in the East but con-tinued to report optimistically on the approach of tracks from all direc-tions. The Burlington, Cedar Rapids and Northern Railway reached Albert Lea in September. It fed into the Illinois Central, opening travel all the way to New Orleans. The Minneapolis and St. Louis link was completed in November. It was now possible to have oysters shipped in all the way from Maryland or to travel there and eat them on Chesa-peake Bay. The former, of course, was more affordable, and hosting an oyster supper became a popular trend in rural hospitality.

The Speers had never lost touch with their extended family even when they depended on ox-drawn wagons, and better roads and the faster speed of horses eased those connections. Marietta kept a close enough relationship with her age-mate aunt Harriet, Robert's youngest sister, that they married brothers and settled in Janesville, Wisconsin. Railroad travel increased the frequency of family visits. As the century wore on, Moscow's correspondents routinely included train trips in the township news. Speer relatives had settled along the border of Fillmore County, Minnesota, and Howard County, Iowa. I imagine it was on a visit to these folks that Amanda found a beau. I picture her at a dance in the Chester town hall, standing along the wall with cousins, shy but hopeful. A young man, dark-haired like Amanda, shorter than she might like but with a muscular build, tosses flirtatious glances her way before daring to approach her. I'm guessing his eyes caught her attention—large and knowing under thick, manly eyebrows. Eyes like his look out from generations of family photos.

Amanda Speer married John Register on May 29, 1879. His arrival introduced an irascibility into our family history that his grandchildren recalled as rigid expectations, father-son fistfights, and speechless grudges. Nevertheless, Robert and Mary saw fit to deed most of their land to Amanda in 1881 on Robert's retirement from active farming. John became the farmer and head of household, but Amanda's name appears in the county plat books.

Maybe it wasn't an Iowa dance. Maybe John Register simply turned up in Moscow, one of many men going door to door in search of work. Maybe the Speers or their neighbors hired him, and Amanda admired the tanned muscles his rolled sleeves revealed when she carried water out to the fields. Labor disputes and unemployment in the East may not have reached the Upper Midwest, but they did have a spillover effect: An article in the *Standard* on July 26, 1877, announced the arrival on the Mississippi of a steamboat carrying six hundred harvest hands. It warned that this crowd, augmented by railroad strikers looking for work, would soon swarm across the landscape: "With this army of laborers, will come a horde of thieves and plunders [*sic*], and our people may as well be prepared for them. It isn't necessary to distrust and abuse every dusty and travel-stained stranger who applies for work, but it is a matter of prudence to keep a sharp look-out for them, remove the valuables to a

John and Amanda Speer Register

place of safety, never leave your premises without having a suitable person in charge."

A new boogeyman had entered the popular imagination, a new stock character in our vision of rural America: the "tramp." That is the word news reports used to divide strangers into two types: the ambitious, morally upright workingman Henry Beecher favored, willing to labor for a pittance; and the lazy, work-shirking tramp, "the terror of women and children, a roaming vagabond, ready to commit any crime if time and opportunity serve his purpose." The pioneer farmer's boogeyman had been the greedy land speculator, but the speculators who stayed in town had become leading citizens. Someone else would have to serve as scapegoat for the fears wrought by economic uncertainty and a pace of change so rapid it could turn a village blacksmith into a relic of the past. The tramp suited the purpose and engendered more warnings, more sightings, and even the formation in Freeborn County of an armed Independent Guard: "And who can say from the experience of the past few days, how soon some emergency may arise where the gleam of the bayonet may not be needed to protect the lives and property of our citizens from some lawless mob."

While tramps swarmed in from the east, some furtively hopping those brand-new railroad cars, another threat approached from the west, borne on wind and wing. Ideas for repelling or killing grasshoppers claimed space in the local newspapers after drought and locusts ravaged southwestern Minnesota. Decades later, Elbert Ostrander recalled "the trains of emaciated horses, drawing wagons loaded with families, traveling eastward along the roads—the same settlers who had gone out into the 'golden west' through the preceding years, filled with anticipation of the joys of a home for themselves." As the drought advanced into Freeborn County, the grasshoppers followed. The Manchester Grange passed a resolution blaming the plague on "the wanton destruction of prairie chickens," the locust's natural predator, by "certain sportsmen." Elbert Ostrander blamed both excessive hunting and the tilling of the soil that destroyed bird habitat. "With our native insect-destroying bird-life practically extinct, no more we hear the booming call of the Prairie Chicken in the early morning of the springtime, the countless numbers of the Upland Plover with its shrill and not unmusical cry ending in a long whistle, no more echoes from the hilltops and over the valleys, we are left alone with our feeble devices for our own protection." Despite the dire warnings, Freeborn County did not suffer serious damage from grasshoppers. Its western prairie townships were somewhat affected, but the newspapers reported little damage on the savanna.

The 1911 *History of Freeborn County* identifies 1877 as the year that corn and dairy began replacing wheat as the county's primary agricultural products. You would not know it from skimming the newspapers. W. W. Cargill was building grain elevators alongside railroad tracks, the first in Albert Lea in 1869, the year the trains began running. His Oakland elevator and flat house stood three miles down the road from the Speer farm, an easy jaunt for a horse-drawn wagon compared with the long overland slogs to McGregor or Winona that the county's wheat farmers had made in the early years. Cargill himself had recently moved his residence and business headquarters from Albert Lea to La Crosse, where he could coordinate shipping by both river and rail. The grain business was booming, and his was going big time.

Wheat buyers from the emerging "Mill City" of Minneapolis kept watch on southern Minnesota's harvest. Even before the M&StL railroad had reached Albert Lea, "Messrs. E. B. Andrews and Wm. H. Dunwoody, representing the Minneapolis Millers' Association," traveled as far as they could get, maybe ten miles short of their destination, and then presumably hired livery to go the rest of the way. They stopped at the *Standard* office to ask for statistics on local wheat production. The editor supplied them with figures showing a steady increase in the county's output, from 139,373 bushels in 1872 to 475,220 in 1876. The acreage devoted to wheat had risen four percent in 1877 despite locusts and drought.

Exactly 527½ of the bushels produced in 1877 grew on the Henry N. Ostrander farm in Bancroft on thirteen acres of land. "Not only is the yield enormous," the *Standard* wrote, "but it was probably the cleanest lot of wheat received here this season. . . . Mr. Ostrander never brings anything but clean, plump wheat that weighs 60 pounds to the bushel." The article gushed with admiration: "When a farmer desires to improve his stock, he selects only the best animals to breed from; the culls and titmans go to the butcher; only the largest, well-filled ears of corn are saved for seed. If an extra nice watermelon is cut, the first thought of the careful gardener is to preserve the seeds for the next season's planting. Mr. Ostrander has applied the same principle to the culture of wheat, and for the last four years has been sowing none but the largest and most perfect kernels." Perfection was accomplished by the use of a sieve that Ostrander himself invented. A later account of displays at the county fair boasted that Mr. Ostrander's sieve process "could not be excelled in any clime." It was not excelled in the county, anyway: it won the award for "best wheat seive [sic]" at the fair.

The big changes marked in 1877 also bear on the eventual transformation of the landscape. Now that the Southern Minnesota Railroad had completed its route, the company would want to turn its swamplands into cash. Even without drainage, a wet meadow at the outer reaches of a marsh became suitable pasture by late spring. The availability of pasture and railroad shipping opened new prospects for raising cattle. A brief item in the *Albert Lea Enterprise* of May 10, 1877, stirs the imagination. A local man drove a herd of 220 cattle to Plymouth Center, Iowa, the closest junction with the freight route to the Chicago stockyards, where Philip Armour and Gustavus Swift operated industrial meatpacking plants. After the turn of the century, Albert Lea and Austin would become destinations for slaughter-bound cattle, and the railroads would distribute meat processed locally across the country.

Yet another novelty made livestock farming more feasible. Although others claimed to have invented it, Joseph Glidden of DeKalb, Illinois, had received a patent for barbed wire in 1874. With less effective restraints available, cattle in Freeborn County had roamed freely across property lines. A countywide referendum, conducted by township, addressed the control of cattle and another controversial issue, "license," meaning the sale of liquor. The Moscow town meeting voted, "Cattle to run at large, and no whiskey."

Conditions were ripe for a new development that would call for large-scale drainage. The name it goes by now is "agribusiness." While the much-maligned land speculators of the 1850s and 1860s bought land cheap and sold it dear, these new entrepreneurs held on to the land and profited from a distance. A feature article about Casselton Place, a 20,240-acre wheat farm in North Dakota, won first-page placement in the March 22 *Albert Lea Enterprise*. Its owners lived in New York City, Boston, and St. Paul. Freeborn County was settled enough to hinder an operation that huge, but the railroad swamplands stood ready.

One 1877 invention awakens thoughts of the fantastic. Thomas Edison applied for a patent for the "phonograph," a tinfoil device that recorded and reproduced sound. It would be decades before the Victrola, a competitor's model, claimed its place in the farmhouse parlor. If only Edison had taken his device out into Freeborn County's landscape, think what we might listen for:

> The tinkling of those new pianos and the moaning of those new parlor organs.
> The song of the alert meadowlark, wise to approaching mowing machines.
> The shrieks that went up from the Speer farm when three horses were found dead, possibly poisoned, within a few summer weeks.
> The shush of wheat seeds in Henry Ostrander's sieve.
> The clang and whistle of the first train engine to pull into a new depot.
> The knock of the tramp or the eager worker at the farmhouse door.
> The mooing of cattle coming home from a ramble, innocent of whiskey.
> The Big Marsh itself, bubbling, croaking, lapping, quacking, whistling, rustling, still living, still breathing.

A New Home on the Prairie:
A Speculation

The northern lights were visible in the heavens early in the evening Saturday, and to those who witnessed their lurid beauty they presented a sight never to be forgotten.

—*Freeborn County Standard*, July 20, 1892

Streaks of green and gold and violet light pulsed across the prairie sky as Elbert and Bertha Ostrander sat side by side on the stoop of their farmhouse. Daughter Grace, not yet four, lay stretched across their laps, fighting sleep as she took in the "celestial wonder" her dad had insisted she see. When her eyelids stopped fluttering, Elbert hoisted himself up and carried her to bed. Bertha pushed past them to answer the sudden cry of baby Floyd. Lyle, the middle child, slept on. How lucky they were, Elbert thought as he headed back outside, that Bertha's babies came easily and proved healthy. She had worried that she might inherit her mother's difficulty. Over a span of thirty years, Mary Hord had borne only three living children: Bertha, a son ten years younger, and a daughter barely Grace's age. Any child would be a gift of joy in the Ostrander family, the young parents concurred.

Outside, bedding down the horses, latching the chicken coop door, tucking in his farmyard for the night, Elbert continued to gaze at the splendor in the sky. It stirred contemplation about how he had come to be a farmer and father out on the prairie under this huge dome. Although brother Cornelius had settled in Alden years before, having married a local girl, Elbert had never intended to follow him or to try to replicate his success. Corneal had made a name for himself as a crafts-man and merchant with two adjacent shops on Alden's main street. In one he built wagons and water tanks; in the other he sold watches and jewelry. As if that weren't enough, he had cleared the sod out of Gem Lake and, as Alden's fire captain, saved the burning hotel from inflaming the whole village—all this despite rheumatism and with a melodic whistle as accompaniment.

Elbert was closer to sisters Eva and Armetta, who noticed his inkling for literature and history and urged him to follow them into teaching. He graduated high school in Albert Lea, then studied for and took the teachers' examination. The District 40 schoolhouse south of Alden was more than a dozen miles from Bancroft. The ride took him through prairie grasses that reached his horse's shoulders. It called back the sensation of running through the wheat field at age four to the schoolhouse where his sisters were. After an initial scolding, the teacher let him stay and listen to the lessons. His destiny had been set then.

Elbert's first winter in Alden proved that the "Storm King" was more violent on the prairie. Armetta wrote him worried letters about the bitter winds on the treeless sweeps and reminded him to bundle up and stay warm. But it was Mettie herself who succumbed, at only twenty-three, just two years after they lost Eva to consumption. He couldn't

The District 40 schoolhouse, south of Alden

imagine a sorrow as deep as the deaths of his smart and lively sisters. His new environs took some getting used to. He missed the oak groves of home and was grateful to the early settler who had planted a row of cottonwoods along the section line between his school and the village of Alden. Those trees were his landmark and his shield from the wind as he rode to and from town. He was glad to have learned some Norwegian from his Bancroft playmates, but he had to tune his ears carefully to catch what the Alden Danes were saying. Written out, the languages looked alike, but, the Norwegians claimed, the Danes talked as if their mouths were full of potatoes.

Teaching suited Elbert, and he might have kept it up if it had paid well enough to support a family. That necessity had dawned upon him when a petite brunette of sixteen with a quick but gentle wit turned up during winter term to round out her education. Bertha Hord lived two miles south of the schoolhouse, and after school let out for the year, Elbert found himself rushing up and down those rolling swells. They were married on March 25, 1886, he having given his promise to keep her close to home. Living near the Hords was no hardship. He enjoyed being with them and soon learned that he and Dan, his father-in-law, saw eye to eye on many topics. Dan and Mary had come to Minnesota as youngsters in the years before Elbert's parents arrived. Their families had been neighbors in Illinois. Dan's dad was a Virginian, and Mary's mother was English. Elbert took delight in the peculiar habits of speech that resulted from those origins. They said "s'rink" instead of "shrink," and the alcove where they tucked away seldom-used things was the "clowzet."

So that was how Elbert came to buy eighty acres of land between the school and the Hord farm. Not all of it was arable. He had chosen it in part for the slough that stretched into it from Steward Creek, assuring him of the beloved sounds of marsh wildlife. Of course, that otherwise useless land made the price affordable. He had found a lake nearby that could stand in for his childhood paradise. Like Geneva, Bear Lake was bordered by woods and brush along one side and ran out into marsh and wet meadow on another. It teemed with wildlife as well. But

Elbert and Bertha Hord Ostrander

now both lakes seemed to be threatened by talk of drainage. Just thinking of the rumors he had heard about possible changes in the lay of the land snapped him out of his reverie. He was glad for the reminder of nature's power and beauty that the northern lights had brought. Maybe others would heed them, too. It was easy for some to forget that man was not the ruler of everything but the humble steward of Creation.

And now he would have to go inside and get some sleep in order to tend his bit of earth in the morning. He had no plans to go to church. Elbert had grown up with the Sunday ritual of United Brethren services in his family home, where a few neighbors gathered. During high school, he had followed Mettie to the Presbyterian church in Albert Lea. Yet the pulsing in the sky that beckoned him to stay out a while longer brought him closer to the divine than he felt in Sunday services. He just might be more pantheist than Protestant.

Elbert knew he would never be a serious wheat farmer like his father or even match his success at wheat in corn or dairy. He lacked his dad's persistence. It had been hard to get Henry and Sarah to admit to old age and surrender the homeplace in Bancroft. They had sold it just a month before and moved onto nine acres on the east side of Alden, within easy reach of Corneal and Jennie. To the last minute, Henry had kept up the farm, plowed the county poor farm nearby as he did every year, and presided over the township board. Elbert had planted a portion of his own land in apple orchard and berry patches, and he was looking into horse breeding. His dad's other passions—public service and poetry—spoke to him, however. He had gotten himself elected Alden township clerk, and he wrote down lines and rhymes when he found the time. But something in him would always resist too much scarring of the land.

Elbert took one last, sweeping look across the glowing sky to impress it upon his memory. Someday he might even find words for it. With the solace of his own little slough and the call of the geese on Bear Lake, he would make Alden Township his home. Like his favorite tree on the east shore of Geneva Lake, he was supple enough to bend down and root himself anew on the prairie, but he would never pull up his first roots in the marshes and moraines.

Fire on the Marsh

The wind on Friday blew almost a gale. . . . The clouds of ashes
raised from the burned Moscow marsh resembled a sand storm on
the great Sahara.

— *Freeborn County Standard*, May 22, 1890

The world we humans occupy was born of fire and ice according to
Old Norse mythology, the ancestral worldview of many who first
farmed the land around the Big Marsh. Certainly, ice and fire shaped
Freeborn County. Glaciers carved and mounded its rolling landscape,
and fire held the line between hardwood forest and open prairie. Fire
is both danger and boon to a transitional savanna. Its primary tree, the
bur oak, is evidence of a fiery history. *Quercus macrocarpa*, the north-
ernmost oak on the continent, is known as the "frontier oak" or the
"pioneer oak" because it stands alone or in small groves or "openings"
on the edge of the prairie, as if marching ahead of an advancing forest.
Its deep taproot probes for water in drought seasons, its wide canopy
keeps it stable in heavy winds, and its corky bark resists fire. The bur
oak depends on fire to thrive. Without fire, other species of tree and
brush crowd it, threaten its longevity, and prevent its acorn offspring
from taking root. Prairie, too, needs fire to renew its grasses and forbs
and keep them free of woody invaders.

Before European settlement, Native hunters used fire to manage their
environment, especially to keep grazing land open to large animals such
as bison and elk, whose meat they ate and whose hides provided shelter and clothing. With a new, alien population on the landscape and the
Indians exiled, deliberate, large-scale burning stopped and the conditions for accidental fire worsened. Haying on the marsh left bundles
of dead, dry grass lying out in the open. Cutting the grasses, grazing

livestock, and draining standing water off the land exposed peat soil to the air, making it more combustible.

News of the fire that burned in the marsh for more than a month in the fall of 1889 began with this quiet notice from Geneva: "The marsh, nobody wants to tell how, got on fire near Ole Everson's ten days ago, and there has been quite a number of people ditching around it in order to stop the fire. It burned several feet into the ground." A drought that year increased the likelihood of fire. The same correspondent noted two weeks later: "Rice lake is so dry you can drive across it." County surveyors came by at the start of October to measure the damage. They found 5,500 acres of land—worth $100,000—burned over and 6,000 tons of hay destroyed at a loss of $30,000. "There is no means of saving the hay," the *Standard* reported, "as the fire is in the peat, under the surface, and it is unsafe to drive a team near it. . . . Such a calamity was never before known in the county."

The calamity wasn't over. The peat continued to smolder to a depth of nine feet. Only a flood of rain could put the fire out, and the water would have to soak all that way into the ground. The fire had spread through Riceland and Moscow townships as well. Charles G. Johnsrud, the district's representative in the state legislature, observed the damage in mid-October and estimated the "despoiled land" at eight miles long and two and a half miles wide. No one lived on the burned land, but it had been stacked with "immense quantities of hay." The outlook was dire: "The soil, which was entirely a vegetable formation, is consumed, leaving a bed of clay and in some places sand and gravel, which is now covered with ashes. Throughout the tract are unburned bogs or hummocks, which present a singular appearance. In a season of usual rainfall, the land will again be covered with water, and will constitute a shallow lake, and as drainage is impossible, it will remain a lake perhaps for hundreds of years to come." Usual rainfall, however, would regenerate the marsh in far less time.

Where some saw calamity, others found opportunity. The fire had demonstrated peat's capacity to smolder and shed heat. By the following April, the *Standard* reported, "Andrew Christian, living on section three, Riceland, obtains from his land all the peat he needs for fuel, amounting in blocks to several cords, and besides sells considerable every year. It is very superior in quality, making an intense fire and leaving very few ashes. The cost of digging it is slight, and it is soon cured or dried by piling it like brick. The beds of peat which were burned in the Riceland marshes last year would have supplied the entire county with first class fuel for twenty years."

Reading of the fires that broke out nearly every year through the nineties and into the new century makes me wonder if it was in part fire and its threat to the monetary value of the land that prompted the railroads to sell it off when they did. A description in 1895 of "one of the most terrific and disastrous fires that ever visited the county" makes a sobering case: "The earth was parched and everything on its surface was like tinder, and the fire sped furiously and almost as swiftly as a race horse. Its course was a distance of about five miles and much of the hay, fences and groves were consumed. Probably one hundred cords of wood was burned in the timber along the lake, and much more damage would have been done in the timber if men had not all day fought the fire." The land's new owners saw for themselves the destructive force of fire. This one started near their farmstead, Ricelawn Ranch, on the eastern shore of Rice Lake. It likely bolstered their determination to drain the land, rid it of its wild vegetation, and bring it under the control of farm machinery.

PART III

The Big Ditch

The Alleged Conniver:
Putnam Dana McMillan

Six thousand acres of the "big marsh" in Moscow and vicinity were sold by Greene & Kellar Monday to McMillan & Co., a real estate firm of Minneapolis, who will ditch and improve and put it into the market through the firm named for farming purposes. It will be a great benefit to that part of the county.

—*Freeborn County Standard*, January 14, 1891

P. D. McMillan looked out over the railroad land he had purchased in midwinter and saw that it was "worthless." It lay flat and isolated, inaccessible by any decent roads. The bulk of it was a watery waste in normal seasons, and the recent drought had not improved it. Two thousand of his six thousand acres lay covered in ashes from fires the previous year, and the land's surface had sunk about two feet from the fire's spread through the peat soil. The burned area had sprouted thousands of poplar seedlings. "These seemed to bother us," McMillan recalled twenty-five years later, and so he had the seedlings mowed down. "This was labor lost for the land soon came into bluejoint," a native grass he saw fit to burn away. Nature's gradual restorative process would not suit his plans for the portion of the Big Marsh he now owned. One feature redeemed the view a little: a hummock, known to locals as Hickory Island, covered with about two hundred acres of hickory, oak, linden, and elm. Here, where a squatter had abandoned a small dwelling, McMillan saw the way clear: build on this oasis, then drain the flat land all around.

For a real estate developer, the attraction of land considered worthless was the challenge of making it arable, turning it to agricultural production, and earning some profit on it. McMillan had sought such land after a visit to Holland showed him what the Dutch had done with land claimed from the sea. Land as rich must lie under Minnesota's swamps, he thought, and reclaiming it should prove far easier than the enormous effort the Dutch had undertaken. Nevertheless, his endeavor to drain the Big Marsh would be fraught with both physical and legal obstacles. In the brief history of the drainage he penned at eighty-two, three years before his death, he portrayed himself as persistent and undaunted, even in the face of local opposition. He described his project as "a long, hard and expensive fight" warranted "by the example it has shown others."

Putnam Dana McMillan was no novice at daunting projects. He had embarked on grand missions and suffered immense losses well before moving west to Minneapolis. Born in Maine in 1832 to a venerable New England family, the kind that passes down its surnames as given names, he grew up in Danville, Vermont, where his lineage of judges and military officers assured him a good reputation but not a life of wealth and leisure. He left school at sixteen to clerk in his uncle's store and at twenty succumbed to Gold Rush fever. After a 141-day journey around Cape Horn and a five-year effort at mining and merchandising in California, he barely broke even and returned to Danville to farm, marry, and start a family. The Civil War took McMillan away again. As a first lieutenant and quartermaster, he guarded railroads and warehouses and fought at Gettysburg. Shortly after his safe return, a new adventure called. He moved his wife and young daughter to Argentina, where he had leased a large plot of land and bought two thousand sheep. A cholera epidemic, which took his wife, and the encroaching violence of the Paraguayan War quashed his dream of a sheep ranch. He returned to Danville landless and with little cash, the widowed father of a seven-year-old girl.

McMillan fared better on his move to Minneapolis in 1872 thanks to the growth of the milling industry along the Mississippi. He opened a realty and loan office across the river in old St. Anthony and began promoting the development of Northeast and Southeast Minneapolis. He oversaw the construction of commercial buildings and the platting and building of neighborhoods. He partnered with his second wife's brother-in-law, Albert W. Hastings, treasurer of the city of Minneapolis, who shared in the purchase of the Freeborn County swampland. This land was McMillan's first rural acquisition since the tragic end of his Argentina sheep farm. He showed no intention this time of becoming the resident patron of his new ranch but hired a Swedish immigrant, Charles Lunquist, to manage it while he continued his realty business in Minneapolis.

The McMillans had a substantial house built at 505 Tenth Avenue Southeast among distinguished neighbors: grain miller and Minnesota governor John S. Pillsbury across the street, University of Minnesota president Cyrus Northrop next door, and the university's first president, the historian William Watts Folwell, around the corner. From two to four live-in servants staffed the household, which included a second daughter, Margaret, and a son, Putnam Dana, Jr. Reports of social events at the McMillan home, with wife Kate or his eldest daughter, the artist Emily Dana McMillan, as hostess, became a mainstay of the *Minneapolis Tribune* society page. Emily both bolstered and benefited from her family's social status. She was a portrait painter, and her likenesses of faculty and administrators graced the halls of the university. Wealthy Minneapolitans hired her to preserve their visages in oil. Of course she painted her father, who cut a patrician figure at nearly six feet two with "a soldierly carriage," a Roman nose, white muttonchops, and "a natural courtliness of manners."

By the 1890s, P. D. McMillan, in his sixties, had become a noted public citizen. He presided over the Minneapolis Real Estate Board, served as a trustee of First Congregational Church, helped found the local Vermont Association, donated and raised funds for the University of Minnesota, and served on city boards and commissions. He had even been elected to the Minnesota Academy of Natural Sciences, perhaps for his support of innovations achieved at the university. Kate McMillan served as "patroness" of various civic efforts. The family mingled with the city's elite in the Minneapolis Society of Fine Arts and summered among them as renters at Maplewood Cottage on Lake Minnetonka.

Portrait of P. D. McMillan painted by his daughter Emily, about 1915

Nevertheless, McMillan continued to be spurred on by loss. Adversity became a motif in his life story, as this 1897 profile illustrates: "It requires a courageous heart and the possession of lots of pluck and determination to overcome many hard knocks in life's struggle, especially if accompanied by affliction. Putnam Dana McMillan has had more than his share of misfortune, but he is the offspring of men who shed their blood in the country's cause, and he inherited their sterling qualities." His friend Folwell pursued the theme of failure and recovery in the eulogy he delivered before the Military Order of the Loyal Legion after McMillan's death in 1918: "Twenty years of active insurance and real estate business built up an ample if not an extravagant fortune, which in the disastrous year of 1893, went to liquidate obligations incurred in the boom period of this city. The comfortable home and some assets of uncertain value were not sacrificed. Among these assets were ten sections of swamp land in the northeastern part of Freeborn county." It fell to these lands of uncertain value to restore McMillan's finances and his sense of achievement.

The First Drainage

When McMillan and Hastings set out to drain the land adjacent to their wooded farmstead in summer 1893, their plan aroused little curiosity, let alone consternation. They hadn't suggested draining the whole marsh or disturbing Rice and Geneva lakes. The *Albert Lea Enterprise* characterized their undertaking as a repair project to prevent flooding: "Work has now been done that will probably result in drawing the water off more rapidly than it has before run off, the Turtle Creek having been obstructed with grass and weeds, which will be removed." McMillan and Hastings weren't the first outsiders to buy swampland in Freeborn County to convert to agricultural use. Two years earlier, George Van Norman, a cattle dealer from Milwaukee, had bought the southern tier of Geneva Township from Russell Sage, the trustee for several swamp-owning railroads. Some of Van Norman's land dried enough in the summer to serve as meadow, and he, like the local farmer to his north, Luke D. Holmes, invited others to graze livestock for a seasonal fee. Van Norman's manager, Charles Wilkinson, a respected civil servant in Albert Lea, helped build goodwill.

Drainage was becoming a familiar practice in the county; a number of farmers had dug ditches to keep pesky low spots in their fields from sprouting reedy vegetation. Albert Lea wagonmakers G. A. Hauge and C. Christopherson did a fair business in ditching plows, which they had added to their inventory more than ten years earlier. Their best-selling ditchers, invented by local manufacturer C. D. Edwards, cut a simple ditch 2½ feet wide and 3½ feet deep. When area residents heard the word "ditch," they probably envisioned a narrow groove in the land that allowed excess water to flow away.

Hauge and Christopherson occupied a large brick building on Washington Street near Spring Lake, "a watershed of about 66 acres with no natural outlet" that had become a focus of drainage efforts. Local residents had been using the shallow lake just west of the business district as a garbage dump. City fathers invited Dr. C. N. Hewitt, the secretary of the state board of health, to come and address "the possibility of an epidemic of cholera" and "filthy vaults and cesspools that now endanger our drinking water and disgrace our city." Despite the frightening language, it took years of debate and trial and error to settle questions of ownership, financing, and where to route the flow of water. While the purpose of this drainage was different from agricultural ditching, the case of Spring Lake fueled the idea of a wetland as a nuisance and a breeding place of pestilence.

The drainage of Spring Lake and the McMillan and Hastings project were not isolated events. The prime mover behind the former had been the owner of the land on which the lake sat––before he deeded it to the city. William A. Morin, Freeborn County's most prominent homegrown real estate developer, enjoyed a cordial business relationship with McMillan and Hastings. Morin was banking on the future of agricultural drainage. In 1893, he was preparing to open the Morin Brick and Tile Works, a manufacturing plant for clay drainage tile that employed twenty-five workers by summer 1895. These tiles—hollow cylinders—were laid end to end in three- to six-foot trenches and spaced at narrow intervals, allowing excess water to seep between them into the hollow space. Then they were covered over again with soil. The *Freeborn County Standard* extolled the size, complexity, and likely benefits of the factory, promising that local farmers "will now be able to secure at moderate cost a quality of farm drain tile that is not surpassed by any manufactured." Tiling was still new in Minnesota, and I have found no evidence that McMillan and Hastings tiled their land in the 1890s. They did, however, share dredging advice with Morin and perhaps even a dredging contractor.

Laying tile in a Minnesota drainage ditch, 1910

While the condition of Spring Lake stirred public debate in the city, the project on the Big Marsh drew minimal attention from rural residents, even as McMillan and Hastings continued to buy up land. The citizens of Moscow, including the Registers, were busy forming a cooperative creamery. Temperance claimed the attention of many of the Scandinavians in Riceland Township. Dubious sightings of monster-sized snakes in Geneva Lake kept nearby residents anxious or entertained. Prospects for livestock farming had improved with the recent expansion of the Brundin brothers' Albert Lea meat market into a packinghouse and the opening of George A. Hormel's slaughter operation in Austin. McMillan and Hastings had seen the trend and filled their meadows with three hundred head of cattle. They owned about fifty dairy cows, whose milk was processed at the new Moscow creamery.

The steam dredge that went to work at the source of Turtle Creek in the late summer of 1893 was not as sophisticated a machine as the name might suggest. It was jerry-rigged out of a hand-built, steam-powered boat and an extra-large, special-order Edwards ditch plow. Its V-shaped blade barely widened and lowered the creek bed while clearing out silt and debris. The contraption inspired little fascination among reporters and readers of the local newspapers. The Moscow correspondent to the *Standard* commented, probably tongue in cheek, "We expect to see [boats] sailing down our river in a few days." Farmers along Turtle Creek may have welcomed removal of the silt and vegetation that slowed its flow after nearly forty years of cultivation along its banks. A little cleaning might even restore their river to its natural state.

Much more verbiage was spent on McMillan and Hastings's appeal for a road to be built from the ranch to Albert Lea and another to connect the ranch with the village of Geneva. Under present conditions, they had to route their products eastward through Moscow, then south and back westward to Albert Lea—an extra nine miles by their calculations—unless they were to sell them just over the county line in Austin, a prospect they hoped would light a fire of competitive zeal under the Freeborn County Board of Commissioners. Albert Lea was the more active railroad shipping hub and a preferable location for long-distance road transportation as well. The board rejected their request more than once. Editorial support in the *Standard* and a petition on which C. W. Lunquist had gathered one hundred signatures proved unpersuasive. "Some members of the board stated that it would cost a good many thousands of dollars in damages and the construction work to establish the proposed road, and the sentiment was not favorable to the undertaking," the *Standard* reported.

By February 1894, McMillan and Hastings wrote for help to William A. Morin, who chaired the committee on roads of the Albert Lea Commercial Club, a predecessor of the Chamber of Commerce. They reiterated the need for a "road which will be an absolute necessity for the future development of the large tract of land which always has been of no value, and worse than that an eye sore to Freeborn County." After several weeks of negotiating and strategizing, Morin agreed to accompany them to the county offices to assist with their "road deal." "When you are here we can talk over the present and future value of this land," he added. The correspondence doesn't specify what "this land" is or who might be offering it to whom, in exchange for what.

In spite of Morin's assistance, the road deal remained unresolved. In an open letter to readers of the *Standard* the following September, McMillan and Hastings wrote, "It is an injustice to the county, whose policy could be to encourage improvements instead of blocking them, an injustice to the owners of the land in not giving them an outlet, an injustice to hundreds of farmers who pay taxes and are entitled to a nearer outlet, and injustice to Albert Lea by forcing people to an adjoining county to trade." The only consistent "yea" vote on the county board had been that of the city of Albert Lea's commissioner, Axel Brundin, proprietor of the packinghouse, to whom trade with an adjoining county meant trade with George A. Hormel. In October 1895, the board finally ordered the construction of a south–north road halfway up the boundary line between Riceland and Moscow townships to connect the ranch with the nearest east–west route. McMillan and Hastings had reduced their request.

The texts of the McMillan and Hastings letters, both published and private, reveal an animosity between the Minneapolis investors and the elected protectors of local interest. Hastings kept a low profile, ceding most of the effort to McMillan, who was no diplomat. He comes across as stubborn and disagreeable, speaking about the value of his proposals with moral certitude. He found resonance with his views in Minneapolis from businesspeople and among academics engaged in agricultural experimentation. But he shared little common vocabulary with ordinary southern Minnesota farmers content to live within the means provided them by a quarter section of land. Morin tried to mediate but ultimately advised McMillan, "It is very difficult here as elsewhere to get legislation favorable to Non-Residents, owing to the foolish prejudice existing among the farming population." McMillan did little to counter that prejudice. While the newspapers reported occasional McMillan sightings, neighborly exchanges were rare.

Meanwhile, flax and timothy grew in flat fields that had long been home to marsh reeds. The dredging of Turtle Creek, plus twenty-five miles of ditching across the property, had turned more than three thousand acres of the Big Marsh into Ricelawn Ranch, an agricultural showcase. McMillan and Hastings had not betrayed any intention to drain Rice Lake, but they did raise the prospect with Morin: "Enclosed we send you a clipping regarding meandered lakes and the thought suggests itself that it would be a good speculation to buy up a little of the land surrounding Rice Lake, or buy a quit claim of the lake from the owners who hold riparian rights, and then lower the creek and drain it. We own quite a frontage, and would like to have you purchase the balance and cooperate with us. From work in the creek this year we are positive the scheme is feasable." The newspaper article enclosed bears the heading GREAT DIRT FOR ONIONS/LAND UNDER SLOUGH LAKES.

Morin copied his response in brown ink onto a translucent onion-skin page of his letterpress book. Sadly, the book is so water damaged that the copy is illegible. Only a "Sept." before a blurred date and the term "riparian rights" standing out like high ground in a flooded land-scape identify this ruined page as his reply. Whatever Morin thought of the idea, he did not "purchase the balance" of the Rice Lake front-age, or maybe its owners refused to sell. One of them soon allied him-self with McMillan and remained a stalwart supporter of his drainage projects. Danish immigrant Christian Ulerik Christensen would see his farm on the north shore of Rice Lake expand as the lake shrank. A Seventh-Day Adventist and thus a vegetarian, he coveted that moist, rich soil for growing produce. C. U. Christensen would be the first to test the drained marshland's value for vegetable farming.

The Middle Man:
William A. Morin

W. A. Morin drives the finest team in Albert Lea. They are matched closely, 16 hands high, and can trot in four minutes to the carriage. He also has Andy P., a chestnut colt, one-year-old, by Almont Messenger. This is a toppy, good-sized colt, and the best feeling fellow you ever saw, and when his colored driver, Mr. Ratliff, gets on the cart behind him he thinks he is the best horse in the world.

—*Freeborn County Standard*, February 3, 1892

A pair of Minneapolis realtors could certainly pore through notices of railroad swampland available around the state and settle on a purchase. To be prudent, they might ask contacts in rural Minnesota to recommend choice properties. P. D. McMillan and A. W. Hastings could have found no better counsel in Freeborn County than William A. Morin, a second-generation land speculator and the area's most prominent and successful entrepreneur.

It is nearly impossible to travel across Freeborn County without setting foot on former Morin land. Morin's father, William Morin, an Irish immigrant who came to Minnesota Territory in 1856, owned more land in the county than anyone else upon his death in 1887. He had been coproprietor since the 1870s of the county's first large-scale farm, the sixteen-hundred-acre Morin and Mason Ranch west of Alden. The Morins owned land adjoining the neighborhood where I grew up and under the schools and the church I attended—indeed, they were said to own half the city of Albert Lea. My schoolmates and I played in Morin Park in the former bed of Spring Lake. The Morins owned the village of Alden and its surrounding countryside where my parents came of age. They also financed others' purchases of property. Reading through the extensive collection of Morin family papers at the

William A. Morin, Clark Street at Adams Avenue, Albert Lea, 1908.
He stands in front of a swinging platform on the lawn of his home.

Minnesota Historical Society, one gets the impression that the typical county farm or home was at some time mortgaged to or rented from the Morins.

William A. Morin also held mortgages on properties in Southeast Minneapolis, where McMillan's business flourished. Among his mortgagees was Maria Sanford, one of the first female professors in the United States, who had been recruited to the University of Minnesota by William Watts Folwell, McMillan's friend. In letter after letter, Sanford appealed to Morin in near desperation to allow her more time to pay on her lien-encumbered houses in Southeast Minneapolis and her farm in Steele County. In a few letters, hints of a social acquaintance come through. Even without social intermediaries, business dealings in the Southeast neighborhood could well have brought McMillan and Morin together.

McMillan and Hastings depended on Morin for political support of their drainage and road projects. He lobbied local officials and organizations on their behalf, spoke at hearings, signed petitions, and strategized with lawyers. He joined their efforts in the most practical way he knew how, buying swampland in the affected area. He served for years as McMillan's sounding board, for new ideas about crops to cultivate and for his ongoing frustrations. My efforts to locate P. D. McMillan's personal papers have so far been unsuccessful. The letters that Morin saved offer rare glimpses into McMillan's combative personality.

While the elder William Morin was self made, having earned his living as a railroad engineer in the East prior to speculating in land, William A. enjoyed the fruits of his inheritance as well as his own attentive engagement in business of all sorts, including real estate, manufacturing, mining, railroads, insurance, and newspaper publishing. His correspondence reveals an iron in every fire, no flame too small nor conflagration too large. One moment he was ordering railcars of firewood to be shipped in from forested areas of the state; the next he was chastising an apartment tenant for neglecting to relock the communal toilet after use. People throughout the county sought him out when their hay or their funds ran short. People throughout the country pitched him the latest in building materials or heating appliances. A brief exchange with my great-great-grandfather shows how these dealings worked. Dan Hord, sixty-nine, sent the forty-seven-year-old Morin a note asking if he could use the pasture next to the Alden mill. Morin replied that he could have it for fifteen dollars for the season if he repaired the gap in the fence that allowed people to take shortcuts. Hord wrote back, "I think twelve dollars is enough for pasture but suppose will haf to take it." Was there no negotiating with Morin? Hord didn't jump immediately to fix the fence; he would do it after he finished clearing some railroad ties out of the road.

William A. Morin was undoubtedly the richest man in the county. To secure a loan to build a hotel in 1899, he sent the Minneapolis Loan and Trust Company a two-page list of his Freeborn County properties that showed his net worth to be $300,146.94—about $8 million in current values. That was only his locally based wealth. He omitted his investments in neighboring counties and as far distant as both coasts. Morin bought and sold land in short order and kept watch for projects that might increase its value. A hint of insider dealing shows up in correspondence with a vice president of the Illinois Central Railroad. Morin, an investor and trustee of the IC, sought information about its projected route through Albert Lea so that he could buy up land in the right-of-way. The vice president replied in a coded telegram that read, "Have you fitnessed incensation Parities you should rhetorician them kind as southern as poultice as oppression of comity at offer is nastiness."

Morin came as close to being local gentry as a rural Midwestern businessman gets. He entertained visiting hunters at weeklong camping trips on Geneva Lake. A connoisseur and owner of purebred horses, he traveled to attend races. At age twenty-nine in 1893, he married Katherine (Kitten) Truesdell, twenty. Their sons, William T. and Richard, were educated at Shattuck School in Faribault while the couple traveled extensively and spent winter in warmer climes. Morin ordered a custom-built fifty-five-foot cruiser, which he called a yacht and named the *Albert Lea*. He envisioned many seasons' adventures in Gulf and ocean waters but listed the craft for sale after one year because he was "up against the proposition of having a wife who is not a good sailor and for that reason the boat must go." Katherine wanted to see Europe instead. Although it is not unusual nowadays for Freeborn County farmers to vacation in Florida or Arizona, in Morin's day, the winter escape was a mark of privilege.

Rather than live among Albert Lea's elite along Park Avenue on Ballard's Point, Morin built an elegant house, now a five-unit apartment building, on a large lot near Spring Lake and developed a residential area around it. A succession of live-in housekeepers and cooks hired from the local Scandinavian population staffed the Morin home. His most telling status symbol, unusual in the Upper Midwest, was his employment of a Black servant to attend to his horses and do his driving. Identified in the census as "coachman" and "hostler," Albert Ratliff, fifteen years older than Morin, was born into slavery in Stumptown, Virginia (later West Virginia), and came to Albert Lea in his thirties to join his mother, Chloe, and stepfather, W. H. Butler, who owned a barbershop. His stepbrother, Amos Butler, was a janitor at the First National Bank. The elder Morin was the first to hire Ratliff.

As a rare person of African ancestry in Albert Lea, Ratliff was identified in shorthand in local papers as "the colored man." His command of Mr. Morin's splendid horses, however, earned him a name. In death, he was lauded as "of a most genial and loyal character" and "a friend of all." The *Albert Lea Times-Enterprise* characterized him with an image now cringeworthy: "a splendid type of the lovable and loyal slave of the palmy ante-bellum days." The obituary went on to say, "In this community where he became so widely known the number of people who will shed a tear in his memory is limited only by the number whose good fortune it was to know and to love him."

Newspaper accounts of William A. Morin's ventures portray him as an upright, esteemed, leading citizen who won election to city and county offices. A man of his status on whom so many depended financially would probably also have his detractors. On September 6, 1894, the *Enterprise* opined, "The throwing of stones through the windows of the Morin residence at 2 o'clock one night a short time ago is a most disreputable action on the part of some coward and is but the result of the anarchistic teachings of a certain agency in this town and the whole outfit should be discouraged by every honest man." Whether there was an organized cadre of anarchist vandals in Albert Lea is open to question. What we do know for sure is that Morin was an investor in the *Enterprise* and bought the business ten years later.

Robert Speer Travels through Time

Robert Speer, Frank Ryan, Thomas Morgan and family did the
World's Fair up in good shape.
  —*Freeborn County Standard*, November 8, 1893

Every research project worth its time, its inhalation of dust and mold,
and its microfilm vertigo ought to yield at least one astonishing discov-
ery. Mine was personal. I had squinted hard to envision my great-great-
grandfather Robert Speer coaxing his oxen through sloughs and fords
on his family's pioneer trek to Minnesota Territory. I had pictured him
hunched over his anvil practicing a vintage craft. I had seen the tombstone honoring his service in the Civil War, which certainly branded
him a relic of long ago. But I had never imagined him strolling the Midway at the 1893 Columbian Exposition, the World's Fair. At sixty-six, he
stepped aboard a train to Chicago, along with fellow pioneer Thomas
Morgan's family and another neighbor, and went to see what all the fuss
was about. Mary was presumably too frail to travel.

I remember myself at eighteen scoping out Chicago's old Midway
Plaisance, feeling as if I had made a bold, pioneering move. The daughter of working-class high school graduates, I was intent on making aca-
deme a fitting new home. During orientation week at the University of
Chicago, we learned that our campus was built on the site of the Columbian Exposition. Some of us learned to sing, if sarcastically, the verse of
our alma mater that claimed:

> The City White hath fled the earth,
> But where the azure waters lie,
> A nobler city hath its birth,
> The City Gray that ne'er shall die.

When I looked for remnants of the White City in the Museum of Science and Industry's imposing facade and Frederick Law Olmsted's Jackson Park waterscape or rushed to class along the Midway, I never heard Robert Speer's footfalls behind me or felt his breath on my back. Now I wonder, did the young boy who traveled the Erie Canal by mule- or horse-drawn packet boat ride the Ferris wheel as an old man? Did the blacksmith who fixed traps for his Dakota and Ho-Chunk neighbors gawk at the foreign "natives" on display in mock villages along the Midway? Did the good Baptist take a peek at the exotic dancer Little Egypt? When he gasped at the size of the woolly mammoth modeled and displayed, could he have imagined that a mammoth skull and skeleton would someday be unearthed from the marshlands near his home? What did a farmer who navigated by starlight along Turtle Creek make of the electrically illuminated faux classical buildings and their dancing fountains?

Getting from Moscow Township to the World's Fair was no feat. The Chicago, Milwaukee and St. Paul Railway sold round-trip tickets from Austin to Chicago for $11.43, with daily specials sometimes reduced below $8.00. The Minneapolis and St. Louis Railroad ran excursions from Albert Lea to Chicago's Englewood Station, where hotels had cropped up within walking distance of the fair. The Moscow folks could connect with either of these trains from the Oakland depot just down the road. A ten-day or two-week visit to the fair was the travel package of the year, and many residents of Freeborn and Mower counties took advantage of it, especially after the harvest. The publication of their names stretched the usual news from the townships into long columns. Some sent their impressions back to the local newspapers. The Reverend C. D. Belden, the Speers' minister, who visited the fair at about the same time, took pride in spending Minnesota Day at the Minnesota exhibit, where he saw a display of grains from the south, milling from the Cities, and ores from the north. In competitions much like those at a county or state fair, Minnesota took top honors in agricultural products from flax to cattle.

The exposition's organizing theme was evolution. Exhibits traced a natural progression from the primitive to the progressive, from the dugout canoe and bark raft to the oceangoing steamship, from the ox to an array of steam-powered farm machinery, even, despicably, from the world's "primitive" cultures to the supremacy of Anglo-European America. Everywhere he walked in the White City, Robert Speer was challenged to place himself on that spectrum of time and to realize and celebrate the fact that his own way of life would soon be obsolete.

Eighteen Yoke of Oxen

C. M. Wilkinson is having some ditching done on the [Van Norman] ranch. With eighteen yoke of oxen hitched to a ditching plow, an enormous amount can be done in a little while.

—*Albert Lea Enterprise*, October 18, 1894

Eighteen yoke of oxen! A long chain gang of brute beasts tugs hard at an iron blade wedged deep in the soil. Huge heads, blunt necks, bulky shoulders strain to push their yoke beams forward. Stocky legs lift, step delicately, hooves spread to keep their balance on bottomless peat.

Eighteen yoke of oxen! Thirty-six spines, 36 swinging tails, 72 curled horns, 72 round eyes fixed on their task, 144 hooves, a gross of hooves. Eighteen yoke beams of hard maple or hickory, 36 oxbows made from hackberry or white oak saplings, 200-some feet of clanging chain. Fifty to 75 thousand pounds of cattle, more than 25 tons of cattle.

Eighteen yoke of oxen! One pair after another, they break the soil with their hooves, stir it into a muddy morass. Pies of body-warm manure plop to the ground, get hooved into the mud, warm it and make it more pliable. Peat and manure, drool and sweat. The soil is churned, nourished, thrown aside as the plow blade slices its groove. Once grown over with grasses and reeds, the soil flies in clumps and wads to either side of the plow, mounding up to show where the ditch will run, six feet deep or more, deep enough to swallow a man, deep enough to drain water away from an age-old wetland and leave it dry.

Where would one find eighteen yoke of oxen in 1894? Suited to pull a covered wagon along westward trails and through untrammeled brush-land and sloughs, to break the prairie sod and turn up roots embedded for centuries, the ox had given way to the horse as the primary working animal on a southern Minnesota farm. Robert and Mary Speer drove two yoke of oxen in 1855; five years later, they were down to one pair. By 1870, they owned four horses instead. Who needed oxen in the 1890s with enough land tilled to live on? Someone intent on draining the land without resorting to the steam engine. Horses, with their thinner legs and bonier shoulders, might rear up against the plow's resistance or get mired in the mud.

An ox is made, not born. A steer—a castrated male—allowed to live beyond prime butchering weight grows huge, strong, and patient by age four. A milk cow relieved of calving and the daily dairy cycle can also be put to the yoke and develop oxen strength. Alert Devons with their chestnut red hides and sloping horns; Milking Shorthorns of red, white, or roan; red and white Ayrshires with their lyre-shaped horns and challenging temperaments can be nurtured and trained as working oxen, along with other cattle breeds. "Ox" becomes an honorific name applied to a large, hardworking, uncomplaining servant animal.

If anyone could round up thirty-six oxen ready to draw a man-deep groove in the land, Charles M. Wilkinson could do it. He was not a farmer in the ordinary sense but oversaw George Van Norman's ranch in Geneva and Riceland townships, where he pastured cattle, his own and others, on wet meadows. A livestock merchant and an Albert Lea resident since 1872, Wilkinson was a popular elected official. A newspaper profile offered this breathless assessment:

> As mayor, president of the city council, alderman and now as deputy sheriff he has proven his uprightness, fidelity, capacity, care, good judgment and undoubted worth as an official, as a citizen of the county and as a neighbor and friend and none has ever been more ready and active in helping others with purse and effort or in promoting the progress and welfare of Albert Lea and the county at large or showed a more cheerful disposition and hearty hand in helping the needy or a friend or others worthy who were seeking office or who asked his assistance in promoting any good cause.

Who wouldn't lend or rent an ox to such a worthy man?

The same issue of the *Enterprise* that told of the multi-ox ditching project reported, "Chris Christenson is fixing up the sheds on the C. M. Wilkinson ranch, putting in stantions and otherwise improving them so as to make a comfortable stable for the cows." These would be the two hundred cows Wilkinson had presumably bought after declaring the previous year that he was "figuring on the feasibility and profitableness of starting a large dairy." With more creatures to make use of the marsh's wet meadow in its dry season, it would make sense to expand its size or lengthen its usefulness.

Spring and summer of 1894, however, saw serious drought—the third dry summer in succession—from the Mississippi River to the Rocky Mountains. On July 25, the *Standard* reported, "The pastures are as dry as tinder; the earth to a considerable depth is devoid of moisture, and what grass is left is parched to brittleness and would readily burn if a fire was set to it. This is a serious injury to dairying and will result in quite a scant crop of hay." A forty-seven-day stretch without rain ended in mid-August: "A jubilant welcome to the rain! It has come; all nature glows with its refreshing bounties and all creatures are rejoicing and blessed by its beneficence." Given the uncertainty of the climate, a man of good judgment like Wilkinson must surely have looked at several options. The *Enterprise* of September 13, 1894, announced, "Chris Christenson is breaking on the C. M. Wilkinson ranch. He intends to break as much as possible this fall and sow it to flax next spring. Chris is a worker and ought to succeed in this world." Breaking takes oxen strength. An ox practiced in breaking might be in prime condition to pull the ditch plow by October.

The Minneapolis investors in the neighboring Ricelawn Ranch had introduced a new agricultural enterprise to the county:

> The patentee of a flax pulling machine shipped a machine from Minneapolis last week to be operated on the Hastings and McMillan ranch in Riceland and Moscow, on their Russian variety of flax, which stands about 44 inches high. . . . It works on the side of the grain like any reaper and is provided with a set of arms or embraces which reach into the

standing flax and gathers in 18 inches, pulling the straw up by the roots; a hand-like device scratches the dirt off and lays it on a table, from which a person takes it and piles it in bunches on the ground, when it is bound in the old-fashioned way.

Wilkinson likely watched this demonstration and learned that flax grows well in clay or peat that is sufficiently drained.

"A worker" like Chris Christenson was probably a good ox drover as well. Did he succeed in the world? Which Chris Christenson was he? His is as generic a name as you'll hear in a community of Danes and Norwegians, and news reporters and census takers could be indifferent about the spelling of patronymics: -son or -sen? Christen or Christian or Kristian? How many drovers did it take to work eighteen yoke of oxen? Who steered the plow? Was there spadework to do after the plow had made its cut? Thanks to the drought, Wilkinson had his pick of farmhands: "There are many laborers in this city without employment, more, probably, than at any previous time in the history of Albert Lea. Good men are glad to get work at $1.25 a day, and they would accept $1 rather than remain idle." Let us hope that this "hearty hand in helping the needy" hired many such men and paid them well.

Moisture and temperature determined how many yards that plow could travel in one day, one mid-October day with sunset around 6:30. When the day ended, were the oxen led to a trough, or did they wade into Geneva or Mud Lake, where this new ditch would likely drain? Someone had to soothe their weary muscles, salve the chafing where the yoke had rubbed, trim the cracks in their hooves, and fork them their share of hay before plodding off to supper while the oxen lowed in the dusk.

Eat they must, both oxen and men. Someone had to cook and serve the midday meal when the workers stopped for a rest. Those with no homes to go to needed another meal before bedding down in bunkhouse or barn. Cooking puts women in the scene as well. Lena Larson, nineteen, is listed as a live-in servant in the Wilkinson household in the 1895 census. Imagine her kneading dough, peeling potatoes, frying bacon in the ranch kitchen the previous October. Lena Larson's identity is even more elusive than Chris Christenson's for the same reasons, plus a name change in the event of her marriage.

Eighteen yoke of oxen. A team of men to tend and drive them. A squad of cooks and serving women. Two hired helpers with identities veiled by their common names. One enterprising agribusinessman. One distant landowner. One more drainage ditch transversing the marshy landscape. One more wetland gone.

"The Great Ricelawn Ranch"

Ricelawn, also spelled Rice Lawn, was Freeborn County's first experience with large-scale farming organized on an industrial model, with distant owners, a resident manager, twenty or more workers, and some on-site processing. While neighboring farmers watched it for practical hints that might be useful on a smaller scale, Ricelawn drew the admiration of certain city business leaders. Charles W. Lunquist and his successors as manager hosted visitors fairly often, but an invitation to join P. D. McMillan himself was a rarity. This article in the Freeborn County Standard *of July 17, 1895, is included in its entirety since there is no better way to capture its rapturous tone. An article in the* Mower County Transcript *on August 7, 1895, was calmer in tone and more data driven.*

Reclaimed and Improved at Great Expense, Begins to Yield Bountiful Returns—A Grand Expanse of Wonderfully Fertile Land Perfectly Subjected to the Uses and Benefit of Man—Roads Required to Give It Access to Markets—A Delightful Visit to the "Island" and Inspection of the Great Farm in the Basin of a Vanished Lake.

Last Thursday P. D. McMillan, of the firm of Hastings & McMillan, for many years honorably prominent business men of Minneapolis, and owners of the big Riceland farm, being in the city, proposed making up a party to accompany him on a visit to the place. He met with no difficulty in finding a company to accept his courteous hospitality and it was composed of those who not only can appreciate the opportunity for observation and recreation which such a jaunt affords, but who are also generally primed for a good time and ready to do their share in sociable ways to make it enjoyable for each other and the rest of mankind in general whom by accident or circumstance they may fortuitously encounter. The list included besides Mr. McMillan, a banker who is also an alert and prominent law-maker, a professor, a leading miller, a STANDARD representative and best of all, four ladies, two of them being wives of members of the party. They occupied two double carriages, and besides a quite unusual equipment of good spirits and a plentiful spicing of good humor were provided with other appetizing concomitants befitting the occasion in case hunger should overtake them on the journey.

The weather was supremely auspicious. The sun beamed with good cheer and lent no languor; the air was freighted with the ozone that fills the lungs with the fragrance of health and inspiration; the roads were level and inviting to the willing feet of the steeds, and on either hand the entire distance of sixteen miles the verdure of the trees, of the fields and meadows and the stretches of yellowing grain furnished relief for the vision, refreshment for the thoughts and scenes for contemplation which no artful pictures can equal. The course taken carried the party along the Hayward road eastwardly into Moscow Township, thence back northwesterly and north, by reason of the improvident lack of a laid-out road, at least three miles useless travel, partly across the wonderful basin or depressed plain at last to "Ricelawn," the headquarters of the big and famous ranch. Here, on an elevated tract of two hundred acres, studded thick with oak, hickory, linden and a score of other varieties of trees, which in the times before the coming of the white man, constituted a beautiful island whose shores were washed by the pellucid waters of a great inland sea; here was the spot nature had designed and man had adopted for the initial point of operations for the redemption and improvement of the surrounding plain, and here was built the extensive buildings, the pretty home, the workmen's quarters, the great barn, warehouses and yards for an abiding place and scene of enterprise. Look east and west, north and south. Let the eye sweep from here the grand panorama, and beyond the perfect level of the plain is seen and for miles in either direction the distant shores of the pre-historic lake of which the plain formed the fertile bed; the shores that were lapped by the vanished waters and the rising hills beyond occupied by bounteous farms, peaceful homes of plenty, the buildings studding the landscape and marking the abodes of active life, industry and civilization.

What a picture is this! What a wondrous transformation it typifies! What a serene and restful yet glorious reality the scene presents. It seems that one could never tire of it, and to one who has surveyed and once become intoxicated with its beauty it becomes a perpetual vision, a kaleidoscope of wonder, a dream of changing delight.

The "ranch" consists of about six thousand acres and four years ago was in much of its extent overflowed with the backwater of Turtle creek, which is the outlet of Rice lake at the west, and which flows through it southeasterly emptying into the Cedar river in Mower county. Four years ago the entire tract was a watery waste and was generally considered unreclaimable and of little value. The "island" was tenanted by the sole inhabitant of a rude cabin, surrounded by the mounds and other relics of the long-departed natives whose teepees used to deck the inviting hills and whose canoes parted the waters of the lake as they left in quest of finny or feathered or antlered game. But the incalculable richness of the basin and its possibilities were presented to Messrs. Hastings and McMillan; they bought it and at once proceeded to reclaim, improve and make it blossom and bear fruit until it has been made subject to their uses; as complete as to drainage, as arable and as productive as the rarest acres, in truth, in the world. In fact and in candor, it is to be doubted whether there is another large tract of land in the world so completely subjective to farming and stockraising purposes and as inexhaustibly fertile as is this. But over $60,000 have been expended by the confident and enterprising proprietors to make it so, and to provide the buildings and other belongings. Turtle creek was dredged and drained, and it is now entirely dry; four artesian wells at a depth of 70 to 100 feet were bored and supply abundant and never-failing water; the lowest and what was considered the most refractory land has been put into crops; grain of all kinds is seen, crops unsurpassed in luxuriance are approaching maturity on the

600 acres under the plow; 3000 tons of as fine hay, blue joint, timothy and red top, as any land produces, mostly averaging three tons to the acre, is being cut by a force of twenty men; and in all directions, on almost every acre of the great tract, the hand of man holds easy sway.

This is the first year that returns profit on the investment, and it will be handsome. Hereafter the prospects are secure. The soil composed almost entirely of decayed vegetation, in some places of many feet in depth to the clayey hard-pan, will endure and retain its richness, it seems, forever. It cannot well be exhausted; the drainage is now complete, and all that is required to open this almost limitless expanse of waiting fertility and wealth to the world, and to rightly enable the world and future owners to enjoy and secure its benefits, is good roads.

And good roads are easily supplied, outlets to Albert Lea, and to the railroad less than five miles to the south, can readily and with slight expense be provided. A threshing machine might be driven across any quarter of the land: there are no woods to cut through; all the inhabitants south along the town line between Riceland and Moscow want a road; a road from the "island" leading to the Riceland creamery, saving nearly four miles to Albert Lea, and another leading in from Geneva and Newry is imperatively demanded, and there is no reason or excuse why each of these lines should not at once be laid out. As soon as they are established by law, they can be traveled, for little or no work on them would at present or in the future be required. The county commissioners are at present considering a petition for a north and south road, and they will doubtless at once appreciate its necessity and establish it. The other lines should speedily follow.

Hastings & McMillan, it is fair to say, deserve unbounded credit for their foresight, faith and enterprise in reclaiming this extensive and unmeasurably rich section of the county: they deserve their reward and they will get it abundantly, but they do not intend to sequester it all to their selfish purposes, to greed, nor to shut out others from sharing it with them. They design dividing the tract into farms of suitable size and selling them off to actual settlers, who will build themselves homes and help to populate the county and to add to its magnificent thrift, wealth and prosperity. Thus they will become, as they are already in goodly degree, public benefactors and copartners of the earnest people of Freeborn county in enhancing its benefits and in contributing to the fair fame which it already commands both home and abroad.

Besides their obligations to Mr. McMillan for his gallant hospitality the party joined in repeated thanks to C. W. Lundquist, superintendent of the ranch, for many courtesies extended them. He threw open the doors of his pleasant home to the visitors, piloted them over the farm and in every way possible contributed to the success and interest of the event. Mr. Lundquist is a very busy man, having to manage not only the extensive farming operations, and give care to the 600 head of cattle, a large herd of cows, 40 horses, the sheep and swine, but also to attend to employing his men, the buying of supplies, the sale of products and other duties too numerous to mention. He is a man evidently of excellent executive capacity and one whom it is a pleasure to know.

The sun hung low in the western sky when the visitors were summoned to the carriages for the return trip and all were reluctant to leave the place. The revelations concerning the great ranch, the spectacle of the wondrous fields of prolific growing grain, the prosperous, comfortable and inviting homes en route and the rare aroma, the inspiring mystery and everywhere the glory of effulgent nature, all contributed to excite the spirits, the admiration and delight of the party with their day's experience and to fix its pictures lastingly on the tablets of their memories.

A Change of Hands
Bodes a Change of Lands

It is reported that a syndicate of eastern capitalists have under consideration the purchase of an immense tract of land in Freeborn county, in the towns of Riceland, Moscow and Geneva. The deal, if consummated, will involve $40,000, and the new owners would put in an immense drainage ditch and greatly add to the value of the land. Part of the land involved is what is known as Ricelawn farm, owned by Hastings & McMillan of Minneapolis.

— *Mower County Transcript*, October 26, 1898

By the fall of 1898, P. D. McMillan found himself virtually alone in his intention to expand Ricelawn Ranch. A. W. Hastings had sold nearly his whole share to McMillan and withdrawn from their Minneapolis realty partnership as well. C. W. Lunquist had left to farm his own land and would soon move to Minneapolis to work as a contractor on McMillan's properties there. The Ricelawn house was occupied by a tenant, E. Burt Parker, identified as "the artist" and "an experienced farmer of York state." "Artist," whether fanciful or the simplest term for his vocation, makes me wonder whether Emily McMillan had lured him westward. Maybe he came to the countryside to paint. He proved to be "a gentleman of the first water" who "extends his hospitality to rich and poor alike."

The ranch's productivity and the market value of the drained land had restored McMillan's wealth enough to finance two new buildings in Minneapolis, a two-story brick building at 717–25 Central Avenue and the McMillan Block downtown at Third Street and Third Avenue. Now, with his cash flow reduced, half his swampland awaited reclamation, and his drainage ditches needed frequent reaming of silt and vegetation. A profitable yield on the land already under cultivation wasn't assured, either. Because of the recent dry weather, the *Standard* wrote in August, "all grain is colored quite badly. Barley won't even make good beer, it is so black."

George Van Norman had sold six sections of land in Riceland and Geneva townships to C. M. Wilkinson in 1895. The following year, Wilkinson was elected mayor of Albert Lea. The extra claims on his time may have induced him to cash out the land rather than work it. The prospect of a buyer willing to invest in the entire swath of the Big Marsh piqued both McMillan's and Wilkinson's interest.

The word "syndicate" is grandiose in this case, but it lent drama to a story with its opening paragraph still unwritten: How did investors from Polo, Illinois, find their way to swampland in southern Minnesota? The buyers' name, Barber Bros., was a misnomer by the time of the purchase. Two years earlier, Harvard graduate Henry Barber had died suddenly at forty-one, leaving his share of the family's banking and investment firm to his widow, Mary, and his mother, Lucie, to manage alongside his older brother, Bryant. Henry's entry in *The Biographical Record of Ogle County, Illinois* approaches hagiography. He "was always associated with any movement calculated to develop the highest standard of citizenship." He was "a deep student of finance" with "singularly keen judgment, unimpeachable integrity, and unusual attainments." The single paragraph about Bryant H. Barber is spare by comparison, suggesting shortcomings rather than achievements. Bryant never graduated from Harvard nor went to college at all. "His practical business education was received from his father with whom he was associated in the banking and other business." No word about his judgment, integrity, or attainments. In his mid-forties, he was unmarried and living with his mother.

I don't know whether any Barbers traveled to Minnesota in 1898 to see the deal through. The purchase of the Van Norman–Wilkinson lands was contracted first. In early November, McMillan met with a representative of Barber Bros. to sign over 3,300-plus acres, more than half his holdings, for $50,120, of which $40,000 was paid in cash. He kept Ricelawn Ranch and its approximately 3,000 acres of "improved"

Bryant H. Barber, 1898

land. What the Barbers bought at fifteen dollars an acre was the same swampy land that had cost McMillan two dollars an acre seven years earlier.

The *Standard*'s front-page report on the sale surmised that McMillan had given up on the drainage effort. Barber Bros., on the other hand, would drain and divide their land into small parcels and sell them to would-be farmers from Illinois. "This scheme is of course a speculation, and is likely to net handsome profits," the *Standard* conjectured. Such an undertaking would greatly increase the county's population and tax base.

This rural Minnesota land sale was important enough to be covered in the *Minneapolis Tribune*, which noted that it was "consummated by McRae and Buxton, who receive at this time the unusually large commission of $5,000." Kenneth McRae, a partner with William Buxton in a Minneapolis realty company, also acquired a quarter section of land just south of Ricelawn Ranch, making him an interested party in any drainage plans.

Barber Bros. continued to buy smaller pieces of property adjoining their large holdings. They were not the only ones engaged in a reshuffle of ownership at century's end. William A. Morin bought a cache of swampland, including some of the recently deceased L. D. Holmes's property along Geneva Lake. He, too, would become both advocate and beneficiary of a reinvigorated drainage effort.

By 1899, McMillan had found a new ally to share his enthusiasm about the agricultural potential of drained marshland: Professor Thomas Shaw of the University of Minnesota's Agricultural College. After McMillan brought Shaw to Ricelawn for a visit, the *Austin Herald* enthused, "Professor Shaw says he has never seen a richer soil than is found there, the black loam being of great depth. He is of the opinion that if the Rice lake and the low lands surrounding it, in the towns of Geneva, Riceland, Moscow and Newry, were drained, it would add a round million dollars to the land there."

What's Black and White
and Grazes All Over?

> The dairy cow is queen of the farm and one of the greatest mortgage
> lifters in existence. She is virtually a machine which turns the products
> of the farms into greatest profit. In order to get the largest returns her
> ways and her disposition must be understood.
>
> —Franklyn Curtiss-Wedge, ed.,
> *History of Freeborn County, Minnesota*

My dad, in his eighties, is sitting in his recliner with the *Albert Lea Tribune* folded in quarters to highlight the crossword puzzle. He's complaining that the puzzle is getting easier; it's being dumbed down, he suspects. One clue particularly annoys him: "'Black and white cow,'" he scoffs. "Who wouldn't know *that?*"

Someone whose first impressions were molded along Turtle Creek early in the twentieth century and rarely tested with travel might well believe the cow the most abundant mammal on earth. That person could spot a black and white Holstein in the distance and distinguish it from a solid tan Jersey or a brown and white Guernsey. Where the woolly mammoth roamed in ancient times and Dakota hunters pursued bison and elk a scant half century before, animal life by the 1890s had come to mean a herd of dairy cows grazing calmly on pasture grasses. By 1902, the Freeborn County assessor reported a bovine population of 24,853. The US Census of 1900 had counted only 21,838 humans.

Farmers around the Big Marsh had learned that a wet meadow gone dry under the summer sun made excellent pastureland. Some basic ditching could drain off the spring thaw and cloudburst rains and keep the meadow useful for three seasons. Livestock farming didn't require the extensive drainage that crop farming did, and the rolling terrain of glacial swells and swales didn't inhibit cows the way it burdened the plow. The early European settlers had harvested the tall grasses that grew naturally in the marsh for hay to feed their draft animals and a couple of milk cows over a harsh Minnesota winter. Farmers expanding their herds discovered that nutritious cultivated strains such as timothy and alfalfa could flourish there, too. While conditions were right for dairy farming, it took a mechanical invention to make it profitable: the cream separator, first manufactured by Gustaf de Laval in Sweden in the 1880s.

A popular creation story of Freeborn County dairying tugs at my ethnic pride. It begins with Clarks Grove resident Hans Peter Jensen's 1884 visit to Denmark, where he not only laid eyes on the new cream separator but saw how Danish farmers had pitched in together to form creameries where they turned milkfat into butter without all the laborious churning required at home. No matter that there were similar operations across the border in Iowa and that a Clarks Grove delegation had checked them out; H. P. Jensen and the Clarks Grove Co-operative Creamery have carried a glow as the Adam and Eve of the Midwestern cooperative movement.

Time-lapse satellite photography of the county in the 1890s, had such a thing been possible, would have shown thousands of dairy cows popping up to fill its pastures, and sturdy buildings with brick chimneys and metal cupolas rising in its villages and townships. By 1911, there were twenty-eight creameries, all but one a co-op. If we squint, we might see twenty-eight proud buttermakers, the achievers of a new, respected, skilled vocation, arriving for work. Time-lapse photography would also document the appearance of the most iconic of all Midwestern farm buildings, the big red barn that sheltered the dairy herd for milking, with their feed stored in a haymow under the barn's gambrel roof.

Looking back from the twenty-first century, when corn and soybeans blanket the old cow pastures and what cows remain are fed, washed, and milked mechanically in long, metal containment sheds, the turn of the nineteenth to the twentieth century looks like the Golden Age of the family farm. Some beef cattle and a penful of pigs brought in additional revenue while a flock of chickens provided the "egg money," the picturesque term for a household allowance. Most farms also had some acreage under cultivation in corn, oats, barley, flax, or grasses. They practiced "the intelligent and safe policy of diversified farming," as the author of the dairying chapter in the 1911 county history called it, adding, "there is certain to be each year a good yield of something."

It seemed that the family farm would endure forever, but change was under way, and that queen of a dairy cow held the clue. *The Community Magazine*, a monthly publication for local farmers, carried a recurring feature called the "Testing Association Reports." Readers learned how many gallons of milk and with what percentage of butterfat the cows tested that month had produced. Under each farmer's name, a list appeared: Belle, Queen, Betsy, Midge, Brownie, Blossom, Snowflake, Creamelle . . . each presumably with her own ways and disposition. The McMillan Land Company, the corporate entity formed to operate Ricelawn Ranch, numbered its cows.

The Second Try

If the drain is constructed what was once Rice lake, which has long
been nothing but a swamp, and many acres of surrounding slough, will
be drained and made dry land. The drain or ditch will be an enlarging
of the Turtle river, a natural water way, and will be about nine miles in
length. The cost will be, roughly estimated, from $15,000 to $20,000,
but it will affect about as many acres of land.

    — *The Minneapolis Journal*, October 18, 1901

September 23, 1901, marks the beginning of the end for naturally flowing Turtle Creek, seasonally variable Rice Lake, and the sprawling Big
Marsh. On that date, a group of twenty-one landowners submitted a
petition to the Freeborn County Board of Commissioners for construction of a public ditch and laterals beginning a mile and a quarter
east of Geneva Lake. The main ditch would follow the course of Geneva
Creek easterly from section 32 through 35 to tiny Mud Lake in Geneva
Township, then turn south into Riceland Township to connect with
Turtle Creek, which it would follow across Moscow Township to within
a mile of the county line. From that point on, Turtle Creek would carry
the water naturally to the Cedar River in Mower County. The main
ditch would be nine miles long. No estimate of length was announced
for the many lateral ditches, tributaries that would carry water into the
main channel.

    The petitioners identified themselves as "landowners, whose lands
will be liable to be affected by, or assessed for the expense of, the construction of the ditch and laterals," but they cited a greater motive than
merely improving their own land. They "would respectfully represent
that the public health, convenience and welfare require the establishment and construction of a ditch and laterals." The work proposed
would be "of public benefit and utility." A Minnesota Supreme Court

ruling in *Lien v. Norman County* the year before had interpreted "public
welfare" and "public utility" in broader terms than health. Even if the
immediate result was to enrich a few owners, "the fact that large tracts
of otherwise waste land may be thus reclaimed and made suitable for
agricultural purposes is deemed and held to constitute a public benefit." You might call this a trickle-down theory.

Six months before the petition was filed, the Minnesota legislature
had passed a new drainage law, chapter 258 of the General Laws of
Minnesota 1901, which replaced most of its earlier legislation. P. D.
McMillan immediately sent a note to Governor Samuel Van Sant to ask
for copies of the new legislation. The new law left responsibility for
drainage ditches in the hands of a county's board of commissioners
but spelled out a procedure to follow. The board could not order construction of a ditch until a petition signed by some affected landowners
had been submitted to the county auditor. The petition must explain
the necessity and describe the route of the proposed ditch, and one
or more of the petitioners must post a bond to cover expenses incurred
in case the board did not proceed with construction. The petition
would be distributed broadly and published in three consecutive issues
of a newspaper along with the date of the first scheduled hearing.
When the board "shall be satisfied that all the foregoing conditions
have been complied with," they would appoint an engineer to survey
the route. Chapter 258 decreed that a ditch "may follow and consist of
the bed of any stream, creek, or river, navigable or not," and that ditching may alter and artificially confine that stream as long as its general
direction was maintained. This provision sealed the fates of Geneva
and Turtle creeks.

The petition appeared in the *Freeborn County Standard* on October
2, 1901, with an announcement that the county board would hear comments and make a determination at its regular meeting at ten o'clock on
October 23. The names of the petitioners were included, among them
some resident farmers with Scandinavian names typical of Riceland
and Moscow townships: Gulbrandson, Stoa, Fjeldbroten, Vollum. P. D.
McMillan's name appeared, as did the surname of his former Ricelawn

manager, Lunquist. The signatory was C. W.'s wife, Louise, the only female name on the list. W. A. Morin, who had purchased 920 acres of Geneva marshland days before the filing, signed the petition, as did H. N. (Harris) Brown, a banker in Albert Lea, and L. A. (Lewis) Brown, an Albert Lea dentist. Curiously absent is the name Barber, the landowners set to profit the most from the drainage. The first to sign, however, was Kenneth MacRae, the Minneapolis realtor who handled the Barbers' purchase of the land. The petitioners came to be known collectively as Kenneth MacRae et al. and the project as "the MacRae Ditch" or, more commonly, "the Riceland-Moscow Ditch" or simply "the Big Ditch."

The *Standard* responded enthusiastically and with some exaggeration, citing the area to be reclaimed as thirty thousand acres. The article predicted a fourfold increase in taxes for "school, town, county and state purposes" and labeled the proposed ditch "one of the most important general improvements that has been undertaken in the county in all its history."

Two weeks later, the *Minneapolis Journal* investigated the matter more deeply in an article headlined LANDS TO BE SAVED and 15,000 ACRES TO BE REDEEMED. The *Journal* said nothing about public health or welfare but attributed the project to a growth in land values that had come with livestock and dairy farming. Back when wheat was the primary cash crop, "slough land" was simply left to lie, but the ease of converting wetlands to pasture had made them more desirable. Land worth five dollars an acre twenty-five years before was now selling for between thirty-five and seventy-five dollars. Owners of marshland would certainly profit from drainage.

The *Journal* saw no significant obstacles to the project: "Of course some will protest against this drainage of water surface on the ground that from it vapor arises and rain is produced. There may be some truth in this phase of the question, as the water surface of Freeborn county has almost all disappeared as compared to what it was early in its settlement, but the demands for land are so pressing and this will be so productive when redeemed." Surely the county board would welcome the addition of so much acreage to the tax rolls, especially if Barber Bros. were to bring in Germans from Illinois, perhaps one hundred families of five people each. The *Standard*, likewise, predicted a smooth process: "It is an auspicious fact that all the land owners whose lands are involved have united in the proceedings, and thus the necessary legal steps can be taken without incurring unfriendly opposition or the delays and costs of litigation."

Not all the landowners involved *were* on board, however, as time would tell. The 1901 law specified how the engineer would conduct his survey. Working in one-hundred-foot sections along the entire length of a proposed ditch, he would estimate its width and depth at any point, plus the amount of soil to be removed in cubic feet. He had to then calculate the cost of doing the work. Three citizen "freeholders" whose lands would not be affected by the project would serve as viewers to verify the engineer's report. A list of estimated benefits or damages to each landowner along the route had to then be submitted to the county auditor. Chapter 258 required that the auditor publish and post the names of the affected landowners in good time for the next public hearing and notify all nonresident owners. A "benefit" was construed as additional arable land and "damage" as the loss of land surface. The Speers and the Registers, who farmed in the path of the main ditch, were likely to suffer damages when Turtle Creek was widened. Their names would appear on the auditor's list, but they were not among the petition's signatories. Farmers in and along the perimeter of the fifteen to twenty thousand acres might note changes in their water table and the composition of their soil, not to mention their way of life, but only the gain or loss of acreage mattered.

The county board's October meeting proved anticlimactic. Having found "certain irregularities" in the printing of the notices, the commissioners voted to republish and repost them and schedule a hearing for November 21. In the meantime, they asked J. T. Fanning, a consulting engineer from Minneapolis, to examine the proposed ditch and laterals. He suggested a smaller-scale plan, which the commissioners recommended at the November meeting. Still, the new law required the board to appoint an engineer to survey the proposed route to the digit. They chose a ditching expert, James W. Dappert of Taylorville, Illinois, the Barbers' home state, to conduct the survey and report by March 1. The hands-on work of measuring and calculating was to be done in the depths of winter.

Whether or not the Barbers had suggested Dappert, they had definitely put their money and influence behind the petition. Albert Lea lawyer John F. D. Meighen addressed the October board meeting on behalf of Mary J. Barber and spoke again at the November session, just after returning from Illinois. He traveled to Minneapolis to meet with McMillan as well. Prior to one such trip, he wrote to his kid brother, "We are preparing to build an immense drain in Freeborn county that may cost $120,000."

Meighen's was the highest estimate. The *Minneapolis Journal* quoted the cost, "roughly estimated," as $15,000 to $20,000. The *Standard* upped the ante to between $20,000 and $25,000. The *Austin Daily Herald* and the *Austin Journal* both reported $75,000. No one could guess accurately until Dappert had completed his survey.

Dollar figures continued to surface in conjunction with the most contentious aspect of the new drainage law: It laid out a system for public financing of drainage ditches, authorizing the county board to issue bonds, payable within ten years, with interest up to six percent. The money to repay the bonds would come from taxes charged to affected landowners for benefits accrued. The law spelled out the terms and time frame for collecting these taxes through liens on the benefited property. No landowner welcomes a lien. What if the ditch didn't work? Or what if it was begun but not completed? What if benefits didn't cover costs? What if land values didn't rise? And why should taxpayers who stood to gain little or nothing bear the risk for those who would benefit the most? These questions, seldom cogently discussed in the newspapers, were raised in neighborly conversations, in town meetings, and finally at crowded county board hearings.

New Man About Town:
John Felix Dryden Meighen

I feel in the language of Iago, as Shakespeare makes him speak, that the time has come that either makes or mars me. The opportunities that are before me here are just what I desire and if I can make the most of them, shall be very well satisfied.

> —John F. D. Meighen, letter to his parents, February 18, 1901,
> informing them that he had passed the bar and become a "full
> fledged" partner with Henry Morgan, the mayor of Albert Lea,
> in the firm Morgan and Meighen

John Felix Dryden Meighen was just short of twenty-four, new to Albert Lea, and freshly admitted to the bar when the real estate investors seeking to drain the Big Marsh hired him as their attorney. Surely they had their pick of more experienced lawyers. They must have seen in the young Meighen the character that comes through vividly in the large collection of personal and business papers he left behind: an ambitious man of deep intelligence and broad curiosity, focused on his goals, deliberate in his choices, open to long hours of tireless work, and determined to leave his mark on history. It no doubt helped that he was personable, articulate, and distinguished looking: six feet tall with a long face, high forehead, and large aquiline nose. Barely out of his youth, he seemed to be a man with a firm sense of destiny.

Meighen's many letters to his parents appear on letterhead, precisely dated. The first ones from Albert Lea are labeled "Newton House," the hotel where he ate his meals, while he lived in more spartan quarters. His letter of April 4, 1901, written with conversational immediacy, says, "There is a real estate agent at the other end of this table trying to prove that farm lands in Southern Minnesota will go from $40.00 to $100.00 per acre. He argues that if land is worth $100.00 per acre in Illinois now,

John F. D. Meighen, 1902

and it certainly is, it will reach a value of $100.00 per acre in Minnesota."
I like to imagine that this agent familiar with land prices in Illinois
was in Albert Lea on behalf of Barber Bros. Maybe this very dinner
conversation left the agent impressed enough with the bright, exuber-
ant young attorney to recommend him to his clients.

Meighen had found his way from the University of Michigan Law
School to Albert Lea via family recommendations and connections, particularly those of his maternal uncle Edward Everett "Big Ed" Smith, a
state legislator from South Minneapolis. Both sides of his family enjoyed
prominence in Minnesota. The Meighens were early and influential
settlers in Fillmore County; the general store his grandparents operated
in Forestville is now a historic site. His grandfather, William, served
several terms in the state house and senate, while an uncle, Thomas J.
Meighen, was a frequent third-party candidate, active in the Farmers'
Alliance and the People's Party. John's parents, Joseph and Mary Smith
Meighen, prospered as farmers near LeRoy in Mower County. John was
born in Spring Valley on September 25, 1877, his only sibling a brother,
Thomas Virgil William, sixteen years his junior, whom he mentored
in a steady correspondence. Meighen had earned BA and MA degrees
in literature from Upper Iowa University before law school, and he
continued to be a prolific reader.

His employment secured, Meighen embarked on the life of a young
man on the rise. He joined fraternal organizations, took dancing lessons,
attended the theater, heard touring lecturers, and put in an appearance
at Sunday church services around town before declaring his allegiance
to the Methodists. As a bachelor of social standing, he drew plenty of
attention. His diary mentions the names and initials of women with
whom he walked around Fountain Lake, attended dinners and parties,
or engaged in late-night conversation. He even kept lists of the women
he danced with at social events.

Meighen's was not a lavish life. He rented a room in Mrs. Martin
Blacklin's house on Fountain Street but shared it with another young
attorney, Claude Southwick. The fireplace was papered over to conserve heat, an ill-conceived plan that once set the room on fire. Meighen

contracted his meals with a shifting array of hotels and boardinghouses and kept a record of the costs. He worked long hours at the law office, where he contended with frozen plumbing or ailing stenographers. Henry Morgan was frequently away, first campaigning for election to the state senate and then on senate business, a circumstance Meighen claimed as opportunity: "People know that Morgan is not in the office much now and that I am responsible for what is done. This is the kind of chance that I've been waiting for and want to make some reputation at this time, if possible," he confided to his parents.

The MacRae petition, filed his first September in town and argued at county board meetings and public hearings, brought Meighen's speaking skills to the fore and won him leadership roles in his clubs and lodges. He even became a popular Fourth of July orator at smaller towns in the region. Working for McMillan in Minneapolis and the Barbers in Illinois offered him the chance to travel, but not in leisure or luxury. His 1903 diary records a typical whirlwind trip. He left for Minneapolis at 5:15 AM on a Thursday, spent the day in legal meetings in both Twin Cities, left for Chicago on the overnight *Pioneer Limited*, and arrived at 9:30 Friday morning. He met with Bryant Barber and the drainage engineers and departed at 6:30 in the evening. The train pulled in to St. Paul at 7:20 AM on Saturday, leaving him twenty minutes to board a different train to Mankato, where he had another case pending. He made it home from Mankato by 11:00 Saturday night after changing trains in Waseca. We present-day readers marvel that such efficient train travel was possible. Vacation travel remained Meighen's greatest pleasure, and he drew sustenance from it long after in written accounts of his trips and travelogue talks to lodges and church groups.

A focus on the public J. F. D. Meighen yields an imposing, self-assured man of unusual professional prowess. The candor of his diaries brings the private John into view, a character still in formation, subject to failed aspirations and self-doubt—in short, a person of more depth and essential humanity than the public documents let us see. A major theme in his personal papers is his perhaps too eager pursuit of romance. News of his engagement to a woman his parents hadn't met displeased his mother, to judge from his reply to her quick response. His letter illustrates so well his measured, deliberate approach to life and his lawyerly argumentative powers, as well as his enmeshed relationship with his mother. Written on a borrowed sheet of Henry Morgan's Minnesota Senate letterhead and dated September 7, 1903, it reads:

> Mother's letter with reference to my engagement was received this morning. It, as you must realize, pained me to note your sorrow in the matter, but I think I can fully realize your feelings.
>
> Now, it may be that you are right in this and that my action is an unwise one. If so there is all the time in the world to change. I am "judgment proof," so there is no particular danger to me in breaking my engagement in case that is the best thing to do. And for that matter, I do not apprehend that there would be any especial difficulty in getting

Mary Meighen and an unidentified child at the Meighen home in LeRoy, Minnesota, about 1890

released from it. Sybil is a sensible girl, her parents are well-to-do and there is no especial financial or worldly reason why she should marry me in place of someone else, or desire to keep up an engagement that was not agreeable to both of us.

Be that as it may, there is no danger of any quiet or secret marriage without your knowing about it. I would like to have both of you become acquainted with her at some convenient time so that you can judge for yourselves as to her personality. . . .

I would consider it criminal to marry before having enough money to own a respectable home, and we may both repent before I succeed in gathering together enough for that purpose. In any event I consider it a very proper time to ask for a larger share of the firm dividends. Mr. Morgan goes away for a ten days trip on the Great Lakes tomorrow and, when he returns, am going to talk the matter over with him

Well, I shall come down to LeRoy as soon as we get past the immediate pressure of business and have a long talk with you. You may depend upon it that I shall make use of the best brains I have in determining what to do and shall be guided very largely by your advice.

Meighen's promise not to marry before he could afford a respectable home points to another constant theme in his personal papers. As busy as he was and as wealthy as his clients were, he had difficulty amassing enough money to support the life he aspired to. Every penny was tended, every unexpected expense rued.

One glaring omission in Meighen's personal papers is his impression of the natural world. On his leisure travels, he attended to culture more than nature. As he chugged back and forth to the Twin Cities and Chicago on business and to family in LeRoy, he probably worked on legal briefs rather than gaze out the railcar window at the passing landscape. His frequent walks around Fountain Lake were spent in conversation, not reverie. A rare observation of the Big Marsh appears in a letter to his parents: "We have been having a great amount of rain here, but no cloud bursts. The flat lands up in the north-eastern part of the county look like one vast lake now. I have never seen quite as much water on the surface of the ground before in any place that I have been."

Meighen's relationship to the marsh was practical, untainted by sentiment. His responsibility in the drainage effort was to serve his clients to the best of his ability and, in the process, to achieve a reputation that allowed him to keep perfecting his skill. He stated the obligation plainly in a letter to his parents: "Our client very promptly paid us $200.00 and expenses for our trips to Minneapolis and Chicago, so that we will naturally attend to his interests with care."

The People Protest

We must be taxed to improve the marsh land for rich corporations, that they may become richer, and get no returns from it. If the county would buy the marsh, then it would become public property, but for the public, to improve private property is not right nor just. All farmers throughout the county have to drain their own farms, and we may let Mr. McMillan do likewise.

—Oakland Township news, *Freeborn County Standard*, December 18, 1901

Visions of acres and acres of fertile land, new neighbors eager to till the soil, and dollar upon dollar dropping into the tax coffers quickly gave way to skepticism. The *Freeborn County Standard*, whose editor, H. G. Day, had welcomed the huge reclamation project, became the primary forum for a countywide debate, with most comments opposed to the drainage.

An editorial on New Year's Day 1902 called for a full hearing on issues raised by the drainage proposal: "Much opposition is heard from all quarters of the county, and business men in Albert Lea are becoming stirred up and are joining the rest in remonstrance against the extensive plans to involve the county in an immense bonded indebtedness. It is estimated that the big Riceland-Moscow drain will cost over $100,000, and reliable citizens of the east part of the county affirm that it will cost even more." The editorial called for a fair, measured discussion. Of the skeptics, it said, "They want publicity, and that is their right. If, when better understood, serious objections are still found to exist, there will be no difficulty in finding a remedy. If no such objections exist, and the schemes are found to be wise and safe undertakings, so much the better and all will be satisfied." John Meighen dismissed Day's conciliatory sentiments in a letter to his parents: "The proposed

Geneva-Moscow-Newry drain is the subject of wide discussion in the county. The *Freeborn County Standard*, a weekly newspaper here that delights in being 'agin' the government' has taken a decided stand against it. The *Standard* is, by the way, a populist sheet."

Farmers in the Turtle Creek watershed who would be affected by the drainage spoke out first. A group from Moscow and environs attended the January county board meeting to "remonstrate against the big ditch." An Oakland correspondent identified as "C. B." sent the *Standard* a collection of comments heard in conversations with local people: "The country is drying out too fast anyhow." "The cattle have a hard enough time getting down to water now, without having it dug down still lower." "Does the county reckon the cost of the bridges that would be required to connect parts of a pasture or other land that lie on both sides of the creek?" "Taxing the county for private benefit is objection enough, if there were no other." "The county would much better buy up the big marsh and keep it. Letting it out for hay would bring the county enough for taxes." "Aw! I think I'll ask the county to have those grubs and stones hauled off my east forty—it's a large job for me alone."

The county board was hardly thrilled to bear responsibility for such a massive undertaking. They had already shown themselves wary of P. D. McMillan's intentions eight years prior in their resistance to his appeals for a road from Ricelawn Ranch to Albert Lea. Only one of the five commissioners, Axel Brundin, who had supported the road, favored the drainage proposal from the outset. The rest had voted to delay the process for a couple of months on an advertising technicality. By January's meeting, they saw no choice but to proceed with the survey of the drainage route prescribed by state law. The new statute irked them. By laying out precisely how the county must proceed in response to a lawfully submitted petition, chapter 258 seemed to deprive local officials of any discretion in determining the *worthiness* of the proposal. Following the letter of the law would apparently get petitioners the ditch they wanted with county financing even if the board and local citizens doubted its value. A statement of the obvious—that local residents had lived amicably with the Big Marsh for a half century, haying its grasses, hunting and trapping its wildlife, letting their cattle graze in its meadows, and that they would rather continue than risk unknown consequences and bear financial debt—did not constitute a legal argument. Opponents needed to specify their objections in terms of the statute itself and the details drawn out in the petition.

The first formal objection was written in February for presentation to the March meeting of the county board and signed by "landowners and taxpayers" from Oakland, Moscow, Newry, and Riceland. They believed that damages would be greater than benefits and that the ditch would not work as intended for these reasons:

> That the presence of large beds of quicksand along the proposed route of the ditch will greatly hinder the digging of the ditch and will be a cause of perpetual annoyance to residents along its way and to the towns in the maintenance of it. That the lack of fall from the beginning of the proposed ditch is so slight that, water from above will not be carried into the Cedar river but will back up onto land along the way of the ditch and make useless very much of some of the best land in Freeborn county. And also that the maintenance of the ditch, of the fences along it and the bridges over it, will be a source of continued annoyance and expense to the towns through which the ditch passes, which burden we object to have placed upon us.

"An Old Citizen" writing in the February 26 *Standard* challenged the rest of the county to join in: "I suggest that every town meeting March 11 take a vote for or against the big ditch, and let the county board know how the people stand on the question." At least twelve townships other than those represented in the protest letter submitted petitions or resolutions or reported votes opposing the drainage. The newspapers reported some votes as unanimous, published numbers on others, and merely noted that others had passed a resolution. Of the numbers available, Hartland Township, eight miles west of the beginning of the proposed ditch, showed the highest support for the drainage: five percent, or four of the eighty voters. No groundswell of drainage proponents turned out for the township meetings.

Each township crafted its own petition or resolution. I know this because one person, at least, saw fit to keep carbon typescripts, which ended up in a box labeled "Hollandale" at the Freeborn County Historical Museum. A cover page identifies the contents as documents saved by P. D. McMillan. The Alden petition was signed by the town clerk, E. H. Ostrander, and three supervisors, all of whom signed their names again in the list of citizens, with Ostrander's first. The name of his father-in-law and my great-great-grandfather Dan Hord appears twice on the typed copy. The box also contains a letter to "the Honorable Board of County Commissioners of Freeborn County" from "E. H. Ostrander, Citizen and tax payer," intended to substitute for his presence at the upcoming county board meeting. The other protests in McMillan's collection are from Hayward, Carlston, Mansfield, Bancroft, Shell Rock, Albert Lea Township, and London. The latter is short and sweet: "On motion it was resolved that the Town of London protest against the construction of the proposed Riceland-Moscow ditch (and that there be a few cuss words interlined for them that favor it)."

The township statements follow several lines of argument against the drainage. Some saw possible damage in the exposure of quicksand in the creek bed and a risk of flooding surrounding lands. A shortage of farm labor and the growing number of farms for rent were cited to show that the county had no need of additional land. The fact that adjacent landowners didn't want the ditch was offered as reason enough to vote the proposal down. The high estimated cost of the project led some to doubt that benefits accrued would ever surpass expenses, and there would be continuing costs to the county for bridges and roads and maintenance of the ditch itself. Elbert Ostrander ventured a slippery slope argument: "While the bonding of the county to the extent of $130,000 might not be excessive it will be only the beginning of similar propositions."

The major argument was the legitimacy or morality of putting public funds at risk for private gain. "We are opposed to bonding said

County for any private enterprise whatever," the people of Hayward insisted. The citizens of Manchester wrote, "The said drain or ditch is not a public necessity, neither for sanitary purposes nor for any other public purpose, but will solely and alone redound to the gain of private individuals." Fifty-seven "freeholders" of Albert Lea Township agreed: "We feel that it is not wise to loan Public Credit for the exclusive bene-fit of a few speculators who hope to enhance the value of their nearly worthless lands by the aid, only, of Public works." History has certainly not put these concerns to rest. Echoes of the argument resound today in debates about public financing of sports stadiums.

The county board, meeting daily from March 24 through 27, 1902, received the township documents and put them "on file," but where that file ended up remains uncertain. They also received their first major invoice associated with the MacRae ditch, expenses accrued in J. W. Dappert's survey. They did not make any further decisions. Bound by the procedure spelled out in chapter 258, they waited and watched for the ditch petitioners to trip up on technicalities.

In the meantime, out of public earshot, the proponents' confidence wavered. One large landowner, L. O. Greene, a feed and fuel dealer whose occupation is identified as "capitalist" in the 1905 Minnesota State Census, had concluded that the drainage proposal didn't have "a ghost of a chance." He advised McMillan to cut his losses. Instead McMillan sought William A. Morin's help with the next step after the survey, securing sympathetic viewers: "If they should appoint men who say Black is white and White black, then they could kill it, except we have a right to appeal. No jury in Freeborn Co. would ever lay the ditch, for you could not find one that would not be dead against it from the start."

How to Read a Flying Bundle of Twine

The twine plant generated profits almost immediately.... By 1917 profits were so great that the state's legislative manual went so far as to call the Stillwater Prison "the greatest revenue producing public institution in the world."

—Sterling Evans, *Bound in Twine*

Drainage became John Meighen's specialty, but it was never his sole concern. His law practice took all comers, on issues large and small. On May 16, 1902, a dispute in Alden Township brought him out on location "hunting up testimony" from seven o'clock AM to seven o'clock PM. His diary notes, "Met Merrit [*sic*] Howe, Dan Hoard [*sic*], Oliver Howe, Arthur Stevens, Ostrander." The single name "Ostrander" is curious. It could mean any of three brothers living in Alden at the time—their father, Henry, having died three years earlier—but the mention of Hord, his father-in-law, and Merritt Howe, his neighbor and close friend, points to Elbert. Did Meighen not know his first name? Or was "Ostrander" shorthand for the town clerk who had engineered one of the antidrainage petitions to the county board? Less than two months had passed since those petitions had been filed. The names of the instigators would be fresh in Meighen's memory.

An incident at the Alden depot the following year brought these two together again. Elbert Ostrander filed a suit against the Chicago, Milwaukee and St. Paul Railroad for injuries received when he was hit by a bundle of binder twine thrown from a train. He engaged the law firm of H. H. Dunn, who was representing farmers opposed to the Riceland-Moscow ditch, and sought $2,500 for his pains. The railroad hired Meighen. A pair of references in Meighen's diary ends with a spare "Verdict in Ostrander case $800." I wish that the astute, observant Meighen had commented on the merits of the case or the personality and demeanor of this Ostrander. Was he the poetic sort inclined to turn his vision to sky and landscape, distracted enough to be caught in the path of a flying bundle of twine?

The 1903 *Alden Advance*, where I hunted in vain for more details about the incident, carries several notices about binder twine, enough to sketch out a story that could stray down the rabbit holes of marsh cultivation, forced labor, agribusiness, and international trade. Binder twine was essential to the turn-of-the-century farmer. Used by hand or with the new mechanical binder, it tied up shocks of grain and bales of hay for storage and transport.

Strands of fibrous vegetable material entwined for durability, binder twine could be made of flax, the first grain cultivated on Ricelawn Ranch's drained acreage. Flax fibers were not especially sturdy, however, so flax twine was the cheaper, less desirable variety. A "Special Chicago Letter" from E. T. Grundlach printed in both the *Standard* and the *Advance* extolled the virtues of vegetation abundant in the northern Midwest: "Have you ever walked along the outskirts of a peat bog, brushing your way through numberless, long thin weeds? The rods, reaching almost to your shoulders, are different from any other marsh weeds; they have round, solid stems unlike ordinary flat-bladed grasses and shoot straight up into the air three, four feet or more, without a joint from the root to the needle-like point." Elbert Ostrander, fond of marshside wanderings, had likely brushed through wire grass or tussock sedge (*Carex stricta*) long before he was felled by twine. Grundlach went on to say, "The grass twine men bought up, very quietly indeed, thousands and thousands of acres of marsh land—and the sellers of the waste soil laughed in their sleeves; they did not know what they were giving away and thought they had stolen a march on the rich men. There are about 1,000,000 acres of wire grass in Minnesota and Wisconsin alone, of which only a few acres remain for those not already in the grass twine business." The rest had already been put to use for carpets and furniture as well as twine, an enterprise the owners of the Big Marsh did not pursue. Before long, the domestic resources gave way to the superior sisal and manila fibers imported from Mexico's Yucatan Peninsula and the Philippines, where we can imagine the grasses cut by low-wage labor for foreign entrepreneurs.

The twine most sought by Freeborn County farmers, because of its lower price, had been manufactured since 1890 at the state prison in Stillwater. The supply of "Stillwater twine" barely kept up with demand. By the end of April 1903, the prison factory had produced a record seven million pounds, almost all of it presold. Because large orders often take priority, farmers needing average amounts organized buying clubs. The legislature regulated the sale of the prison's twine. A small amount of each season's product was reserved for farmers not affiliated with buying clubs, and first dibs went to consumers until May 1, when dealers could make their purchases. One of the area's representatives to the state house, William Wohlhuter, sat on a committee devoted to binder twine policy. The other, Ole Opdahl, served, appropriately, on the drainage committee.

Despite the state's efforts to control the binder twine trade, including private manufacturers' output, getting enough for one's own needs could be contentious. I no longer see Elbert Ostrander standing alone daydreaming alongside the tracks. I imagine a melee of farmers come to town, their wagons and horses surrounding the depot. They bombard the freight clerk, demanding their share before he has time to check off the previous buyer in his account book. Meanwhile, the crew chucks bundles off the train while buyers scramble and jostle to claim them. Anyone turning his back for a moment could be knocked down.

However it happened, I think I can guess the injury: a double infection. Competition for twine among rich and middling buyers left Ostrander afflicted with righteous anger on behalf of the common farmer. By the 1930s, he would be attending farm mortgage foreclosure auctions, persuading farmers not to bid on their less fortunate neighbors' property. He traveled to St. Paul to lobby Governor Floyd B. Olson and the state legislature, to whom he dedicated a poem celebrating Minnesota's 1933 farm mortgage moratorium. Whatever residue the hands of laboring prisoners left on the twine infected Elbert Ostrander with compassion for the incarcerated and institutionalized. While the younger of his and Bertha's eleven children were still at home, the family housed a total of thirty-six parolees from state prisons and mental hospitals, who helped on the farm until they found other work. Their son Lee recalled much later, "Some of our hired men he secured as parolees from Red Wing Reformatory. Some were drifters. One was probably a participant in the Haymarket riot. My favorite babysitter at age 4, 5, 6 was Fred Foster, whose release dad secured from the insane asylum at Rochester. He always had peppermints in his pocket which he shared with me."

Such are the dangers of being hit by a bundle tightly twined with social and economic meaning.

A Lone Voice for the Environment:
Fred McCall

It would be anachronistic to read the popular resistance to the Riceland-Moscow ditch in terms of twenty-first-century wetland preservation. The environmental movement was barely nascent, and the early conservationists had only a dawning sense of ecology, the science that demonstrates the vital interdependence of creatures and their habitats.

The League of American Sportsmen, for example, set out to protect the population of game birds so there would be enough for recreational hunting, not because birds had an intrinsic right to exist. Meighen's law partner, Henry Morgan, attended the league's national meeting in Indianapolis in February 1902 just as the ditch protesters began to speak out. The next year, President Theodore Roosevelt established Florida's Pelican Island as a bird reservation, the first of fifty-one federal bird sanctuaries and four national game refuges created during his presidency. The National Association of Audubon Societies incorporated in 1905, bringing together groups of citizens who sought greater respect for the wide variety of avian life. The impetus for some was excessive sport hunting; for others, it was the use of feathers to decorate women's hats, which threatened to do to birds what men's hat fashions had done to the beaver. The value of bird habitat was gaining recognition, but an obscure marsh in the Midwest didn't draw national attention.

In the final fifteen or so years of Elbert Ostrander's life, as public awareness of nature's importance grew, he understood himself to have been a conservationist all along—someone who found solace in nature, lived simply to cause little damage to his plot of earth, rued the harm that others inflicted, and mourned the loss of creeks and lakes and woods he held dear. He read and contributed to *Fins, Feathers, and Fur*, inaugurated in 1915 as the conservation-minded publication of the Minnesota Game and Fish Commission.

One man in the county was prescient enough to warn of the irrevocable harm the Big Ditch might cause to the environment. He was Fred McCall, the seventy-year-old postmaster of Twin Lakes. An Irish immigrant by way of Canada who had settled in Nunda Township in 1856, McCall was a tinner by trade. He posted this letter to the *Standard* in January 1902:

> If the drainage question was not of momentous consequence to southern Minnesota I would not request space for this, or any other, article on that subject in your valuable paper. But as 98 per cent of all vegetation is the product of air and water, and being so distant from the great lakes, or any other large body of water, our only reliance for plant food has been and ever must be on our swamps, sloughs and small lakes, every one of which every summer day sends out in vapor at least two tons per acre of their surface in water, which moistens and cools the atmosphere by day, and nightly descends in dew to nourish and invigorate all vegetation, and every swamp, slough or lake drained destroys a vast amount of plant food. It is a fact, notwithstanding our improved culture and seed, that for the past 35 years the yield per acre has decreased in almost exact ratio to the increase of drainage.
>
> The Moscow slough is of vastly greater value to the county as it is than it ever could be if drained. In all probability the products of that slough and Rice lake, of which it is but a continuation, have in the few past years exceeded a million dollars in value. It has produced a great amount of timber for many miles around. It has hatched more fish than ever has been hatched by our costly state fish hatchery, which with the millions of aquatic fowls and the fur bearing animals shot and trapped there by Indians and whites, must have been of great value.
>
> It has produced a luxuriant vegetation and never-failing crops everywhere within the radius of its influence. Fellow citizens, will you submit to have this county bonded for $75,000, or any other sum, to have that

slough drained and your crops deprived of plant food? I hope not, for
if this drainage is not stopped southern Minnesota will in a few more
years be a barren waste.

McCall's numbers might be questioned, but the general idea set
forth in his letter found corroboration the following week from engineer N. Y. Taylor, who "caused a stir" at a statewide meeting of county
surveyors and engineers by calling for a prohibition on the draining of
meandered lakes. The *Standard* summarized his argument: "In his
ignorance—Mr. Taylor said—man has tried to improve upon the conditions of nature, and in some cases, the attempt has proved disastrous.
Years ago, when lakes were plentiful, drouth was unknown in Minnesota. Now it is a phenomenon ever recurring and at shorter intervals.
Mr. Taylor said the drouths are due to two things—the cutting away of
forests and the draining of lakes, and the draining of lakes is the more
mischievous of the two."

Fred McCall had sounded the alarm before. A more modest proposal in 1895 to enlarge the channel of Lime Creek to keep Bear Lake
from spilling onto farmland had roused him to write, "We think private
avarice should not be allowed to rob the public of these beautiful lakes,
and the man that will ask the people's money to pay for such piracy is
utterly devoid of conscience and has more brass in his face than brains
in his skull. If the lowering and draining of our lakes are not soon
stopped the fertile fields of Minnesota will be an arid desert."

Drainage proponents dismissed his arguments as more fanciful than
scientific. When prose failed to convince, McCall turned to poetry.
Here, for the sheer appreciation of the "future generations" he addressed,
are stanzas five through seven of his poem, "To the Old Settlers":

But if we let the lakes be drained,
And forests all defaced,
That soon would make this fertile land
A black and barren waste.

Protect the lakes at any cost,
Keep them full flowing o'er,
Plant trees on every place you can,
The moisture for to store.

And then the land will richer grow,
With each succeeding age,
And be for millions yet unborn,
A fruitful heritage.

Counterarguments

January and February in Minnesota are hardly suited for a meticulous outdoor survey, but at least the marsh and creek were frozen enough to walk on. The winter of 1902 turned out to be milder than usual, causing concern about summer ice storage. Fountain Lake, where the city of Albert Lea cut its ice, was frozen to a depth of only thirteen inches, so the blocks set aside were smaller than ideal and at risk of thawing. The moderate temperatures, however, allowed the survey crew to do its work in efficient all-day shifts.

James W. Dappert had set out on January 20 with County Engineer Frank Fisk as his assistant and six chainmen, two stake setters, a rodman, and two teams of horses with their drivers. They worked in one-hundred-foot segments along the proposed course of the MacRae ditch and broke for midday meals, reimbursed by the county, at farms along the way. The chainmen earned thirty dollars each for their labors; the rodman's work was valued at forty. Engineer Fisk received $130 for his services. Dappert's fee, which included many borings deep into the frozen ground, ran to $638.90.

For two days prior to the survey, Dappert had "consulted" and "conferred" with John Meighen. Although his survey was to be an objective measure of the physical dimensions of the ditch, he had a stake in its construction. Educated as a civil engineer, Dappert had worked on buildings, mines, and irrigation systems in Kansas, Colorado, and New Mexico before starting his own business back home in Illinois. The specialty he developed in the drainage of agricultural land had taken him all over the Midwest and to upstate New York in the previous fourteen years. Yet an Illinois history containing a profile of Dappert identifies the ditch "in South Minnesota" as one of the most impressive projects on his résumé.

The crew finished its survey the second week of February, and Dappert returned to his wife and six children in Taylorville, where he would review the measurements, make the requisite calculations, and draw up plans to submit to the county board. If the commissioners voted to undertake the project, they would put Dappert's plan out for bids. Freeborn County citizens, meanwhile, composed the petitions and resolutions opposing the drainage that they presented in March.

In response to the protests, Meighen wrote to Dappert, Bryant H. Barber, and Barber's hometown lawyer, John C. Seyster, to suggest an educational campaign promoting the value of drainage. Dappert sent a long letter, which Meighen circulated to local newspapers. The *Standard* made no mention of it. The *Albert Lea Enterprise* acknowledged receipt but wrote, "We are compelled to omit publishing it in full owing to its extreme length." The *Evening Tribune* printed excerpts, calling it "a private letter to J. F. D. Meighen." Only the *Alden Advance* gave it the two columns it required, under the heading "That Moscow Ditch." The letter is not the number-laden report Dappert made to the county board but rather a persuasive text meant to put objections to rest.

"The proposed system of drainage is practical and feasible," Dappert assures readers. The "numerous borings" he has made over the whole marsh reveal that "the surface soil is a black, decomposed vegetable compost, varying from two to eleven feet in depth, and underlaid with a blue, or greenish blue boulder clay" that he deems "practically impervious to water." The soil throughout is suited to ditching and promises "a good hard bed." He dismisses concerns about quicksand by describing the sand he found as "a true water-bearing sand, being coarse-grained and mixed with gravel, pebbles, and in some cases with boulders." It is "nowhere of great depth" and everywhere underlain with blue clay. "I cannot understand what the land owners conceive a quicksand to be," he adds, "unless they regard the loose slushy muck within the creek bed to be a sort of quicksand." That muck could be easily dredged.

There are no plans to drain Geneva Lake, Dappert promises, only the areas where it overflows the land. To the concern that drainage might diminish rainfall, he explains that the sources of rainfall are the Gulf of Mexico and the Atlantic Ocean, while the small lakes of Minnesota "have no effect whatever on precipitation."

At this point, the letter turns from the scientific evidence to the agricultural benefits of the drainage, its effect on the local economy, and the validity of the drainage law itself. It waxes prophetic in its description of how the land would change: "It must of necessity advance greatly in value as it becomes very productive; then it becomes too high-priced to hold for a fixed investment and it will be sold out in small tracts and every quarter section will be owned by a man who resides upon it, and all over this marsh will be dotted with houses, with barns, school houses and creameries, and looking down over this valley from the west will be one of the finest sights ever witnessed."

Within days of Dappert's letter, County Attorney A. U. Mayland offered his legal opinion. Noting that county boards had often refused ditch proposals that didn't promote public health, convenience, or welfare, he alleged that chapter 258 "was passed to force their hand." By omitting the requirement to show public good, the law allowed that "any person by making and filing his petition, accompanied with the proper bond, can take his neighbor's lands against his will and use the same to drain his own lands, and furthermore assess the lands of his neighbor for the cost of draining his own land. . . . It seems to me that the said act violates one of the fundamental principles of our laws and is therefore unconstitutional."

The county board had already questioned the constitutionality of the law for depriving them of decision-making authority. Mayland's opinion bolstered their objection, but they were spared from having to act on it. A group of Polk County taxpayers had filed a writ of certiory to prevent their county board from condemning lands for a drainage project that would benefit only private persons. The Freeborn County Board could sit tight and wait for that case to be resolved. They heard Dappert's report at their July meeting but postponed the next step, the appointment of three local viewers, until October. "They seem agin' us," John Meighen wrote in his diary.

Nature stirred the controversy with worrisome variations in the weather. A drought early in the year impelled the wag submitting Moscow news to the *Mower County Transcript* to joke, "The Turtle creek is nearly dry. The fish are calling for rain and the frogs are going to and fro inquiring of one and another about where they can find the big ditch." May brought a torrent of rain, and stormy weather continued into the fall. One weekly account reported, "The total rainfall was more than six inches, the lakes are filled to a high mark, all streams are torrents and low lands are flooded as in the early days before the county was settled." Rather than declare a disaster, it concluded, "Except on overflowed land, however, the rain is considered a great benefit to crops and no more than the land requires."

Elections were coming up, and the mood of the electorate was easy to read. Ole Opdahl, running for the state house, urged the county board to refuse the MacRae petition: "These men bought the land for what it was worth, and if it is as easy to drain as they say, why do they not go ahead and drain their land without asking the aid of the county?" Henry Morgan promised that if elected to the state senate he would work to restore county boards' discretion over drainage matters. Without naming names, he questioned the validity of the proposal brought by his law partner Meighen's clients: "I am not in favor of draining or improving private property at public expense, and am opposed to any and all legislation having this object in view and shall vigorously work against the same." The day Morgan's statement appeared, Meighen spent hours addressing envelopes and stuffing them with educational slips favoring drainage. In the evening, he deployed his girlfriend, Sybil Koontz, and her younger sister, Lulu, to help him complete the job.

Meighen had solicited a statement from County Commissioner Brundin and spent two August days ghostwriting it after an evening's discussion. It was so lengthy and detailed that the *Standard* reduced its font size to fit it into three columns on one page. It bears evidence of Meighen's easy eloquence and thoughtful argumentation. The text strikes a careful balance between defending the county board's caution and advocating for the drainage, first reviewing the 1901 law and showing step by step how the county board had complied. "We have been criticized by the friends of the drain for not hastening matters and we have been criticized by others for doing what the law commanded us to do," it notes, soft-pedaling Brundin's disagreements with fellow commissioners, "but we have steadfastly endeavored to safeguard the interests of Freeborn county and are willing to submit our acts to the candid judgment of the citizens of this county." The letter tries to soothe taxpayers' fears of the costs of the drain by spelling out the financing process and assuring readers that the land's value would rise by multiples of two or three. Brundin would never ask the county to pay to drain the land of private landowners, but he has no objections to the county's loaning them money. The letter reminds readers that "our supreme court has repeatedly held that surface water, in sloughs, swamps or elsewhere, is a common enemy, and that owners may get rid of it in the best way they can so long as they do not unnecessarily or unreasonably injure others." Although the letter appeared in plenty of time to influence the county board's October deliberations, the commissioners again postponed the appointment of viewers.

A Minnesota Supreme Court ruling on November 7, 1902, quashed the Polk County taxpayers' writ of certiory and upheld the constitutionality of chapter 258. To the claim that the law undermined the county board's authority, it answered that in the case of an "imperfectly drawn" statute—unclear writing, technical errors, omissions—the court would infer the legislature's intent from the whole rather than throw it out. It left the determination of public benefit to the Polk County Board to settle after following the procedures set forth in the law.

The Freeborn County Board could delay no longer. On December 1, they appointed three viewers, established county residents in their forties, to follow the route of Dappert's survey and appraise damages and benefits to property along the way. They were T. P. Jensen, a Danish-born boot and shoe dealer in Albert Lea who had been conferring with Meighen and other drainage proponents, and farmers George D. Frisbie of Moscow and A. H. Skaug, a Bancroft Norwegian. Lulu Koontz, not Sybil, sent Meighen a dozen chrysanthemums in congratulations.

Another swampland controversy wound up the year on a different note. Under the heading FOUNTAIN LAKE FOREVER, the *Standard* expressed its joy that "Fountain lake will be preserved and remain forever to benefit and bless the people of Freeborn county and endure unimpaired to contribute to the glory of Albert Lea and the pride and joy of its people." A landowner's claim for flood damages had been denied. "The issue involved the existence of the lake as a natural body of water," the article explained. "The jury found that it is a natural, a public body of water, and that the city had a right to maintain and protect it." One might argue that Rice Lake and the Big Marsh were natural bodies of water, too. At the time of European settlement, Fountain Lake had been an "unsightly" marsh clogged with eight-foot stalks of wild rice. The dam that turned it into a classic, lovely sheet of water had saved its life.

The Moscow Farm Prospers

John Register has a gang of carpenters building a $3,000 dwelling home on his big farm. He says it will cover so much land that there will be no room for the big ditch through his place.

—*Mower County Transcript*, June 11, 1902

Robert Speer lay cradled in the stillness of winter in the bed where he had slept for a near half century. His log house had grown larger, his family had added a generation, and his thoughts lingered on the familiar here at the center of his ebbing life. Amanda and the granddaughters tended to him, and Marietta had come from Wisconsin to help. Dear Mary fretted over him, too, but her diminished mind could make little sense of his sallow skin, his immobile body.

In the hours he spent alone, he listened. Beyond the bustling in the house around him, he listened for the calming sounds he knew: the horses stirring and huffing in their stalls, the milk cows lowing, the cackling of one hen arousing the whole flock. He listened for the wilder sounds: the red fox cracking the crust of the snow as it dove for a field mouse beneath, the mink setting its stealthy paw on the frozen creek, the muskrat rustling the dry grasses of its lodge, unwittingly luring the mink. He listened, too, for the occasional breaks in the quiet: the howl of a wolf in the Moscow woods, the haunting call of the few overwintering geese drawn to the open water of the mill pond.

Human footsteps crunched the snow along the Turtle, four pairs of feet measuring the length of the creek for its impending destruction. One pair was outfitted in sturdy boots: the shoeman, Jensen, from Albert Lea. One was the engineer, Dappert, who had passed by the year before. Skaug was another. The tramp tramp of their feet could almost be taken for the approach of death. The fourth man, George Frisbie, would indeed help carry Speer's body to the grave.

Death came on January 29, 1903, sparing Robert Speer, at seventy-five, any further worries for the fate of lovely Turtle Creek, the expansive marsh, and the remnants of the timberland that had drawn him to this piece of the frontier. He left the place in good hands. Sons George and DeWitt had departed on their own journeys, so it had fallen to Amanda and her enterprising husband, John Register, to carry on after Robert's retirement. They had done well, despite concern that his son-in-law's impatience made him ill suited for farming. Among the sounds he heard on his deathbed were the hammers enclosing the frame of a fine new farmhouse that would make of his own home a storage shed.

Robert Speer left one hundred dollars to each of his surviving children except for Amanda, who already had her share. He left her his parlor organ, willed his harness and buggy to grandson Bert, and reserved the rest for his "beloved wife Mary Speer," who lived another eighteen months.

Amanda and John had expanded the Speer claim by 240 acres. They had taken up dairy farming and built a barn dedicated with the requisite barn dance in the summer of 1892. John served as a director of the creamery and was cited as "our leading dairyman" in 1900 after earning

Threshing on the Register farm, 1918

Moscow's biggest creamery check. The Registers owned a few beef cattle and were successful crop farmers as well. The year 1901 had been unusually productive. They had sold timothy seed by the hundred-weight, shipped a railcar of flax out west, and pronounced their potato crop the best ever. Later they planted an orchard of Charlamoff apples.

The new house promised to be "one of the finest in the vicinity," according to the *Austin Daily Herald*. Over the two years it took to complete it, the Moscow and Oakland contributors to the *Herald* and the *Transcript* reported loads of lumber arriving, casings put up, and plastering going on inside. It was no mansion, just a tall, three-generation farmhouse with an open porch, like others rising on productive family farms in the first two decades of the twentieth century.

Their move into the house in February 1904, along with a new Story and Clark piano, enhanced the Registers' way of life. To celebrate their twenty-fifth anniversary that May, they threw a party for fifty friends and neighbors. The new house accommodated the Moscow Musical Club and the Ladies Aid of the Oakland Baptist Church, and housed

Register farmhouse, Moscow, Minnesota, between 1910 and 1914. Family members, left to right, are Lida Register, Eliza Register Wortley of Kansas, Lee Ostrander, Roy Register, Amanda Register, and John Register

visiting relatives from Chester, Iowa; Janesville, Wisconsin; and faraway McPherson, Kansas. Property tax lists showed the Registers to be among the wealthiest of Moscow's farmers, although their farm was no competitor to Ricelawn Ranch.

Amanda and John implanted their hopes for a prosperous future in their children. They sent oldest daughter Hattie to Albert Lea College for Women, a Presbyterian school to which she traveled back and forth on holidays with a Hormel girl. She left school early, however, to marry and move to Austin. Daughter Anna caught herself a butter-maker-in-training, Peter Christiansen, who secured a creamery position in nearby Lansing. John and Amanda saw their sons as heirs to the farm and designed the house with space for an extended family, not like the cramped quarters they had shared with Amanda's parents. When Roy and Leslie needed surgery in quick succession, their father took them to the Mayo hospital in Rochester.

The sour note in the Register family was eldest son Bert, or Robert, named for his grandfather. He frequently stumbled into trouble. He let his horse wander away and go missing overnight while he danced at the Moscow town hall. He got in the way of a "vicious cow" and broke his arm. Shortly after his grandfather's death, Bert was arrested and hauled off to Albert Lea for shooting a neighbor's dog. He was acquitted and had apparently earned some sympathy. As the *Standard*'s Moscow correspondent put it, "There are several other dogs around here that should be registered in the same way." By August 1903, John saw fit to disown or emancipate Bert. The legal announcement is terse: "I hereby give notice to all persons that I have this day given his time to my minor son, Robert D. Register, and from date I will not be responsible for or pay any debts which he may contract and I will not claim or hold any of his earnings." In time, Bert moved to Kansas to work for his uncle Lyman, but he returned three months later after "some experience he will not soon forget. He was drugged and robbed of his watch and money in Kansas City and had to remain in a hospital several days before he could resume his journey homeward." Hapless, vulnerable Bert—"nervous" in the family's vocabulary—would keep landing wherever refuge was offered. In retrospect, Robert Speer's endowment of harness and buggy looks like an act of knowing grandfatherly affection.

While Bert's condition was a sorrow, Roy and Leslie were sturdy, smart young men. John and Amanda had every reason to believe that the land they had inherited and tended so ambitiously would be a lasting legacy for their descendants. Yet that dreaded ditch threatening to eat into their land marred their vision of the future.

Meighen in Court and Courting

Spend evening in office until 12 midnight working on brief in drainage case. So many callers during day that one cannot work.

—John F. D. Meighen, Diary, January 4, 1904

The years 1903 through 1905 tested the mettle of young attorney J. F. D. Meighen. While he gained competence in his profession, his personal life remained unsteady. His diary chronicles, in brief notations, a struggle to keep it all in balance.

The viewers sent out in January 1903 to calculate benefits and damages to the land along the proposed ditch filed their majority report in early March. Meighen had noted in his diary the week before that "the viewers are agin' us in the drainage proposition." Indeed, Frisbie and Skaug found against the drainage. Their calculations showed costs and damages of $150,734.70, exceeding benefits of $136,018.55. In addition, they deemed the ditch "impracticable" due to lack of fall in elevation along its course and the quantity of sand in Turtle Creek.

The third viewer, T. P. Jensen, issued his minority report three weeks later. Meanwhile, County Auditor I. L. Ingbritsen had published the legally required notice listing the owners of the affected lands, Amanda Register, John Register, and Mary Speer among them. Jensen's calculations favored the ditch, the main difference being his valuation of land in Rice and Mud lakes after drainage. He estimated thirty dollars per acre to Skaug and Frisbie's seventeen dollars. Noting that Turtle Creek grew wider and deeper as it flowed, he contended that straightening its channel would increase its fall. He also cited the standard public benefit—ridding the area of a "nuisance" dangerous to health.

The day Jensen released his report, Meighen was in Chicago meeting with Bryant H. Barber. He had taken his mother along and spent time between meetings dining out, seeing a play, and taking a five-dollar carriage ride. He composed a letter to the Freeborn County Board meant to nullify the difference between the majority and minority reports: Mary and Bryant Barber declared their intent to take responsibility for any drained land in Rice Lake that might be left with its assessments unpaid. They promised to buy up to 850 acres at the highest estimated value if need be.

As soon as Meighen got home, he began preparing for the April 6 county board meeting, which opened at two o'clock with a reading of the viewers' reports. Meighen spoke on behalf of Mary Barber, urging adoption of the minority report, while Bryant Barber stood by to underscore the guarantee in their letter. H. H. Dunn, representing area farmers, endorsed the majority report. William A. Morin, P. D. McMillan, and others spoke until adjournment at six o'clock. "Hearing was a farce," Meighen wrote in his diary. The board reconvened the next morning with Dappert's testimony. Commissioner Wohlhuter then introduced a resolution to "refuse to establish and construct said ditch" and to order the petitioners—namely McMillan and Morin, who had posted bond—to reimburse the county for the expenses of the survey and review. Meighen objected to the resolution, as did McMillan and Morin. A vote was taken, with all in favor of Wohlhuter's resolution except Commissioner Brundin. BIG DITCH KNOCKED OUT, the *Standard* headline read the next day. Meighen wrote in his diary, "All smoothly for a while. Then Morin threw in a bomb which smashed things." What Morin did to bear blame for the MacRae petition's failure remains a mystery.

The ditch petitioners decided to appeal the board's decision and dispatched Meighen on a whirlwind trip to Minneapolis, St. Paul, and Chicago to build the case. McMillan added new personnel to the effort, including his son, Dana (P. D., Jr.), just twenty-one and a student at the University of Minnesota, and attorney and fellow Vermonter Henry C. Belden, with whom Meighen conferred often. Meighen worked on the appeal most of every day and courted Sybil Koontz in the evening. On a Saturday in April, with McMillan and Belden in town for consultation, he "felt very dead all day." He had danced with Sybil at the Knights of Pythias lodge until well after midnight. Fortunately he had no Saturday evening plans. "Retired at 8:00 PM as I felt worn out," he wrote. He spent Sunday in the country, visiting the farmers who had signed the petition and eating dinner at C. U. Christensen's. He must have caught up on his sleep because he reported, "Quite a pleasant day."

Meighen drafted two separate appeals for the May term of the Tenth Judicial District Court, one on behalf of Mary Barber alone and the other for McMillan and twelve others. They were similar in substance, disputing the viewers' conclusions, charging them with prejudice, and reiterating arguments about public utility and benefit. Just as he completed that work, the New York production of Henrik Ibsen's *Ghosts* starring Mary Shaw came to town. He and Sybil went to see it and finished the evening with a dance at the Elks Club. "Sybil that Ghosts bad," he wrote, but didn't say whether she faulted the performance or the play's taboo subject matter.

Nothing happened in May court. The case was deferred until the next session, and Meighen used that time to file for a change of venue. He cited newspaper coverage to show that public opinion in the county was biased. Meanwhile, it rained and rained. "Such a May deluge was never before known to the oldest inhabitant," the *Standard* claimed. Water stood in the fields delaying spring planting. The Moscow correspondent described the path across the marsh as "awful damp." "The question is asked on every hand: What will we do with our low land?" None of the township reports suggested ditching Turtle Creek.

During the lull in court action, Meighen and his mother took a "recreative and sight-seeing visit" to Colorado, where they encountered Sybil's parents, Mr. and Mrs. Henry Koontz of the American Mercantile Company, who were also traveling in the area. Upon his return in September, Meighen asked Sybil to marry him. The news made the *Standard*: "The pleasing announcement of the engagement of Miss Sybil Koontz and J. F. D. Meighen is made public. They are among the first of the estimable and popular young people of Albert Lea and their prospective union is recognized as most fitting to be made." Meighen showed less enthusiasm in his diary: "Home all day. Official Bd. meeting in evening. Russell Abbott borrowed $3 yesterday. Presented Sybil with ring during evening. Did not accomplish much in office. Found flaw to Henry Stenerson's title. Draw Wallum mortgage."

After a Sunday together reading Hawthorne aloud and playing fan tan and whist, the young couple found the drainage case encroaching more and more on their engagement. John was back in court on September 21, and Sybil left in October for a month-long visit with relatives. He traveled to Minneapolis and St. Paul and came home to work piling up in the absence of his partner, Senator Morgan. Court resumed on November 20, and his diary notes tersely, "Drainage hearing." Some stirrings in his personal life claimed more space. November 19: "Called on Etta during evening." November 21: "Met a friend at cor. of Pres. Ch. at 10:30 pm. Singular coincidence." November 22: "4–5:15 with Sybil. Last 15 min. was nerve trying. 6:30–7:30 E. L." November 23: "In evening donned my spike tail and a white tie, called for Sybil and listened to and looked at dainty Dolly Varden, fragrant as a summer garden." A nationwide tour of the popular comic opera had come to Albert Lea, and Meighen seldom passed up a cultural opportunity, no matter the strain on his and Sybil's nerves.

Work on the drainage appeal ramped up after Thanksgiving, with Dappert and the McMillan forces meeting at district court in Austin and out on the marshy landscape despite the chilly weather. Meighen recorded more tense moments with Sybil, but as he got ready for a December 22 hearing, she agreed to do his Christmas shopping. He spent Christmas with his parents in LeRoy and continued on to Chicago to meet with Bryant Barber. He sent Barber a bill for $436.76, then wrote in his diary ten days later, "Wonder why Barber is so slow about paying up." Meeting his clients' demands in record time was no guarantee of quick payment. Fortunately Morgan had agreed that Meighen should receive two-thirds of the firm's income while he was handling the bulk of the work. The same day he noted that agreement in his diary, he wrote, "'The man who marries for money, earns it.' Sparklett."

One month after the hearing, on January 23, 1904, Judge Nathan Kingsley of the Tenth Judicial District issued his order in the Riceland-Moscow drainage appeal. He left standing the county board's refusal to construct the ditch but did not rule on its merits. The list of affected landowners that the county auditor circulated had turned out to be incomplete. That technicality was enough to defeat Meighen's effort. Within days, the temperature fell to thirty-five degrees below zero, and the water closet in his office froze.

His primary task in the following months was an appeal to the Minnesota Supreme Court. Amid work and business travel, he squeezed in a few evening hours and weekend lunches with Sybil. On Valentine's Day, he wrote his parents,

> Informed Sybil some time ago that my parents looked with extreme disfavor on our engagement. She suggested that such a view was hardly fair to her by reason of the fact that neither of you had ever met her except for a few minutes, and asked me to invite you to Albert Lea. Informed her that I would do so, but that I doubted very much whether you would accept the invitation. Am writing this to you, so that you will be fully informed of the situation. Our engagement is getting on the ragged edge and bids fair to go to pieces before long.

The stresses of law and romance began to take their toll on Meighen's mood. "Feel rather pessimistic and agin' the universe," he wrote on March 19. Events of the next few days did not disperse the clouds. March 20: "Someone took my coat while at Sunday School. Day ended in rain. No calling today—. Discovered to my pain that bank bal. is overdrawn some $200.00." March 23: "Get my wrist scratched in a somewhat unusual manner during evening." The month ended with a fateful personal decision: "Dissolved a contract with Sybil—a thoroughly painful and sad evening's work on my part—."

His mother may have felt vindicated for her misgivings about Sybil, but Meighen's blue period continued. Money was coming in slowly, and Morgan was still absent, not on senate business but because of his drinking, which was eroding the partnership. Local farmers still looked askance at absentee landowners' desire for public funding. Although Meighen paid no attention to the circumstance in his diary, a series of socialist meetings drew hefty audiences to the Moscow town hall, in the area most actively opposed to the drainage.

Meighen's spirits lifted with the summer sun and his debut before the state supreme court on June 21, 1904, at age twenty-seven. He didn't get to introduce the appeal, listed as "P. D. McMillan et al. vs. The Board of County Commissioners of Freeborn County." That privilege fell to seasoned attorney Henry C. Belden, who had served just two years as a district judge yet still bore the title "Judge Belden" as an honorific. H. H. Dunn answered for the opposition, and then Meighen got his turn. He celebrated by eating lunch at Schiek's and enjoying "a good strong sleep" at the Windsor Hotel. The *Minneapolis Journal* conjectured that the case would go to the US Supreme Court because of disputed provisions in the state drainage law.

The Minnesota Supreme Court announced its decision on July 15, but it went unrecorded in Meighen's diary. He was on to new efforts at courting: "Attend Chautauqua with Marie Southwick. Suppose some of my friends will talk some." The supreme court settled no big issues, ruling only that the county board's refusal was indeed subject to appeal and that the calculation of benefits and damages could be contested. It referred the case back to the district court.

As Meighen began preparing for a new round in district court, P. D. McMillan turned to William A. Morin for help. He was afraid the county board might "bamboozle" H. H. Dunn into taking the case to the US Supreme Court, where Dunn would "get cleaned out of his boots without any doubt." "Cannot you do something so no appeal will be allowed and this case allowed to proceed on its merits," he urged Morin, adding, "I do not fear the outcome but I hate the delay."

"Feel rather pessimistic," Meighen confided to his diary on New Year's Eve. The district court session was scheduled for January 16, 1905, at the Freeborn County Courthouse—not the neutral venue Meighen had sought, but Judge Kingsley had recused himself in favor of Judge

Lewis of Ramsey County. McMillan brought in two more former judges to lead the charge: Robert Jamison, who had been the private secretary of Governor Samuel Van Sant, and James M. Taylor of Illinois, "an expert on drainage law and proceedings." Meighen stood third in the ranking. Dappert, McMillan, and landowner L. O. Greene testified first. Dunn and County Attorney Mayland had lined up more than a hundred witnesses but called instead for a dismissal on technical grounds: the names of five affected farmers had been left off the latest legal notice. On January 24, after Meighen had sat up late trying to find a way around that omission, Judge Lewis dismissed the case. Had the error been overlooked, other obstacles stood in the way: threatened injunctions from Geneva citizens who feared for the future of their lake and from Mower County farmers whose lands might be flooded.

That evening, rather than mope in defeat, Meighen attended a Knights of Pythias meeting and was impressed enough with the new ceremonial robes to mention them in his diary. The MacRae proposal was dead, but it had gained Meighen enough stature to be invited to draft legislation and to testify before the state senate and house drainage committees. His major work through the spring was revising the state drainage statute. When summer came, he went rowing and lay in a hammock "talking slush" with Marie Southwick, his roommate's sister, who would prove no more compatible a mate than Sybil. Notoriety and new romance didn't assure him a decent living. "Am running behind at the bank must do something to brace up," he wrote. "Very little money coming in. A great deal going out."

One loyal woman who stood by him through his bumpy courtships, his overloaded schedule, and his financial hardships won occasional credit in his diary. She was Anna Svanberg, his stenographer, who not only stayed late in the office and spent extra hours at the courthouse transcribing documents, but also lent a sympathetic ear to his personal worries. The two of them might have made a good match, but the prospect went unmentioned. She stuck by him until her marriage in November 1906.

The Winning Strategy

With the MacRae ditch case dismissed and no appeal forthcoming, objecting farmers looked ahead to spring planting with renewed confidence. They might have cheered the David and Goliath finish—a tiny technical oversight had curtailed the big landowners' plans—but they would probably have preferred a definitive ruling on the issues they raised. Some kept up their campaign of persuasion. Elbert Ostrander stopped by Meighen's office in the months after the dismissal to "consume time," as Meighen put it. He was carrying an extra burden of sorrow. A lightning bolt had struck his barn the previous autumn while five of his children were playing in the haymow. Seven-year-old Cora was killed instantly, while two other daughters suffered serious burns. His son Floyd had died at age seven four years earlier, and the loss of children became a recurring theme in Ostrander's poetry.

Life on the Big Marsh and along Turtle Creek continued in rhythms familiar and natural after fifty years of European settlement. The township news told of good fishing and successful trapping. C. U. Christensen sold "exclusive trapping rights" on the Barber lands in all four of the marshy townships. Two enterprising Moscow residents built a hunting lodge along the marsh in time for the fall migration. Families, church congregations, and groups of young people enjoyed warm-weather outings along the creek: "Some of the young people of Oakland picnicked on the banks of Turtle Thursday chaperoned by Mrs. N. A. Shipton. The time was delightfully spent in games, horse back riding, swimming. A bountiful lunch was served consisting of fried chicken, sandwitches, salads, deviled eggs, pickles, honey, cake, cookies and ice cream, which were partaken of with zest and at a late hour all returned to their homes tired and happy."

News of the Big Ditch disappeared from local papers for nearly a year, but the effort to drain the Big Marsh had not gone dormant. Ongoing consultation in certain quarters kept the vision alive. P. D. McMillan had his soil tested to make a case for its value and sent the results to William A. Morin, whose help he continued to solicit. "Still it is of great 'Public utility' as a hunting ground for Muskrats," McMillan scoffed. Getting the drainage accomplished is the primary subject of John Meighen's diaries from January 1905 to halfway through 1907, alongside the ups and downs of romance, plays and Chautauqua lectures, his work toward new degrees in the Knights of Pythias and the Masons, and travels with Mother.

The day after Judge Lewis's ruling, H. G. Koontz, the father of Meighen's erstwhile fiancée, Sybil, had called to suggest a "farmer's ditch," which Meighen understood as "presumably a smaller ditch." Drainage of low spots in cultivated fields was becoming routine. Farmers dug or paid for their own ditches or banded together with neighbors in joint efforts. Others contracted with the county to control overflow from lakes adjoining their property. These petitions generated their own disputes over property rights or damage to the landscape. As a known drainage lawyer, Meighen helped resolve such "nuisances." Maybe a smaller-scale ditch would be more acceptable than the huge canal the MacRae petition had called for. By the end of April, McMillan, too, saw the merits of a more modest approach. He told Meighen he would like to cut Engineer Dappert's plan by half. His intention was made public, but no details were provided.

Reducing the ditch to a size less threatening to the farmers in its path became one element in a new three-pronged strategy. Meighen was already at work on the second, writing a new state drainage bill and testifying on its behalf before both houses of the legislature. McMillan had been consistently frustrated in his dealings with Freeborn County officials. He saw the county commissioners, except for Axel Brundin, as obstinate, ignorant adversaries standing in the way of progress. Chapter

230 of the Minnesota Statutes of 1905 passed unanimously in April after
a bit of amending. It shows Meighen's hand at work in its meticulous
detail and in several provisions intended to soothe McMillan's frustrations. It included a procedure to override a dismissal of a petition based
on simple failure to give proper notice. Any single petitioner could
apply for a rehearing within one year. It mandated that any county official who "refuses, or willfully neglects" to perform the duties prescribed
in the statute "shall be guilty of a misdemeanor." Did the McMillan
forces suspect Auditor Ingbritsen of deliberately omitting landowners'
names from his list? The statute also gave the county board authority
to correct and change the findings in a viewer's report. It ordered the
county to repay bondholders who provided surety for a failed petition if a ditch was later constructed along the same route. McMillan
and Morin were, in the meantime, refusing to reimburse the county for
the costs of the MacRae ditch survey. The statute also omitted from
legal protection any meandered lake that was "normally shallow and
grassy and of a marshy character." Rice and Mud lakes fit that description; Geneva Lake was open enough at its center to be spared.

The surest way to get the Big Marsh drained was to bypass the reluctant county board altogether. The solution was the "judicial ditch," an
entity created in a preceding statute and refined in chapter 230. A ditch
that crossed county lines fell under the jurisdiction of the state district court. Extending the ditching of Turtle Creek into Mower County
would put its fate into the hands of the judge of the Tenth Judicial District. Because McMillan counted judges from other districts among his
friends, he might have an easier time convincing this gentleman than
trying to enlighten a benighted crew of farmer politicians. There was
not one fellow New Englander on the Freeborn County Board, just
two Norwegians, a German, a Yorker, and one friendly Swedish meat
dealer.

The third prong in the new strategy was a change in the cast of char-
acters. The resentment toward wealthy outsiders that had plagued the
MacRae petition would not be allowed to derail a new one. The signatories to a new petition would all be local. Even though McMillan and

the Barbers stood to gain the most, their signatures were unnecessary as long as others could be found to replace them. Fourteen local folks played the visible ditch proponents in the next act of the drainage drama. They signed a brand-new petition for a judicial ditch and filed it with the clerk of court of the Tenth Judicial District on January 4, 1906. The drama was directed, however, and its illusions created by two local attorneys and a fleet of strategists from the Twin Cities, Illinois, and Iowa who worked behind the scenes on what Meighen called "the drainage scheme."

The "farmer's ditch," besides being smaller than the initial proposal, would presumably be sought by farmers. The first to sign was indeed a Geneva farmer, Norwegian-born Hans J. Eid, and the proposal became known as the Eid petition. Only four more farmers' names appeared: Herbert F. and Mary C. Haynes, Eid's neighbors; Andrew Brown, a Riceland Creamery officer; and Frank W. Scott, a young widowed farmer who was a friend of Meighen's. Three signatories had also joined the MacRae petition: Louisa C. Lunquist, who still owned a 160-acre farm adjacent to Ricelawn Ranch, and the Brown brothers, Albert Lea residents. Harris N., a banker, and Lewis A., a dentist and druggist, also dealt in real estate and mortgage loans. Harris relocated to Minneapolis before the petition was heard in court. Lewis and Meighen became close friends and spent many summer evenings walking around Fountain Lake or rowing upon it, especially when Meighen was short a girlfriend. The remaining signatories lived in Albert Lea, although some owned land near the marsh: Hans Eid's brother Bent, a salesman; Carl L. Swenson, a bank cashier and city councilman; Thorvald V. Knatvold, a former state senator; John G. Sharp, a windmill manufacturer, and his brother James E., a well driller, who could expect demand for their services to grow after drainage; and Henry G. Koontz, president of the Albert Lea Mercantile Company. Two significant local names from the 1901 petition were absent from the new version: C. U. Christensen, who remained active behind the scenes, conferring often with Meighen and hosting the out-of-town players; and William A. Morin, who was spending longer segments of the year traveling.

The drainage scheme operated almost entirely in a clandestine manner. Newspapers did not report its tactics or its progress. We know of it now only because J. F. D. Meighen tracked it in his diary. Whenever Meighen traveled to Minneapolis and St. Paul or to Chicago, he met with some configuration of a team of eight strategists. Two of them, McMillan and Bryant Barber, had a huge investment in the success of the petition. Another, James W. Dappert, was, like Meighen, doing his job, applying his engineering skills when hired. True to the ethic of his profession, he supported agricultural drainage as a matter of progress. He and Meighen became good friends even though Dappert was nearly twenty years older. Absent from home and his large family for weeks at a time, he sought Meighen's companionship and confidence. They shared meals, took evening walks, and discussed personal concerns, such as the "wandering" of a Dappert son.

The name Isaac S. Struble spread across the plat maps as he bought up parcels of marshland. A lawyer and former congressman, Struble represented the Western Investment Company of Le Mars, Iowa, or so he said. Once the ditch was under way, he would transfer his land to Barber. Struble had grown up in Polo, Illinois. Milton M. Trumbauer, the head cashier of the Barber Bank, did much of Barber's legwork, traveling to Freeborn County to meet interested parties and persuade the hesitant. McMillan brought to the team the two Minneapolis lawyers he had engaged earlier, former judges Henry C. Belden and Robert Jamison.

The eighth strategist is a puzzle. On Sunday, July 2, 1905, Meighen noted in his diary, "Confer with Dunn in re tactful handling of new drainage scheme." He reported to Barber after they met again the following Wednesday. Not quite six weeks later, Meighen met Howard H. Dunn at 7:45 AM at Chicago's Union Station to take him to a meeting with Barber, Trumbauer, Struble, Dappert, McMillan, and Jamison. I imagined a lopsided negotiation with a lone, travel-weary lawyer representing the interests of the farmers in the path of the ditch. Whatever his intent at that Chicago conclave, Dunn ended up switching sides. He, not Meighen, filed the petition and bond with the clerk of district court. Meighen took a copy of it to H. G. Day for publication in the *Standard*, as required by law. On a trip to Minneapolis in April, Meighen saw Jamison "in re Dunn's pay." We can only speculate whether the pay in question was a payoff or an hourly fee. By the time the petition was heard in court, Meighen and Dunn were both identified as the petitioners' attorneys.

In the second issue in which it carried the petition, January 17, 1906, the *Standard* published an editorial endorsing the drainage. Unlike the previous effort, it noted, "the undertaking is begun and will be prosecuted by Freeborn county citizens." The ditch would not be as large or expensive as first proposed, and placing it under Judge Kingsley's control "will insure the legality of all the proceedings and also be a guarantee that all men concerned and all interests will be justly treated." The editorial announced that "the Standard is decidedly of the opinion that as the project is now undertaken, it should be carried to a successful consummation and we believe that when this is done it will be the greatest and best public improvement ever made in Freeborn county."

The strategy was already working, even convincing that "populist sheet." No outcry followed in the *Standard*, only an observation by the Oakland correspondent that "the Moscow Riceland ditch case excites the people here in general." Farmers along Turtle Creek still opposed its ditching, but their view was rarely represented in the *Standard* this time around. The public forum seemed to be shrinking in size and diversity. Ray C. Blackmer, the editor-publisher of the *Freeborn County Times*, another outlet for rural voices, retired in 1906 and sold the paper to C. S. Edwards and W. A. Morin, owners of the *Albert Lea Enterprise*. The merged *Times-Enterprise* carried rural news but mostly of the one-line who-visited-whom variety—little of the cheeky commentary associated with the township correspondents to the *Standard* and the *Times*. The *Alden Advance* showed waning interest in events at the other end of the county. The *Evening Tribune*, first attempted in Albert Lea in 1897, had taken nearly a decade to establish its footing. Its four pages allowed little space for probing local controversies. Evidence of discontent turned up instead in the *Mower County Transcript*, published by the Rev. C. D. Belden in Lansing, the border township about to be crossed by the last three miles of Judicial Ditch No. 1. That's where I learned, in successive reports of Moscow news, that the new strategy had not appeased John and Amanda Register, Belden's parishioners at the Oakland Baptist Church.

All went smoothly, as Meighen noted on several occasions in his diary. James Dappert was hired once again to survey the route for the main ditch and its nine laterals, aided by County Engineer Frank Fisk. His report proved the smaller "farmers' ditch" a fanciful palliative. Dappert lengthened the laterals and enlarged the main ditch, justifying those changes as wise and practical engineering: "The whole plan of drainage contemplates full and final drainage and not merely 'surface drainage,' and when completed, will enable the development of the marsh areas into a high class of farmlands as fertile and as well drained as the higher lands in their vicinity, it being certainly good policy to make the drains amply large, and especially amply deep to perform the drainage at once, rather than halfway perform the work now, and have to deepen and enlarge the drains in a few years." Judge Kingsley appointed three viewers who reported back, in unison, that benefits would exceed damages. The clerk of district court, not the county auditor, published a full description of the project and a list of affected landowners in the December 22, 1906, issue of the *Standard*. He also set a hearing for the Freeborn County Courthouse on January 28, 1907, at ten o'clock in the forenoon.

In the meantime, attorneys H. C. Carlson and A. W. Wright collected formal objections from the affected landowners. John and Amanda Register, due to receive damages of $552 for loss of land, submitted the boilerplate version, which listed several objections. It challenged the assessment on grounds that the benefits were "grossly excessive" and the damages "entirely inadequate." It called the laying of the ditch "a taking, injuring and damaging of the objector's property for public and private use." It questioned the constitutionality of chapter 230 because it imposed "an unjust and unlawful tax" for improvements in which the taxpayers were "not in any way interested or concerned." Finally, it would drain two meandered, navigable lakes "of beneficial public use of a substantial character for fishing, boating, hunting, water supply and navigation." In addition to the boilerplate objections, B. J. Stoa, a Moscow farmer who had signed the MacRae petition, opposed the ditch because its high banks would make it inaccessible to the cattle he watered in Turtle Creek. Also, the creek divided his property, and its widening and deepening would require him to go miles out of his way to get to the twelve acres that lay opposite his homestead.

The *Evening Tribune's* reporter proved to be the best observer of discontent in the courtroom. The article opens,

> Monday was the long-looked for day that Judge Kingsley was to hear the Moscow-Riceland-Geneva ditch proposition and at an early hour in the morning people began gathering at the court house and when the time arrived for the opening of court nearly fifty of the farmers who have interests involved were on hand, most of them in opposition to the proposed improvement. Judge Kingsley was in his place, Reporter Denison was ready for business, Clerk Hayes with his broken left arm was doing as well as he could, Sheriff Subby was ready for emergencies and County Attorney Peterson was ready for anything that turned up requiring his assistance, while a large array of attorneys looked anxious and interested.

The reporter circulated in the crowd, which included John Register, and found "great dissatisfaction over the movement." The article ends with a prediction that the objecting farmers would continue to fight the ditch. "There are many grounds for objection given and all seem to think they have excellent reason for kicking. The indications are there will be long litigation over the manner [*sic*]."

Court decorum didn't allow much "kicking," however. When Judge Kingsley asked if there were objections to "the validity or regularity of the proceedings," A. W. Wright, the Mower County Attorney, called

the current ditch law unconstitutional in that it converted private property to public use. The judge listened to the argument, then overruled
Wright's objection, which did not address procedural irregularities, and
"brushed one bugbear away," as the *Tribune* put it. Freeborn County
Attorney Norman Peterson objected on behalf of the county board
that the ditch would drain Geneva Lake, protected public waters. Deputy Auditor Wilbur of Austin objected to the drainage of Rice Lake,
which he described as a navigable body of water used for hunting and
fishing, the breeding ground for fish in the Cedar River, and the principal source of the Cedar's water supply. None of these objections was
seen as germane to the judge's question.

Hearings on the Eid petition continued for three weeks. As the testimony neared its conclusion, H. C. Carlson withdrew the objections of
L. P. Lawson of Geneva and John and Amanda Register of Moscow,
"but he made objection to the ditch being constructed on the part of
other interested parties." I doubt the Registers had been persuaded that
the Big Ditch was a fine idea after all. Two events may have drawn their
attention elsewhere. First, the husband of a recently deceased niece
had been found gassed to death in a Minneapolis hotel room. There
was a funeral to attend and grieving and comforting to do. Then their
seventeen-year-old son Leslie "had the misfortune to get a severe kick
from a horse" and spent two days in bed. Even without these distrac-
tions, I can imagine John Register running out of patience, certain of
his cause's demise, saying "to hell with it" and heading home. Elbert
Ostrander would likely stand strong in the face of opposition and at
least claim the moral victory. The record doesn't show whether he was
present at the hearings.

On February 19, 1907, Judge Kingsley approved the Eid petition
and ordered construction of the ditch. The court continued to meet to
resolve individual objections to the viewers' assessments of benefits
and damages, the last gasp of protest. In the end, the *Evening Tribune*
offered a bit of sympathy for the losers: "It is unfortunate that such an
improvement cannot be pushed through without having a bad effect

upon others who are in no need of the ditch and will have their premises injured more or less by the digging of the drain, but the law is sup-
posed to make the way plain after the evidence has been heard and
those who know Judge Kingsley are satisfied he will do what he consid-
ers is right in the matter."

Notices advertising the job of constructing the ditch went out on
March 6. The France Dredging Company of Mansfield, Ohio, offered
to do it for $114,133.79—$50,000 less than Dappert's estimate of the
cost. The privilege of opening the sealed bid envelopes went to John
F. D. Meighen, who had seen the project through from day to day almost
since his admission to the bar in 1901. He was not yet thirty years old.
Governor John Johnson honored Meighen's work by appointing him
and Freeborn County Engineer Frank H. Fisk Minnesota's delegates to
the National Drainage Congress in Baltimore, at which Dappert would
represent Illinois. Meighen was expected to address the congress on
drainage law. At the last moment, however, he canceled his trip because
he felt "drowsy." He did make it months later to a state convention
where he spoke on "Construction of Drainage Laws by Our Courts."
His reputation as an expert on the subject continued to grow.

BIG DITCH A GO, the *Standard* proclaimed on April 10, 1907. It
would take two years for the ditch and its laterals to be constructed, but
its chief proponents could rest easy. P. D. McMillan moved his Minneapolis office into larger quarters. Meighen and Morgan bought 241
acres of Geneva marshland from J. G. Sharp, a signatory to the petition.
Meighen set off for Ireland via Liverpool with his father in July and
stayed away from his office until September 2. He left his work in the
hands of his new stenographer, Arra Jeffries, who proved herself as proficient a law clerk as a typist. Bryant H. Barber and Milton Trumbauer
departed for Liverpool in November, although it appears they stayed
for only two days before boarding a different ship back to New York.

Liverpool figured in John Register's life, too, as the port from which
his mother, Harriet, and his siblings left their homeland to join his
father in Ohio three years before John was born. I imagine him nagged

by regret and anger as the Big Ditch approached his land. The memory of watery places that lodges in the cells of the body carried the residue of his ancestors' losses: those fen folk, the scrappy farmers, eelers, and fishermen whose lives were upended by drainage, their children turned into laborers and then, after the floods, emigrants. Nothing was certain but his own stubborn will.

Rice Lake and the Big Marsh
Go Down the Drain

Ain't I glad I've got my garden patch high and dry down here where I'm not goin' to get converted into a fish pond by the Moscow ditch business. You bet when all that water runs off all at one rush it's goin' to make lively scramblin'. The folks up to Austin don't seem to wake up to realize that they're goin to get caught bad in this flood from the Turtle but they are. You just wait until the flood of the Turtle backs up on the Cedar and there'll be no letoff for the water comin' down thru Austin.

— Farmer Ben's Column, *The Mower County Transcript*,
February 27, 1907

Local skepticism and outright opposition had held off the Big Ditch for five and a half years, but in the end, wealth and political influence prevailed. Still, it would be another six months of eager or wary anticipation before the transformation of the landscape began. Two new dredges had to be assembled to dig the lateral ditches, which would be sixteen feet wide and eight feet deep, nearly fifteen times greater in volume than the scratch C. D. Edwards's original ditching plow made in the earth. Work began at the end of August, fittingly, on the Hans J. Eid farm in Geneva Township.

The main ditch required a machine of monstrous size. Fourteen carloads of mechanical parts were expected to arrive in Clarks Grove, the closest railroad station to the head of the ditch, and this wasn't the whole of it. The dredge's wooden frame would measure forty by one hundred feet, requiring enough lumber to build a house. A man identified as "Mr. Blair, an experienced ship-builder," erected the dredge on high ground on the Everson farm in section 35 of Geneva Township, near the present site of the village of Hollandale. The hull weighed

375 tons and the dipper and its arm twelve tons. Someone—maybe Mr. Blair, or E. H. Cowan, the project foreman, or Harvey C. Cogdal, the big dredge's engineer—named it the *Swamp Angel*.

Before the dredge could begin its work, it had to be moved from the construction site into Geneva Creek, which had been dammed to create a pond large enough to accommodate the *Swamp Angel* and its fleet of supporting vessels. The launching was scheduled for October 8, 1907, even though the dredge was not yet fully equipped. It would be another two weeks before O. Goodnature delivered its boiler, hauling it through the village of Geneva behind his threshing engine. But the ceremonial moment had been arranged, and the France Dredging Company had hired carriages to transport public officials and the local elite from Austin and Albert Lea. Seventy-five people gathered to witness the launching.

The reporter from the *Standard* rode out from Albert Lea in a carriage with Cowan, John Meighen, and the banker Alfred Christopherson. They arrived at one of the lateral ditches, where Cowan invited them onto a boat "about as high as a minute" and rowed them to one of the smaller dredges, regaling them along the way with "skittish stories of how deep the ditch was." They watched this dredge scoop mud and took "kodac" pictures before continuing to the dammed-up pond, where the guests were treated to dinner. The sight and size of the main dredge astonished the reporter, who submitted this account under the headline "SWAMP ANGEL" TRULY AN INLAND WONDER:

> Say, it was a Leviathan. It contained great timbers that must have come from the big forests of faraway Washington. Some of the machinery was on the deck, but not nearly what will be there. She was poised upon the ways already to be slid into the water. The crew of men were making everything shipshape so that there might not be the slightest defect in the launching. So at 2:20 PM the huge craft took to water. There were several standing on the deck and they could not feel the slightest shock when she struck the surface of the basin. . . . To give even a further idea of what the machine is it may be added that the dipper arm is 46

feet long. The seams used up a mixture of 700 pounds of tallow and 1,000 pounds of oakum. The machine when working will be electrically lighted, steam heated and will work 22 hours a day. Mr. Cogdal of the company says . . . that within a few years people may ride everywhere across the now impassable swamp on dry roads and witness rich and far-reaching fields of grain on every hand.

A less reverent *Austin Daily Herald* reporter commemorated the launching with a parody of a Henry Wadsworth Longfellow poem:

She starts, she moves,
She seems to feel
An awful pain, for hear her squeal
As slipping through the Freeborn mud
She utters forth one sputtering blub
And falls into the prairie ditch.

Switching to prose with tongue still in cheek, the reporter watched the reactions of a group of Mower County residents:

They had read Longfellow's "Launching of the Ship" and they went with their souls attuned to the sweet sentiments of such an occasion. They expected to see the proud ship bedecked with Flags with the daughter of a Freeborn County Commissioner standing at the prow holding aloft a ribbon decorated bottle of champagne to break over the bows as she slid down the ways and sent the waves dashing upon the strand of Deer Creek [*sic*]. But there was no sentiment about the contractor. There was not a flag flying, not even a bottle of root beer, however appropriate such a beverage might be in christening a dredger that is to root its way across the prairie. The launching was a business proposition to the contractor who is 73 years of age and who has built and launched 133 other dredging machines. The ways were greased with the cheap oat grease that could be found in the market and when the ponderous mud digger slid into the water there was no hand clapping, no God speeds, just "Gosh! But she went in fine," from the Auditor of Freeborn County.

"The ponderous mud digger" may have slid in fine, but "hers" was no tender touch. The ditch it cut would be sixty-five feet wide and twelve feet deep. Where curves in the creeks along the route proved inconvenient, the *Swamp Angel* would push through the adjoining land to divert the water into a new, straight channel. Despite the petitioners' assurance of a smaller "farmer's ditch," the 17.7-mile main ditch and its nine laterals, the longest nearly four miles, would appear to a heavenly angel like a huge surgical scar across the northeastern quarter of Freeborn County. Engineer Dappert had proposed the removal of 1,739,779 cubic yards of soil along thirty-three miles. In its first season of work, from late November 1907 into mid-January 1908, when the ground froze too solid for digging, the dredge advanced about two miles along its course.

An article in the *Herald* described how the excavation was done:

The engineer has seven levers to attend to. He pushes one over and the great arm of the machine with an iron scoop bucket on the end plunges down through the twelve feet of water. He pushes another lever and the bucket is given a sweeping and upward stroke and another lever raises the arm. For many feet on either side the waters recede as a great mass of earth is brought to sight far more than the bucket will hold. Out of this is cut two and a half yards of earth, cut as clean as from cheese. The engineer pushes over another lever and the arm swings far out over the bank of the ditch. A man on the swing arm pulls a cable and the mud is dropped. The engineer swings the arm back and the work is repeated. After a time it becomes necessary to move forward. The engineer by a lever raises the anchors, two geared posts. The long arm of the dredge is let down as far forward as possible and is used on a forward anchor to draw the dredge forward to its new station.

Ten men in two shifts kept the dredge running day and night. "A big boiler, a powerful engine, power driven windlasses and a dynamo for arc and electric lights" made this pace of work possible. The *Swamp Angel* dug its course from spring thaw until freeze-up, moving forward about one hundred feet every twelve hours. The crew cooked, ate, and slept in a boat that followed the dredge, while Mr. Cowan, the project manager, lived with his family in a house in Albert Lea. A second "boarding house boat" served the crews at work on the lateral ditches. The workers aboard were skilled employees of the France Dredging Company, with homes in Ohio, Indiana, Illinois, and Iowa, to which they returned while the dredge sat idle in the winter. Some turnover occurred during the two years it took to complete this massive job, and county newspapers reported the comings and goings. Engineer Cogdal resigned seven months short of completing the Big Ditch. The newspapers kept track of frequent mechanical breakdowns as well. Despite their round-the-clock labors, the crew found time for leisure, especially while they waited for replacement parts. The dredge even fielded a baseball team that played against Moscow's.

The Big Ditch had been touted as a moneymaking opportunity for local folks. A wagon, a team of horses, and an enterprising spirit could turn a young man free of farm chores into a deliveryman. Merchants scrambled to fill those wagons with food and other provisions. The dredge's boiler required a steady supply of coal. A Moscow woman, Mrs. J. Todd, cooked on the mess boat. Local labor built temporary dams along the course of the ditch to control the flow of water while the dredge scooped out the soil. The dredge knocked out seven bridges that had to be replaced after it had passed.

All this activity turned the construction of the ditch into a spectator sport. A glimpse of the electrically lighted *Swamp Angel* clanking and crawling through the darkness could tingle the spine. Parties of local dignitaries arranged excursions to the dredge. One group gathered at the starting point and traveled down the ditch in a little steamboat for five and a half miles to the dredge itself. "Foreman Cogswell [*sic*] proved a most pleasant host and showed the visitors every courtesy," they attested. He even offered them "a splendid dinner" in the crew's quarters. Ordinary rural folks made excursions of their own: "Frank

Baker and mother and Howard Ross, also Miss Anna Johnson, all of Riceland, took dinner at Gene Lowry's Friday and all went to see the big steam dredge in the afternoon," the Moscow correspondent to the *Herald* reported. P. D. McMillan himself turned up from time to time to check on the *Swamp Angel*'s progress.

While the waters of Rice Lake drained into the wide, muddy-sloped channel of Judicial Ditch No. 1, destroying waterfowl habitat, local sportsmen, aware of the irony or not, organized to make the county the "more favorite resort" of migratory birds. The Freeborn County Game Protective Association distributed 350 pounds of wild rice seed to be sown in other lakes. Two months before the drainage was complete, the *Standard* claimed, "Reports from the country all agree that this is the greatest year within the memory of the oldest inhabitants for all kinds of feathered game, including prairie chickens, ducks, woodcock and snipe." Such abundance of ducks and snipe, dependent on shallow, reedy waters, was about to fade into memory. Coincidentally, 1909 marks the introduction of the pheasant as a game bird in Freeborn County.

The *Swamp Angel* dug its last fifteen feet of the Big Ditch in Lansing Township on November 6, 1909, and then dug out its own harbor alongside, where it would sit until spring. The France Dredging Company would disassemble it for transport to the site of its next contract. The ditch's completion passed without ceremony—no carriages delivering special guests, no expressions of awe, not even a description of the water's flow—only a brief mention in the local papers. O. A. Anderson, who had replaced Cogdal, predicted that spring floods would be "more severe, but of shorter duration, as the excellent drainage will carry the water off at a rapid rate and make the volume of water at the Cedar much larger at one time than ever before."

The results of the drainage came clear in the next publication of county plat maps. Turtle Creek appeared as a diagonal line with a few straight jigs and jags. Rice Lake was gone, replaced by rectangles labeled with owners' names and acreage figures. The north half of Riceland section 15, formerly the middle of the lake, was marked "J. F. D. Meighen."

The *Swamp Angel* Plays Cupid

Sadly, my ancestors weren't the sort who saved their correspondence for future generations to peruse. A treasured letter survived, however, tucked among family photos passed on to my dad. When he died, we shoved the box into my sister's attic until someone had time to look through it. I'm thankful that I was that someone and that I didn't wait years longer. It's a love letter, or what might pass for a love letter in the mind of a shy farm boy writing to a young country schoolteacher. "Dear Grace," it begins. "Thot I would send this to remind you of the dredge." The letter is penned in brown ink across two picture postcards of the *Swamp Angel* in Turtle Creek. In the first photo, the dredge's size can be measured against a building on the bank. Black smoke trails from its tall smokestack. The second postcard shows it knocking a bridge loose with its scoop as two men—workers or creekside cheerleaders—gesture with upraised arms.

"How goes school this week?" the sender, "L.A.R.," asks, then confesses, "I'm lonesome without 'you.' Guess they will move the other bridge tomorrow." A little news of the dredge segues into good wishes: "Hope you are well and so you can walk by this time, we have been planting corn today will be down after you Friday night." What would prevent her from walking? The letter ventures a bit more romance: "Don't suppose you ever get lonesome do you?" and closes, "Lovingly yours." I can't help but wonder whether the farm boy's faulty syntax dismayed the schoolteacher. Maybe her heart fluttered instead at the word "lonesome" and whatever reminders the photos of the dredge offered her. I imagine the young couple strolling through the countryside at

Swamp Angel digging out Turtle Creek and removing a bridge, 1909

night, arm in arm, the dredge's electric lights standing in for a full moon. Maybe at a distracted moment she slipped in the mud and twisted her ankle. Did he carry her the rest of the way? I hope he was as taken with her twinkly blue eyes and her easy laugh as he was with the dredge's mighty arm and scoop.

Leslie Register, twenty, wrote these postcards to Grace Ostrander, nearly twenty-one, on Tuesday, May 18, 1909. They had spent the previous Friday evening and Saturday together at the Ostrander home in Alden Township, a visit noted in the *Austin Daily Herald*'s Moscow news column. They had watched Grace's brother Lyle perform in a high school play. Leslie presumably slept over, bedded down among the three Ostrander boys.

During the workweek, Grace, who had taken the brief teacher-training course in Albert Lea the summer before, taught at the one-room Freeman School (District 96), a mile and a half east of Moscow village. The story handed down in the family is that Grace boarded with the Registers. It was common for teachers to circulate among neighboring households, living for several weeks with each. The Registers, however, lived two miles west of her school in a different district, Moscow 29.

The Moscow correspondents to the *Transcript* and the *Herald* kept watch on this budding courtship. It appears that Grace first became friends with Lida Register, Leslie's younger sister. It's an odd pairing. Lida has come down in family legend as the prime example of Register orneriness, while Grace was known for her sweet, exceedingly patient disposition and affectionate humor. Grace "Sundayed" with Lida on October 11, 1908. She had probably attended the Moscow Musical at the Freeman farm next door to her school the night before, where Lida played the piano. If she did, she also heard Leslie sing a solo. Grace attended a Saturday night Hallowe'en party at the Moscow town hall and stayed at the Registers through Sunday. Lida, in turn, spent Thanksgiving with Grace's family in Alden. By mid-December, it was Leslie who traveled to Alden "to spend a few days with friends." In February 1909, "Mr. Ostrander with his little son and daughter of Alden came

Friday and stayed till Saturday with the John Register family." Was it a rare Minnesota marriage negotiation? How did the two men get along? John, the prosperous farmer, could be boastful, and Elbert, content with a bare-bones existence on eighty acres of prairie, could be arrogant in his moral judgments. Whatever the parents thought, the young couple's ardor prevailed. Newspaper readers would have no trouble interpreting Leslie's "flying trip to Alden" in March. It didn't require an airplane.

Leslie and Grace were married on September 1, 1909, at the Albert Lea home of Dr. Russell B. Abbott, a Presbyterian minister and president of the Albert Lea College for Women. A wedding announcement in the *Transcript* described Leslie as "a young man of excellent principles and character" and Grace as "a young lady of winsome ways, with good education" who would make "a worthy life companion." The dredge, having done its romantic business, had just finished its course through Moscow and crossed into Mower County.

After a honeymoon in the Twin Cities, the newlyweds moved into John and Amanda's big house. Brother Roy and his bride, Isabel Overlie, had recently moved to Rush City, where Roy apprenticed in buttermaking. Grace returned to Alden for the birth of her first child, Vivian Grace, in November 1910, probably to benefit from her mother's expertise. Bertha had borne her tenth, but not her last, child the year before. Grace and Leslie's second child, Gordon Leslie, was born in the Moscow house in January 1912, the first member of the third generation to claim birth on the Speer farm.

Leslie contracted with his father for a share in the farm and worked alongside him until the end of the war in 1918, when John and Amanda made a cultural leap to a bungalow in Minneapolis, where they lived out their lives. Leslie got first dibs on buying the farm at market rate, with large loans from a bank and from John himself. He jumped full bore into farming and followed his parents' example, including traveling to Nebraska to buy beef cattle. The future looked secure with a well-established farm, a growing family, and elder son Gordy, my father, eager to follow his dad or hired man Clint Arett everywhere.

Leslie and Grace Ostrander Register, 1909

Vivian, Alan, and Gordon Register in front of the old Speer house, about 1916

The farm's prosperity was shockingly short lived. A precipitous drop in farm commodity prices in 1920 put Leslie and Grace and many other farm families in jeopardy. According to my dad, whose memory was rich but not always accurate, the bank gave them a year's grace on loan payments. The story goes that John Register, allegedly less forgiving, blamed Leslie himself for the straits into which he had fallen and showed him no mercy.

The economy didn't recover, at least not for ordinary farmers. The farm recession merely segued into the Great Depression of the 1930s. Until the end of his life, my dad retold the story of his family's farewell to Moscow Township. He recalled in detail how he, a ten-year-old, drove the horse-drawn wagonload of household goods while his dad drove the Fordson tractor on the ten-hour, twenty-five-mile move to their new home on the edge of Alden, a smaller house on eleven acres where first Henry and Sarah Ostrander and then Dan and Mary Hord had retired. Dan had died in March of 1922, and Mary was moving to Iowa to live with her younger daughter. The Registers' exile from Eden altered more than their economic circumstances. "It was like the spirit went out of him," my dad once confided about my grandfather. "He was never the same after that." Grace, on the other hand, had learned from an early age how to find joy and meaning in subsistence.

Huge changes were taking place across the country in the relation between farming and industry, one of the most significant being large-scale, mechanized food processing. While area farmers struggled to hang onto their land and livelihoods at the start of the 1920s, East Coast investors bought the packinghouse that had begun its life as the Brundins' City Meat Market. By the time Gordy and other disinherited farm boys came of age, Wilson's in Albert Lea and Hormel's in Austin stood ready to offer them a different sort of living.

I can't blame my family's loss of the Speer/Register farm directly on the drainage of the Big Marsh, although Judicial Ditch No. 1 certainly aided the industrialization of agriculture and the rise of agribusiness. In contrast to those terms, the monosyllabic "farm" sounds as simple, yet as nuanced, as the word "home." When I read Leslie's love letter to Grace, though, and look at those postcards of the dredge, I have to ask whether the particular configuration of my genes owes something to the *Swamp Angel*.

The New Model Farmer

P. D. McMillan was down to Austin Monday, from the big Rice Lawn
farm west of Moscow. He says he has 200 acres of as fine flax as one
would wish to see which will thresh over 20 bushels to the acre.

—*Mower County Transcript*, August 24, 1910

The mud had barely dried on the *Swamp Angel's* scoop when P. D.
McMillan turned to farming his land with renewed energy and closer
attention. By the end of 1909, at age seventy-seven, he had sold his
realty business in Minneapolis, which was renamed Boardman and
Ware, and installed himself as president and general manager of the
newly incorporated McMillan Land Company. With headquarters in
Minneapolis and shares listed at one hundred dollars, its sole business
was the agricultural development of land in Freeborn County. All its
officers were named McMillan: his wife, Kate, sixty-six, was appointed
vice president; their daughter Margaret, twenty-nine, secretary; and
son, Putnam Dana, Jr., twenty-eight, treasurer and superintendent.
Emily, forty-nine, still living at the family's Tenth Avenue home and
traveling to New York and Paris to perfect her art, was the only family
member without a post.

An early order of business was laying a four-hundred-foot railroad
spur 3.8 miles west of the Oakland depot to handle shipments to and
from Ricelawn Ranch. It received herds of cattle plus the carloads of
seed and the large machinery required to produce the great volumes
of flax and other products to be shipped back out. Three carloads of
drainage tile arrived, too, "for a start" at a government-sponsored project "to test the efficacy of tile when laid under scientific directions."
Government sponsorship presumably included taxpayer support.

Much of the news about Ricelawn Ranch now came directly from
McMillan, who began turning up on the streets of Albert Lea and

Austin and stopping in at the newspaper offices to report on acreage and bushels. In the spring of 1910, he hired George Dearmin of Moscow to build a summer cottage on the ranch. P. D. himself informed the *Transcript* that he had built a "bungalow" at the farm and that his family was spending the summer there. An ad ran in the *Austin Daily Herald* for several issues: "WANTED—A good girl for general housework, in the country. Four in family, wages $6 per week. Address M. McMillan R.R. No. 4 or telephone Moscow 29–21." One family member was missing. Maybe Emily opted out of summer sojourns as well as board service. Or maybe she brought easel and oils to the farm while Dana—P. D., Jr.—kept up his busy schedule as a wheat buyer for the Washburn Crosby Company in Minneapolis. He had been hired there within months of his 1903 graduation from the University of Minnesota.

The McMillans got a late start that first summer, but in 1911, they had settled in by mid-May. A large gasoline-powered traction engine was already at work day and night pulling ten fourteen-inch plows, breaking twelve hundred acres of land to be sown in flax. "He has a carload of seed and will go into the business on a large scale," the *Transcript* reported, "and he has unbounded faith in the productiveness of the land that was lately worthless." McMillan had also leased 160 acres to the University of Minnesota's agricultural school for experimental farming "on account of the remarkable fertility of the soil."

By July, reports of the farm's success rivaled those published when Ricelawn began in the 1890s. The *Standard* gushed,

> The crops . . . are of most bountiful proportions and phenomenal excellence and in truth are entitled to go on record as among the most notable ever produced in Minnesota. . . . [The flax] will yield 30 bushels or more to the acre—think of it! The 135-acre barley field is equally remarkable. The heads are like those shown in the catalogues. . . . Altogether the great fields are a marvel to look upon, and Attorney J. F. D. Meighen who saw them Sunday, says it will well repay anyone to make the trip to view them.

Dean Wood of the University of Minnesota's agricultural school "pronounced the crop to be the greatest of all in the northwest, and attri-
butes the fact to the peculiar virtues of the subsoil, the like of which is
scarcely to be found elsewhere in the state."

McMillan's days as resident patron in Freeborn County weren't
entirely sunny, however. On his way back to Minneapolis for the state
fair in September, he stopped in Albert Lea to reiterate a long-held
grievance. He still didn't have the road he wanted. The county board
had connected the ranch to the existing east–west route, but McMillan
still demanded his own shortcut to town. He argued that Albert Lea
was missing out on thousands of dollars annually, not only the profits
to be earned marketing his products but also the money spent by
his thirty employees, who shared in a three-thousand-dollar payroll.

P. D. McMillan on Ricelawn Ranch

The benefits were going to Austin even though McMillan preferred to do business in Albert Lea. Many of those employees, however, were Moscow residents already in the habit of going to Austin, which lay just across the county line, closer than their own county seat twenty miles distant.

In a thank-you note to John Meighen for the gift of one of his travelogues, McMillan complimented Meighen on his "facility of writing" and suggested that he "write up the history of Rice Lake past, present and future." McMillan penned his own account in February 1915, five handwritten pages entitled "History of drainage of Riceland Marsh." As with any work drawn from memory, it contains factual errors—his purchase of the land is misdated by ten years—and glossy oversights—construction of the ditch proceeded "without a skip or fault." Its tone reflects the author's unyielding claim of foresight and his disdain for those who objected to his project.

The history seems to have been McMillan's last hurrah. His name disappeared from the county papers, and he and Kate no longer graced the society page of the *Minneapolis Tribune*. McMillan died of myocarditis at his Minneapolis home on Sunday, April 7, 1918. He was eighty-five years old. His obituary in the *Minneapolis Journal* credited him with the drainage of fifteen thousand acres of land in Freeborn County. The notice in the Freeborn and Mower county newspapers was curiously spare: a two-paragraph press release identifying him as a leading contributor to the growth of Minneapolis and "a descendant of illustrious ancestors of Colonial and Revolutionary times." It said nothing about the drainage.

Leadership of the McMillan Land Company ceded to son Dana, who completed the tiling and tilling of the property and remained enthusiastic about the peat soil's potential. It is hard to say whether pride of ownership was matched by hands-on involvement. His duties at Washburn Crosby were demanding: buying wheat and vastly expanding the company's grain storage capacity across the country. He was named director in charge of grain operations and appointed to the company's board of directors in 1921. The company newsletter noted that he had "won the reputation of being one of the best grain men in the world" and that he would be the youngest board member and its only bachelor. When Washburn Crosby bought out other milling companies and reorganized as General Mills in 1928, Dana McMillan became a vice president.

McMillan's salaried job, his management of the family land company, and food-supply work in Washington as a dollar-a-year man during World War I gave him enough insight into the economics of farming and food production to venture a public stand on agricultural policy. He opposed price supports and production quotas and wrote articles suggesting a simpler solution: taking marginal cropland out of production, even if it meant a government buyout of privately owned farmland. His Freeborn County land would not suffer that fate. In a memo updating his profile for General Mills, he wrote, "The farming operations of many city growers are not noted for their profits, but this development and operation has proved very profitable."

Dana McMillan retired from General Mills in 1947 with a lifelong directorship. Over the next two years, he sold 1,750 acres of the McMillan farm in small plots to working farmers, following the pattern George Payne had established for Hollandale in the 1920s. He contracted with a canning company to grow vegetables, mainly asparagus, on the remaining 650. The name Ricelawn Ranch faded from memory as locals resumed calling it Hickory Island.

McMillan's passion in retirement was art. He became president of the Minneapolis Society of Fine Arts in 1948 and began collecting. He divided his time between a summer home on Lake Minnetonka and a winter home in Santa Barbara, California, where he died at seventy-nine on April 7, 1961, the forty-third anniversary of his father's death. His obituary in the *Minneapolis Tribune* credited him with helping "to develop the Hollandale area into the largest vegetable-growing region of the Upper Midwest." His sisters had predeceased him and, like him, left no progeny. The McMillan presence in Freeborn County had come to an end.

The Victor's History

Turn, ye student, to the history of Freeborn county of 1911 . . . and read
from pages therein of the magnificent blessing that has been bestowed
on all of the people thereof by the desecration of the laws of nature.
Read of the consignment of all of the objectors to outer darkness,
which is the final destiny of all dissenters by the powers that be, and
you, now in possession of the facts as revealed after the lapse of a
quarter of a century will pronounce that prophecy as mythical as the
story in ancient history of the wanderings of Ulysses.

—Elbert H. Ostrander, "Connivings of Dishonest Men Cheat
Nature As Well As Fellow Beings, Writer Avers," *Freeborn
Patriot*, July 19, 1935

Most precious among the victor's spoils is the privilege of shaping the
story. When Franklyn Curtiss-Wedge enlisted local lights to write for
his *History of Freeborn County Minnesota*, he included the expert on agricultural drainage. Most of the book's text bears no particular author-
ship; the writers are grouped under "assisted by" on the title page. The
section entitled "The Drainage of the Riceland Marsh" (515–20), however, carries an endnote attributing "this able article" to John F. D.
Meighen, who is "prominently identified with the legal and statutory
aspects of the drainage ditch proposition." Besides giving credit where
due, the note lets readers know the article has a point of view.

The *History of Freeborn County*, a tome that sits heavy and unwieldy
in my lap, was published in 1911. The dredge had scooped its last muck
from the bed of Turtle Creek on November 6, 1909. That left little time
to make a fair assessment of consequences. Meighen's piece opens with
a triumphant image, a display of farm products at the 1910 Freeborn
County Fair: "The flax, corn, sugar beets, beans, potatoes and other
vegetables composing it were excellent specimens and attractive in
themselves, but the particular object most viewed was a large placard

announcing that the entire exhibit had been grown by C. U. Christensen, a farmer of Riceland Township, in the bed of Rice Lake, where
up to the year before the musk rats and wild ducks had ruled for centuries." We are left to imagine the former rulers banished, the losers along
with the "conservatives" who believed the marsh could never be successfully drained.

To be fair, Meighen devotes two full pages of scarcely five to quotations from the township petitions and resolutions lodged in protest
against the 1901 MacRae ditch proposal. He dismisses them quickly:
"Today, after the lapse of ten years, most of these objections seem
highly amusing, but at that time they were seriously urged." He singles
out two individuals in the opposition: "A citizen of Twin Lakes"—the
unnamed Fred McCall—who believed "the drainage of our marshes
would diminish the rainfall and make Freeborn county a desert," and
"one taxpayer in Alden," whom he quotes as saying, "It will be only the
beginning of similar propositions, as there is hardly a township in the
county but will petition your honorable board for the establishing of
a drain within its border." Although logicians look askance at slippery
slope arguments, the taxpayer, Elbert H. Ostrander, was right. Freeborn County was soon crisscrossed with public ditches and its surface
underlain with miles of drainage tile.

The years between the 1901 and 1906 petitions, Meighen writes, "had
educated the public greatly on the question of ditches. Many of the
most active opponents had been converted into equally active friends."
That would be true of H. H. Dunn, but resignation, not a change of
heart, accounted for the silence of many opposing farmers. Those concerned about the expense to county taxpayers may have backed off and
let the ditch happen, but they hardly became activists in its support.

Meighen's account gives "particular credit for this magnificent public improvement" to P. D. McMillan and B. H. Barber. He takes care to
mention James W. Dappert and Frank H. Fisk, the engineers whose
work "added twenty-four sections of most fertile soil" to the county's
farmland. Judged by his own values and his own definition of progress,
Meighen himself deserved more recognition than he claimed for a job

well done. His sharp, strategic legal mind; a work ethic that brought him to the point of exhaustion many nights over; and his loyalty to the lawyer–client relationship, even when payments lagged, made him essential to the drainage of Rice Lake and the Big Marsh. Quite a feat for someone whose most frequent diary entry reads, "Did not accomplish much."

The article by Elbert Ostrander that alerted me to this history never questions who won but charges that victory was dishonestly gained. Ostrander alleges deliberate fudging in the measurement of the fall of the ditch and a discrepancy between the ditching contract and the ditch's actual dimensions. He alludes to an unnamed coconspirator in the falsification who was silenced by commitment to an insane asylum. There, denied access to liquor and morphine, the man regained his clarity of mind and sent Ostrander "a very insistent message" to come and see him. The source confessed that he had accepted a bribe to move the survey stakes. Ostrander arranged for his release, but other parties insisted that he be sent to a fraternal order rest home in the East. As far-fetched as the story sounds, it matches the circumstances of

Elbert Ostrander in front of the Hazle Hotel, Alden, Minnesota, about 1910

County Engineer Frank H. Fisk's death en route from the Rochester state hospital to the Elks National Home in Bedford, Virginia. Fisk was indeed committed for treatment of alcoholism on October 16, 1915, and discharged two years later "unimproved." I wish I could say who brought his case to the Freeborn County probate court, but I know only that he had made the Albert Lea Elks Club "his headquarters" and that his behavior there had become unruly.

As exciting as it might be to uncover a murder mystery, none was alleged, and the charge of "connivings" is enough to pique my interest. Ostrander claims that the ditch was extended into Mower County not to improve its efficiency but "for the sole purpose of circumventing the taxpayers." The statute that placed jurisdiction for multicounty ditches in the district court, refined with Meighen's help, did deprive voters of a representative voice in the matter. Hiring an attorney to write legislation to suit one's private interests sounds shady, although we tolerate it now as "lobbying." Using local stand-ins to petition for a project that benefits absentee owners seems disingenuous, even though legal. It's troubling to read of Meighen's meetings in Chicago and Minneapolis with strategists who had no stake in the drainage and no attachment to the landscape it altered. One of the participants, Isaac Struble, even disguised his alliance with the Barbers to dupe those who sold him land. Area farmers were not privy to these meetings, nor were their interests represented. The secrecy that protected the drainage scheme fits the very definition of "connive," "to cooperate secretly or conspire."

I am never surprised when the wealthiest people win. Those who could afford to buy thousands of acres and assert their private property rights enjoyed several advantages in the fight. They could buy expert legal advice and pay for lengthier preparation for court. Money and social affiliations gave them access to political power, to the hearts and minds of legislators and judges. How could a farmer with a mere eighty acres, like Ostrander, or even one with a flourishing half section, like John Register, stand up to McMillan's and Barber's forces? The sanctity of private property didn't protect local farmers from having ditches reamed through their fields over their objections.

It's dismaying to learn how much the drainage victory depended on mere procedure, on correctly following the steps sketched out in state statute. Except for vague acknowledgments of "public welfare" and "public health," Minnesota's drainage laws allowed little room to consider the wisdom of a massive change in the landscape. Fred McCall's warnings were only opinions of no legal merit. Where competing cultural values might cause conflict, rules of procedure hold sway. But procedure is not value free. Those with greater political influence lay it out, write the rules, and build the path to victory. Even the county board recognized the tyranny of procedure and played by its rules, finding one procedural error after another to delay the inevitable.

One of Ostrander's arguments was radical in his day: natural resources are "the common property of all people." Although the idea has more adherents now and a little more legislative grounding, applying it successfully to any one wetland, any one forest, any one mountaintop threatened by industrial or commercial development still requires money, lobbying power, and an intricate familiarity with legal procedure.

Underlying Ostrander's lament is an ethos ingrained in the local rural culture. The Big Ditch's opponents judged the project not just by its cost or the changes it wrought, but by a moral code that clashed with the interests of industrial agriculture: McMillan and Barber bought land—lots of it—that they didn't intend to live on. They expected to reap the rewards of the harvest without working the fields themselves. They demanded public roads and ditches that would bring them private gain. They set out to alter a landscape endowed by nature with a bounty of water and game and beauty that others shared in, raising questions about what can be owned and about the meaning of stewardship. In short, they challenged the tenets of right living and neighborliness that ordinary county farmers trusted in.

I have wondered whether this conflict of vision can be traced in part to the geography of westward migration. We hear of the Yankee ingenuity and individual drive that built American industry and established cities in the Midwest. Many of the prominent entrepreneurs in early

Minneapolis were, like P. D. McMillan, New Englanders. Among the Easterners who settled in Freeborn County, however, Yorkers predominated: yeoman farmers from upstate New York with simpler ambitions to live securely on land they worked themselves. I offer this distinction not as conclusion but as hypothesis.

Some reader is sure to ask whether the drainage opponents engaged in sabotage or violence, and if not, why not? I have found no evidence of any, but it could have gone unreported. Strong words and arguments were probably the extent of the protest. If the objection to the Big Ditch did indeed stay within the limits of reason, the cause may have been cultural. The dominant ethnicities in Freeborn County are Scandinavian—specifically Norwegian and Danish—and Yorker. For both groups, consensus and community cohesion are prime values. The Dutch underpinnings of the Yorker migrant culture showed up again in the neighborly loyalty of the Dutch American farmers in Hollandale. Consensus in Scandinavian culture has long kept the progeny of Vikings from killing each other. They need only read the Icelandic sagas to see how badly things go when conflicts are allowed to flare. Of course, the desire for consensus can easily lead to resignation and the avoidance of confrontation, especially in the face of a dogged entrepreneurialism that runs against the grain. This cultural trait is known as "Minnesota Nice," which newcomers and visitors misread as passive aggression.

And so we take our vengeance in words, after the conflicts are over. Elbert Ostrander wrote his critical account a quarter century after the drainage. And here am I, with neither bricks to toss nor a gun to fire, another eighty years later. I am sorry, heartsick even, that this vast wetland was drained and its natural beauty and utility destroyed. Yet I don't begrudge the citizens of Hollandale their fruitful years on the drained land, nor do I fault the fine ditch inspectors and drainage engineers who maintain the Turtle Creek watershed and, as one described his task, keep the water flowing downhill. We all partake in this quiet history of tremendous, mind-boggling, earth-shifting change.

The Mysterious Fall of
Bryant Barber and Other Endings

Bryant H. Barber remained a stranger in Freeborn County even as residents took to calling his vast property the Barber Marsh. In Polo, Illinois, on the other hand, he was the familiar local banker and wealthy citizen. Besides the family bank, he owned a hotel and a large farm north of town where he had raised high-grade driving horses until the growing popularity of the automobile reduced his profits. He dealt successfully in the stock market and traveled to Chicago often to tend to his investment in the Railway Exchange Building and other property. Barber played a civic role as well, serving on the Polo school board and as a trustee of the Independent Presbyterian Church.

Barber lived in a style that displayed his wealth. In 1901, he and his mother moved into a classical revival mansion designed on commission by the architect Joseph Lyman Silsbee. It still stands on a parklike corner lot next door to the somewhat more impressive Silsbee house Barber's late brother Henry had built ten years earlier. Both houses are listed on the National Register of Historic Places for their architectural value. Bryant Barber owned two automobiles, one a Stevens-Duryea roadster, and employed a chauffeur to take him on leisurely drives.

On one such excursion on November 16, 1917, Barber asked his driver, Otto Olsen, to stop the roadster at the end of the bridge over the Rock River at Grand Detour, Illinois, eighteen miles from home. He wanted to walk across. He often requested stops like that, so Olsen thought nothing of it—until he looked up and saw Barber's coattail sliding over the bridge railing. A passerby had seen him drop but couldn't say whether he had jumped or fallen. The two men raced to the water's edge, but neither could swim. Barber's body was never found. He was wearing a heavy, fur-lined coat that probably pulled him under.

Polo's *Tri-County Press* expressed its shock, then turned immediately to "whispered conversations" among the worried populace, who had "given into his custody every dollar they had in the world." Whether Barber's death was an accident or suicide was open to conjecture. Some claimed that he had never fully recovered from an illness he had suffered in 1907—an inflammation of the spine plus melancholia. The bank panic of 1907 had cost him his hotel and a chunk of his stock portfolio (1907 was also the year construction began on Judicial Ditch No. 1 and the year Barber spent only two days in England before returning home). Others said he had resumed his normal behavior and had been visiting his farm and coming to the bank regularly. Recently he had "cleaned up heavily on U.S. Steel," offsetting his earlier losses. Through it all, he had steered the Barber Bank on a steady course, working at home during the difficult years. Bank employees attested that "on Friday last he was in unusually good spirits for him and much more talkative than usual, and they cannot bring themselves to believe that he contemplated suicide when he left the bank for his afternoon ride." A few saw the good mood as relief at having decided to end his life. One statement leaps off the page: "Mr. Barber had no close friends and no confidant [*sic*] in this city who can shed the least light." He had business colleagues, but socially he appears to have been a loner.

The next week's paper offered a motive for suicide. The Barber Bank, the accounts of which Barber kept "beneath his own hat," was insolvent. He had said he was leaving instructions in his will for a trust company to assume management of the bank, but the only will found named his eighty-five-year-old mother as executor and sole heir. Papers documenting his Chicago investments had disappeared. "Bryant H. Barber has added another disgusting chapter to private bank history," the newspaper concluded.

A brief mention of Barber's land in Minnesota alluded to a suit brought two years before by his sister-in-law, Mary J. Barber, regarding payment on a $100,000 mortgage bearing $30,000 interest. He had been trying to negotiate another loan. He had also disputed whether the acreage held in his name was truly his responsibility or belonged to the family partnership.

An earlier exchange of letters with William A. Morin suggests that Barber's commitment to the drainage project had begun to wane after the Eid petition was filed in spring 1906. Morin was displeased about having to share responsibility with McMillan for the surety bond when Barber owned the most land, so he wrote and asked for help. Barber, who worried that McMillan might sell his land and leave him hanging, replied,

> I am not at all set on having this improvement go through. If the other interested parties are not willing to do their part, and people generally in Albert Lea and the locality of the lands do not wish to encourage so valuable an investment being made, I am quite willing to drop it and that it be left in a very indefinite state, and I am very certain that if we are not called upon for the money to pay for our part of the improvements, that the funds placed in other lines of investment will yield a far better return.

Whether his letter was sincere or a petulant threat to take his ball and go home, Barber didn't follow through on his intent to improve the land. Eight years after completion of the Big Ditch, the drainage of the Barber lands had not produced the fertile farmland promised, and no new settlers from Illinois had shown up. The project had turned lakes to marshes and marshes to meadows, but achieving arable land required more extensive ditching plus tiling. Lack of maintenance on the ditches had allowed willow and cottonwood to grow and slow the flow of water. A good deal of the Barber Marsh was still muck. Bryant H. Barber apparently had neither the financial means nor the physical and emotional wherewithal to complete the endeavor. His death opened the way for the Payne Investment Company of Omaha, Nebraska, to buy the marshland and transform it into the agricultural colony of

Hollandale. Finally the word "reclamation" fits: George Payne's efforts restored value to land that had been left ruined.

⌒⌒

An untimely death five years before Barber's suicide brought long-desired improvements to John F. D. Meighen's life. On May 21, 1912, William A. Morin died of heart disease at forty-eight, leaving his wife, Katherine, thirty-six, and two adolescent sons. Among the women an Albert Lea attorney still single in his late thirties might court, the widowed Mrs. Morin was certainly the wealthiest. Meighen had continued to struggle financially. The day before Judicial Ditch No. 1 was finished, he had written in his diary, "Seems to me I'm hardest prest for money than at any time since Ann Arbor days." He was, however, caught up in an "intense" romance. Several names crop up in his diary, but some seem to be clever aliases for one fiery teacher at the Albert Lea College for Women. That relationship finally came to naught because, a female friend later advised him, he "had permitted [the] 'psychic moment' to lapse."

Katherine took the initiative in the summer of 1915 by inviting Meighen to join friends at the country club. Over the following weeks, he accompanied her to dinner and dances, on canoe rides, and to a woman suffrage meeting. He kept his reserve, in part to protect his reputation: "Suppose being too friendly with a widow is bound to be misconstrued. Folk will conclude that I am after her money and incidentally her. But she is bright and interesting in any event."

The pace picked up the next year. By March, Mrs. Morin had become Katherine, and by May Kitten, the nickname her friends used. Meighen had grown serious enough to consult his mother about the wisdom of marriage before talking to Kitten herself: "Mother is more sane about her than I expected. Wishes naturally that she were younger. Fears that with change of life, affection for me may vanish." He proposed in June, but Katherine hesitated. She said yes in September but later withdrew her consent. Meighen's 1916 diary concludes, "One more sweetheart episode seems closed." All was not lost, however.

Since both traveled often, many opportunities for letter writing
arose, and Meighen's letters to her survive. They show a fond mix of
romance and intellectual companionship. He told her about his work—
"a day of datum planes, gradients, benchmarks, stresses and drainage
engineering generally"—and waxed eloquent about its pleasures: "I
rather enjoy tramping about along the soft banks of a newly built drainage ditch, especially where there is quite a bit of peat in the soil. The
waters ooze into the channel from a hundred pores. The green fresh
grass comes up where the marsh reeds and muskrat houses once held
sway. There are interesting tile outlets to inspect and at times interesting insects to fight." The same day he wrote that letter, Meighen sent
Katherine a formal business letter reporting progress on negotiations
over some Morin property in Maryland.

They married on December 27, 1917. Katherine proved to be a cre-
ative businesswoman as well as a supporter of philanthropic and civic
causes. She formed and presided over Shoreland, Inc., an upscale residential development on property known as Morin's Bluff, on the north
shore of Fountain Lake. She donated the Morin home on Adams Avenue to the YWCA and moved into one of the first houses in Shoreland
Heights, at 107 The Fairway. Meighen sold the respectable house across
the lake that he could finally afford and joined her there.

Meighen continued to aspire high, work hard, hold leadership posi-
tions in lodges, attend cultural events, and take on civic responsibilities
that came his way, both local and statewide. Fittingly, he became judge
of the Tenth Judicial District and served from 1920 to 1923. Like his
colleague in the drainage scheme Henry Belden, he carried that honorific title the rest of his life. Although I never knew him personally, I
learned to recognize the tall, dignified older man with the erect bearing
I saw around town as Judge Meighen. I knew that he was important and
a respected leader in the community.

The turmoil over the Big Ditch did not fade away, not even after it
was renumbered Judicial Ditch No. 24 and called the Hollandale Ditch.
Conflicts arose over maintenance and expansion of the drainage, especially when it could not contain the spring thaw or a heavy rainfall. The

John F. D. Meighen, seated by his office window, looking down on the
businesses lining Broadway in Albert Lea, 1952

period from 1946 through 1949 was especially contentious, with Austin residents and farmers around the original marsh affected by flooding. Meighen continued to be the ditch's advocate while the objecting farmers turned to Albert Lea attorney Lyle Ostrander, Elbert and Bertha's oldest son. The Ostranders had mortgaged the farm to put Lyle through law school, on the condition that he help educate his siblings.

J. F. D. Meighen died at home of a heart attack on April 17, 1957. He was seventy-nine. His old flame Sybil Koontz never did marry. She took care of her father until his death, then moved to the Twin Cities in 1935 to work with the Children's Home Society and the Unity Settlement House. She lived to be ninety-four. Another hardy woman, Katherine Meighen made it to ninety-five.

~

The last decade of Elbert Ostrander's life saw a kind of blossoming, even in the midst of the Great Depression. The need he noticed all around him drew him further into social justice work, and he found allies in political movements stirring. He published both poetry and prose in local newspapers, in the countywide *Community Magazine,* and in *Fins, Feathers and Fur,* a predecessor to *Minnesota Conservation Volunteer.* His favorite topics were wildlife (especially waterfowl), conservation, beleaguered farmers, and public education. He also wrote accounts of historical incidents. "Connivings of Dishonest Men" was not Ostrander's only lament for a Freeborn County wetland. In "Passing of Bear Lake," published in the *Community Magazine,* he mourned that lake's destruction. His familiarity with Bear Lake, where he hunted and camped with his family, drew on close observation: "The wild rice has vanished. The pickerel grass and water celery exist only in straggley patches. The snail beds are not, and the water level has been so lowered that the ice no longer heaves in midwinter as formerly when it piled up in a long windrow and left an open rift of running water flowing from one section of the lake to another, thus aerifying the waters of the lake. Instead, the water now becomes putrid, making it impossible for life to exist under present conditions during the winter months."

Ostrander neither sought nor claimed prowess in farming. The property was nearly always indebted, and none of the children could afford to take it on. Grace turned her eleven acres in Alden into a replica of Elbert and Bertha's farm: a field of strawberries, a devil-may-care yet prolific orchard, a rundown chicken coop, and litter after litter in the smelly outbuilding we grandchildren knew as the "cathouse." At heart Grace was a teacher, and she returned to a country schoolhouse in middle age. Her siblings worked in education, public health, and criminal justice. The self-identified black sheep, Lloyd, defied the family's ethic and got rich turning California desert into suburbs. He kept a tight grip on every dollar he made, especially the one he claimed was his first, which he kept in his wallet and showed off at the slightest prompting. Family and friends received an annual account of his wealth in his Christmas letters. In old age, he eased up and gave some away. The Ostrander Auditorium at Minnesota State University, Mankato, bears his name and portrait. I have read my work there with both pride and embarrassment.

Elbert Ostrander was revered in memoriam at my house as my dad's kind, witty, fun-loving, self-educated, justice-seeking, politically engaged granddad who always championed the underdog. He had offered a refuge with those qualities to adolescent Gordy whenever tensions in the Register household felt intolerable. Never mind that he lectured Conger Germans on American patriotism during the nativist furor of World War I or thought Indians savages because of the events that coincided with his 1862 birth. Of course he wasn't perfect, and my portrait of him is not meant to be a hagiography. Years ago, my sister and I, intrigued by his writings, asked his surviving children for stories about him. A twenty-page handwritten letter from Lee, born in 1907, offers delightful anecdotes about a happy, egalitarian family life and lengthens the list of his parents' virtues. Lee let slip two negatives about his father: he was egotistical, and his sense of humor was caustic enough to make enemies. The most critical words came from youngest daughter Marvyl. "My dad had no business keeping my mother pregnant all those years," she fired. "Somebody should have stopped him." She recalled tiny Bertha left at home with a malfunctioning kitchen hand pump and wood-consuming stove while Elbert was off in St. Paul politicking.

Elbert Ostrander died of pneumonia on April 17, 1937, exactly twenty years before Judge Meighen's death. He was seventy-four. His last poem, dictated to his daughter Elsie from an oxygen tent, ends, appropriately, on a watery motif:

> The waters of Styx run dark and deep,
> And now I lay me down to sleep.

I have searched the Internet up and down to find those lines in case he cribbed them from some other poet, but so far they haven't turned up.

PART IV

Restitution and Restoration

From Booty to Beauty

Hanging on a gallery wall at the Minneapolis Institute of Art is a painting of Christ's crucifixion that could agitate the faith of a Protestant raised on Warner Sallman's blue-eyed, silken-haired *Head of Christ*. The MIA's Christ is swarthy and gaunt. The cross and segments of his body are outlined in thick swipes of black paint. Vivid patches of wine red, teal, and royal blue shine through the dark overlay. Christ appears to be moldering into the muddy earth. Art historians will explain that the black outlines and rich colors mimic the stained glass windows the French Expressionist Georges Rouault worked on as a young apprentice. Yet the piece suggests the mortal reality of death and decay, not the lofty transcendence of a church sanctuary. A curator at the MIA once called the painting "splendidly turgid."

I have long carried in memory the image of Rouault's *Crucifixion* and other famous works of art. As a lucky student in Albert Lea High School's pioneering humanities program, I received an education in art history equivalent to a course at a fine liberal arts college. Our class took a field trip to the MIA that may have implanted the memory of this painting. I wish I could say for certain. And I wish our astute teachers had known enough to point out the credit line on the gallery label that reads, "Gift of the P. D. McMillan Land Company." The name meant nothing to us then. The Hollandale kids would not have known that the wealth that purchased the painting grew out of their home soil. Those of us with family origins along Turtle Creek had no idea that our encounter with this painting might serve as recompense for damage done long ago. The Rouault, donated in 1955, was the second

gift of three from the land company, and it is the most widely reproduced. The first, presented the year before, hangs on the same wall:
Egon Schiele's *Portrait of Paris von Gütersloh*. A small cast bronze sculp-
ture, Ernst Barlach's *The Avenger*, stands in an adjacent gallery. These
three are only a small share of the art I claim as "ours."

Putnam Dana McMillan the elder emerges from the historical record
as a combative man of steely confidence who acted on privilege and
scorned objectors. His son, Dana, who benefited from his father's investments but also earned wealth in his own career, was of a different sort.
A director of the MIA described Dana as "shy and retiring," "an orderly
man who lived a beautifully ordered life." He "related himself to the land
in a wonderfully simple and direct way," and his summer home in Orono
on Lake Minnetonka was "a microcosm of the Minnesota landscape he
loved so well," with rolling green hills, the lake, and, yes, marshland.

Dana McMillan bought art in his retirement not simply for the pleasure of ownership but to build a legacy to share with others. He sought
the advice of the chief curator, Richard Davis, and went to New York
in the fall of 1947 to select works that would cohere in a collection of
modern European art. Those he bought were the avant-garde of their
time, some even shocking departures from tradition. Elected president
of the Society of Fine Arts in 1948, Dana McMillan helped Davis engineer a change in direction to "let the new generation in."

He had planned all along to bequeath his collection, motivated by
a desire expressed in his will "to discharge the social obligation of one
who has been unusually fortunate in his financial rewards." Yet those
who knew McMillan saw a deeper urge than noblesse oblige or guilt
assuagement. The curator responsible for incorporating the bequest
into the museum's collection understood that "it is hard to give, yet it
also immortalizes, extends and justifies one's pleasure. And nothing can
be more just than to give if what can be given may have the value and
dignity of public property." This is a different sensibility than the one
that led McMillan's father to expect the county to drain his land and
build him a road to Albert Lea.

Upon Dana McMillan's death in April 1961, the Minneapolis Institute of Art acquired its very first Picasso works, a drawing entitled *Reclining Nude* and the well-known painting *Woman by the Sea*, which hangs in the same gallery as Rouault's *Crucifixion*. The bequest included a late Monet rendering of his Japanese bridge at Giverny, which Monet himself described as revealing "the instability of a universe transforming itself every moment before our eyes." The twenty-eight works bequeathed are nearly all paintings produced between 1890 and 1930. Fauvism and expressionism are the collection's major visions.

Still more gifts were forthcoming. McMillan's will singled out several cousins and friends for cash or allotments of stock. He left stock to the First Congregational Church in Minneapolis, Carleton College, and the Santa Barbara Museum of Art. The remainder was divided three ways: one-quarter to the University of Minnesota for professorships and fellowships, one-quarter to the Congregational Board of Foreign Missions in memory of his mother, and one-half to the Minneapolis Society of Fine Arts to be held in an endowment, the McMillan Fund, in memory of his sisters. Half of the fund's income was to buy art and half was to maintain the museum and finance a pension fund for its employees. The fund's value at its inception was about one million dollars, nearly eight million in 2015 dollars.

McMillan had excellent reason to honor his sisters' memory. While he won praise for his generosity, they were his inspirations and models. Emily, who lived to be ninety-three, preceded him by decades as a director of the Society of Fine Arts. Twenty-one years his senior, she had first left home to pursue art when Dana was a toddler. She studied in James McNeill Whistler's studio in Paris and got to know artists Pierre Bonnard and Édouard Vuillard. The portraits she painted back home in Minneapolis respect traditional expectations of accuracy and likeness, but her use of color and texture shows the influence of her avant-garde contemporaries. Dana McMillan attributed his interest in twentieth-century European art to Emily and her excitement about its experimentation with form and color.

Margaret McMillan Webber had set a precedent as a donor to the Society of Fine Arts. When she died in 1951, Dana was in his fourth year of collecting. While her interests tended toward Asian art, her bequest may have spurred him to be still more generous. A search for her name on the MIA's collection website yields ninety-five images. They include about forty nineteenth- and twentieth-century Japanese paintings, a few French impressionists, Minnesota artist Dewey Albinson's *St. Croix Rapids*, and a special collection of Persian art that was newsworthy at the time. Margaret's wealth can't all be traced to the soil of Freeborn County. At forty-seven, she married a sixty-seven-year-old widower, Charles C. Webber, an implement dealer, who predeceased her by seven years. The implements he manufactured and sold were of the John Deere brand. John Deere himself was Webber's grandfather.

Although the P. D. McMillan family is extinct, its name lives on in an art museum, an institution seemingly far removed from swampland and drainage ditches. I don't believe an act of philanthropy atones for the destruction of a natural landscape, but it does make me more inclined to look for redeeming features: the bountiful vegetable harvests the peat soil produced, the rich memories enjoyed by people who grew up in Hollandale's heyday, the determination of those who keep the Turtle Creek watershed thriving. What I most enjoy about the McMillan bequests is knowing that private gain enabled by public funding and the legalized appropriation of others' land has been put back where it belongs: in a place accessible to everyone, with no admission charge. I can go to that beautifully ordered place whenever life seems chaotic. On clear, comfortable days, I might rather seek the company of redwings and egrets at a wetland preserve, but on dreary or turbulent days, I'll be wandering the Minneapolis Institute of Art, stopping to ponder Rouault's *Crucifixion*, which my family helped pay for.

Wo Wacintanka

The news came quietly; a friend forwarded a mass e-mail from the Minnesota Department of Natural Resources that I might not otherwise have seen: a new wildlife management area in Newry Township was to be dedicated in a public ceremony on June 6, 2013, and it appeared to include the farthest northern reach of the old Big Marsh. I almost didn't make the dedication. Dark clouds swarmed thick and low that morning, and the forecast included thunderstorms, some severe. Since my journey from Otranto to the flooded streets of Austin, I'm cautious about driving to southern Minnesota in uncertain weather. At the last minute, my legs simply walked me to the car.

I exited Interstate 35 at Geneva and drove east on high alert, nearly the only car on the road. Eight miles later, balloons at the roadside, cars parked in a field, and a tent shielding people on folding chairs from the misting rain told me I was there. Rick Erpelding, the DNR staffer with hands-on responsibility for the new WMA, said the area felt remote even to him, a man experienced with lone fieldwork in woods and wetlands. I tried to conjure up the presettlement landscape as he described the place to us: 553 acres of rolling topography with oak savanna and twenty-five existing acres of wetland on 300 acres of hydric soil subject to seasonal saturation or flooding. "A couple of ditches" had drained some of it for crops and cattle grazing.

Erpelding's charge was to restore the landscape, and he posed the question, "Restore to what?" Not to the postglacial tundra or primeval forest. The Dakota name chosen for the WMA, Wo Wacintanka, which means "the action of hope" or "to persist in spite of difficulty," suggests taking clues from the landscape itself. (The choice of name, although a thoughtful acknowledgment, was merely symbolic. The land would not be returned to the Dakota people.) Persistence could be seen in the hazelnut, nannyberry, compass plant, and fringed brome growing up from the soil. Wetland restoration was under way, and Erpelding had begun burning the oak savanna's woody understory and planting the prairie portions of the land with locally native seeds. Before yielding to the next speaker, he urged us to avoid walking in one area not far from the tent: he had spotted a blue-winged teal nest hidden in the grass shortly before the dedication.

Carroll Henderson, the DNR's nongame supervisor, introduced himself as the person in charge of "everything you can't shoot." He offered more signs of persistence: bald eagles and bobolinks and the trumpeter swans and sandhill cranes that had already stopped to nest. An association with the Jay Hormel Nature Center in Austin would encourage birders and kids' nature classes to enjoy the area, and it would be open to hunters of deer and other populous game in season. There would be no roads or mulched paths or boardwalks or parking lots, however. We could follow the firebreaks or the trails the deer made. Wo Wacintanka is intended, above all, for wildlife.

Other speakers followed, among them the benefactor, John C. Goetz, a Minneapolis lawyer. He had donated the land with the rare proviso that it not be sold without his or his heirs' approval. An urban investor in rural real estate, he had bought the land in 1995 intending to rent it out for farming. He soon became aware—with advice from the DNR—of its unusual condition. The oak groves had not been bulldozed; wetlands had been left undrained and slopes unleveled. Goetz praised the former owner's stewardship. He told us that Alvin Christianson, a bachelor farmer born on the farm, had lived there with his unmarried sister until his death. Goetz bought the land from the estate after Christianson's sister moved to a nursing home.

Erpelding encouraged everyone to walk the land but warned us that wood ticks were plentiful. I was neither dressed nor sprayed to deal with that single scourge of life among beautiful bur oaks. Heavier raindrops and a darkening of the western sky spurred me to head back north. Yet I stood a while and took in the rise in the land to the south, the comforting softness of waving grasses, the dark grandeur of fully leaved oak crowns. Noting that we were in section 15 of Newry Township, I calculated the distance to the Speer farm in Moscow's section 22—seven miles due south, across moraines and marsh and the edge of the old Moscow woods. Someday I would come back and try to envision the landscape as the Speers first saw it.

The cash value of Goetz's donation—$664,000—triggered a matching expenditure for wildlife habitat elsewhere via Reinvest in Minnesota. The program pays owners to enroll marginal farmland in a conservation easement. Some run for a specified number of years, but the program encourages perpetual easements. Dana McMillan, who proposed buying marginal land as an alternative to price supports and subsidies, might have approved. The Board of Water and Soil Resources reported 117 RIM projects in Freeborn County as of November 29, 2012, but a 2015 RIM map shows few within the Big Marsh.

Reinvest in Minnesota is one of a dozen or so government programs that offer financial incentives to take land out of production and restore it to wetland, prairie, or native timber. The financing is offered mostly in response to need, calculated by watershed or larger region. After the floods of 2008, millions of dollars were released for wetland restoration as flood control in the Cedar River watershed, of which Turtle Creek is a part. Unfortunately, these programs shift with the farm economy and political winds. No overriding vision of restoration governs public policy. Restoring a wetland is more difficult than just letting nature take its course. It means digging up tile, plugging ditches, and rooting out established crops. Even with that done, it takes about eight years for a wetland to become self-sustaining.

I would be remiss not to mention Freeborn County's dean of wetland restoration, my shirttail relative Bill Bryson. For decades, Bill nurtured an eighteen-acre marsh on his farm a mile and a half east of Alden. He rerouted drain tile to let a pasture revert to wet meadow and deepened two potholes to make them more appealing to ducks. The marsh is aswarm with feathered and furred wildlife and a favorite site for Audubon Society excursions and school field trips.

Bryson's efforts almost came to naught in 1970 when the Freeborn County Board decided to build a road through the marsh. Again and again they served him with road easement forms, and again and again he refused to sign them. The county then summoned him to a condemnation hearing. In the meantime, the state legislature had passed an Environmental Rights Act that emboldened Bryson to challenge the order on grounds that the proposed road would, in the language of the legislation, "materially adversely affect the environment." After five years of arguments, lower court decisions, and appeals, the Minnesota Supreme Court ruled in Bryson's favor. He in turn granted the state a perpetual easement to preserve the marsh as a DNR wildlife management area.

The experience turned Bryson into an advocate for wetland restoration, a contributing writer to conservation magazines, and a popular speaker. Up until his death at eighty-seven, he was ready to engage anyone in conversation about the value of wetlands. He carried folded copies of his articles and speeches in his pocket, as I learned firsthand at my aunt Vivian's funeral. Although they shared no genetic connection, I see a bit of Elbert Ostrander in Bryson's argumentative demeanor and his relentless concern for environmental justice.

The Minnesota Supreme Court ruling in *County of Freeborn by Tuveson v. Bryson*, filed June 18, 1976, did more than spare Bryson's "little duck pond" from a gravel and gasoline intrusion. It undid the equation of swamp with wasteland that had governed Minnesota's drainage law since statehood. The justices quoted Aldo Leopold's *A Sand County Almanac* in basing their decision on a "land ethic" that "enlarges the boundaries of the community to include soils, waters, plants, and animals." The ruling makes an eloquent case for wetlands:

> To some of our citizens, a swamp or marsh land is physically unattractive, an inconvenience to cross by foot and an obstacle to road construction or improvement. However, to an increasing number of our citizens who have become concerned enough about the vanishing

wetlands to seek legislative relief, a swamp or marsh is a thing of beauty. To one who is willing to risk wet feet to walk through it, a marsh frequently contains a springy soft moss, vegetation of many varieties, and wildlife not normally seen on higher ground. It is quiet and peaceful— the most ancient of cathedrals—antedating the oldest of manmade structures. More than that, it acts as nature's sponge, holding heavy moisture to prevent flooding during heavy rainfalls and slowly releasing the moisture and maintaining the water tables during dry cycles. In short, marshes and swamps are something to protect and preserve.

For the Birds

Elbert H. Ostrander got me into this swamp of a project. I took to blaming him whenever other obligations pulled me so far from the work that I lost its flow and forgot its pleasures. So many arcane facts to trace. So much dizzying microfilm to read. So many brittle documents to turn over in the hunt for one revelatory gem. So many experiences missed while fumbling through the sepia dimness of the past. So many failed attempts at a succinct answer to the dreaded question, "What are you writing now?" Did ancestral pique justify my preoccupation with a topic as dreary as drainage ditches?

In one such funk on an otherwise fine October day, I decided to have it out with the man. If he was going to dog me into continuing one of his half-baked pursuits, he could at least throw me a story line or a fertile metaphor. I was planning to drive to Albert Lea anyway for the funeral of a friend's elderly father. Talking to the dead might be appropriate. If I set out early, I'd have time to unload my complaints at the Ostrander gravesite in Alden cemetery. It was only twenty miles out of the way.

Racing to Alden on Interstate 90 is unnerving, so I took the familiar route on old US 16. As I neared the turn into Alden, I checked the time and saw that I had too little for a conversation, even one with no responses. I turned south instead, toward the place where Elbert and Bertha had raised their brood. I hadn't been that way in decades, probably not since family rides up and down "ticklebelly hills," past the sites that figured in my parents' younger lives. Dad liked to check out the Ostrander farm, long out of Ostrander hands. A drainage ditch had carried away his granddad's slough.

Nothing along the road looked familiar. Huge metal containment sheds loomed on the west side. Where a house and outbuildings used to mark the site of the Ostrander farm, a small rambler stood alone. The distance between farmsteads was greater than I remembered. I gathered these impressions quickly because a truck was breathing down my neck and the road was painted with a yellow no-passing line.

I finally reached the Conger junction, where I could turn east toward Albert Lea and the funeral. The truck sped on unhindered, and I stopped for a last look at the Alden prairie. I couldn't pull off the road because the fields were plowed to the pavement—no shoulder, no roadside ditch of goldenrod and milkweed, no fence wound with wild grapevines. Bertha's parents, Dan and Mary Hord, had farmed at this junction, but I couldn't remember which plot was theirs. The farmstead on the northeast corner looked occupied and well maintained. An object of a shape my mind first registered as "angelic" hovered above the yard like a remotely controlled flying device. I watched it float in place until it flapped a pair of wings and perched in a tree. I would confirm its identity when I got home to my bird books, but it looked like a red-tailed hawk, a large one. My dad would have called it a chicken hawk.

I drove on through Conger, a sad collection of mostly empty buildings where a small grain-elevator-and-creamery town used to thrive, and felt comfort return as I left the prairie for the curves and woods around Church and Eberhardt lakes. The lovely little Pickerel Lake Methodist Episcopal Church stood as a sentinel of the past, offering the illusion of a country idyll.

At US Highway 69, I turned north toward the funeral, with just enough time to stop at a favorite childhood destination, the hilltop park alongside Pickerel Lake. A second large bird of the day had alighted on the gravel just ahead of me. At the crunch of my tires, it arose and beelined across the park to a safe roost. I had watched enough eagle cams to know this bird, a juvenile, at first sight. Bald eagles on Pickerel Lake?

As I pulled back onto the highway, I looked toward the slough where I used to watch tadpoles. It was covered in a snowy white. Egrets stood motionless in the ring of reeds. Egrets lifted their long legs and waded in tense concentration. Egrets stretched their necks and thrust their beaks into the water. Egrets perched in the trees that half encircled the slough. Each spring I anticipate my first sight of an egret standing alone in a marsh, a sign that has become a sort of totem. I had never imagined egrets in such abundance. And then I saw, floating on the clear surface at the center of the slough, a flock of white pelicans.

It was the fall migration, the gathering of the flocks for the long flight south to a place where, Elbert Ostrander liked to think, migratory birds spend their time pining for their true home in Minnesota. I felt as if I were reading one of his poems, not in words but in the images that inspired it. None of these birds was familiar from my childhood, when the largest birds around were pheasants and mallard ducks and the raucous crows that were said to flock to Albert Lea in the wintertime like swallows to Capistrano. Mourning doves woke me on summer mornings, but I rarely spotted one. Even Canada geese were tiny specks forming a V in the sky as they passed our landscape by.

What Grandpa Ostrander was trying to tell me wasn't immediately clear, but I finally got it back in Minneapolis. As if to hammer the point home, a "crow" flying ahead of my car as I approached my driveway landed on a tree and turned its profile toward me, showing its true colors: black, white, and bright red. It was a pileated woodpecker. Maybe I had put the wrong emphasis on the headline over the drainage diatribe in the *Freeborn Patriot*. Did he really want me to investigate the "connivings of dishonest men?" I'm sure he never doubted their culpability. Now my attention fell on the words "cheat nature." This work of mine, so often slowed by a frustrating tangle of facts or a fascinating slide down a rabbit hole, is honestly for the birds. And so I dedicate it to the birds that once swarmed in thick clouds over Rice Lake and the Big Marsh, and to the birds that are coming back, flitting across the fields of corn and beans from one wetland oasis to another. Mine is not, after all, just another gloomy story of rural decline, but a promising story of restoration, as birds and humans find their way home.

Acknowledgments

In November 2008, I met with Pam McClanahan, director, and Ann Regan, editor in chief, of the Minnesota Historical Society Press to try out a book idea that had begun to pursue me. I told them about my great-grandfather's essay critical of the drainage of the Big Marsh and showed them the postcards of the dredge my grandfather had sent my grandmother when they were courting. When I asked if they thought the drainage story worth investigating, Pam responded, "Do you need to be struck by lightning?" In the years of research since, conversations with Ann have focused on what matters most: finding a coherent story in the chaos and writing prose people want to read.

Many keepers of the historical record have been generous in aiding my search: the staff at the Gale Library and the Hubbs Microfilm Room at the Minnesota History Center, especially the never-daunted Debbie Miller; Linda Evenson, librarian at the Freeborn County Historical Museum, whose memory should be digitized; Vivie Loverink of the Hollandale Heritage Huis; everyone at the Hennepin County History Museum and at its neighbor, the library of the Minneapolis Institute of Art; Susan Wakefield of the General Mills Archives in Minneapolis; Betty Obendorf of the Polo (Illinois) Historical Society; Martha Vickery of the Minnesota Department of Natural Resources; Ruth Ann Montgomery of the Janesville (Wisconsin) Public Library, who met me at the side of a highway in her work clothes of skirt and sandals, then crawled through the brambles of an abandoned cemetery to help me locate tombstones; Freeborn County Recorder Kelly

Callahan, the go-to local history buff; Jeanne Herman and her colleagues in the county auditor's office; and Steve Penkava of Jones, Haugh & Smith Engineering Co., where the old maps and ditch surveys are kept.

Participation in the monthly researchers' group convened by Debbie Miller at the Minnesota Historical Society and also guided by Hamp Smith has been of tremendous benefit. There is no encouragement like the empathy of fellow obsessives. We have listened to one another's progress reports, speculated about meanings, cursed the obstacles, and rejoiced in our serendipitous finds. Mary Hawker Bakeman, Paul Maravelas, Thomas Shaw, Sue Hunter Weir, and Carrie Zeman have earned an extra measure of gratitude by offering specific help. One research colleague deserves my utmost thanks: Carol Veldman Rudie, a Hollandale native studying land use in the area over time. Carol and I have exulted over arcane bits of data, taken road trips to our shared landscape, and spent hours at Sebastian Joe's coffee shop gossiping about long-dead players in the drainage scheme.

Current and former Freeborn County residents have provided me with information, suggested resources, told me stories, and/or driven me around to their favorite places: Neil "Gunnar" Berg, Mike Bradley, Dennis Dingemans, Donald Draayer, Betty McKee GreenCrow, Janet Reichl Heidinger, Ray and Elaine (Winjum) King, and Ken and Kathy (Hanson) Muilenburg. Thanks to Jackie and Roger Jacobson for inviting me in to the old Speer/Register house. And thanks to Ken Muilenburg and the other volunteer firefighters who saved it from destruction back when it was the Greibrok place.

For helping to fill out the Register history, I thank my far-flung relatives Penny Register Jones; her husband, Mark Jones; Dara Swanson Hoffman; and Phyllis Hoffman.

Two writer friends read pieces of the book in progress: Morgan Grayce Willow, whose poetry and prose on the meaning of place I greatly admire, and Sara M. Evans, whom I count on to delete the apologies and understatements we know as "chicken-selling."

Ann Regan, managing editor Shannon Pennefeather, and copyeditor Tom Dean have earned my genuine gratitude for their attentive and respectful reading of the manuscript. I offer them apologies as well for my profligate use of commas.

I did not apply for funds to support this project, but I am grateful to the Franklin D. Roosevelt administration for the most reliable writing grant I've ever received: a monthly check from Social Security.

Source Notes

To trace the stories of settlement and drainage and learn about the people involved, I read local newspapers. These papers often blended news and opinion, and they did not always verify information. I have checked facts against other documentation and read several newspapers' reports on a single incident, and I note discrepancies and uncertainties when it matters. Here are the newspapers I used most often, along with the abbreviations by which I cite them: *Alden Advance* (*AA*); *Albert Lea Enterprise* (*ALE*) and *Times-Enterprise* (*T-E*); *Evening Tribune*, Albert Lea (*ET*); *Freeborn County Standard*, Albert Lea (*FCS*); *Freeborn County Times* (*FCT*); *Austin Daily Herald* (*ADH*); *Austin Register* (*AR*); *Mower County Transcript*, Lansing (*MCT*). I read these papers on microfilm at the Minnesota Historical Society (MNHS) and at the Freeborn County Historical Museum (FCHM). *FCS* is also available on the Minnesota Digital Newspaper Hub, and *MCT* on the Chronicling America website of the Library of Congress.

For personal data on people in the story, I conducted searches on Ancestry.com that brought up census listings, immigration and military records, and the like. Several times I had to ward off Ancestry's efforts to add W. W. Cargill to my family tree. I read death certificates at MNHS, used the newspaper index and obituary files at FCHM, and read published biographical sketches at Hennepin County History Museum (HCHM) and online.

This story could never have been pieced together without access to two large manuscript collections at MNHS: the William Morin and Family Papers and the John F. D. Meighen and Family Papers. The

Morin correspondence file contains rare letters from P. D. McMillan, who, as far as I know, did not leave his own collection behind. Meighen's diary reveals inside information about the drainage pursuit that exists nowhere else.

In a few instances, I have veered away from fact and into imagination, but only with reference to my own ancestors. My speculations arise out of oral family stories and preserved memorabilia. Readers will know when I'm taking a flight of fancy. I don't intend to mislead anyone or distort the truth.

Notes

Notes to Prologue

The scene with Amanda is imaginary, although the names and family circumstances are true. I'm not sure about the horse, though. That could be Amanda's wish. The Speers had no horses—only oxen—before the war. The Minnesota Cavalry would likely have kept its horses.

page 4   Geneva Lake: Elbert H. Ostrander, "Connivings of Dishonest Men Cheat Nature as Well as Fellow Beings, Writer Avers," *Freeborn Patriot*, July 19, 1935.

Notes to "Hollandale: An Introduction"

page 7   Wetland loss: Thomas E. Dahl and Gregory J. Allord, "History of Wetlands in the Coterminous United States," US Geological Survey, National Water Summary on Wetland Resources, USGS Water Supply Paper 2425, http://water.usgs.gov/nwsum/WSP2425/history.html; Minnesota Department of Natural Resources (DNR), Minnesota Wetlands Conservation Plan, Version 1.02, 1997, http://files.dnr.state.mn.us/eco/wetlands/wetland.pdf.

page 7   Pollution alarms: Dennis Lien and Dave Orrick, "Minnesota Farm Drain Tiling: Better Crops, but at What Cost?" *Pioneer Press*, August 31, 2012, http://www.twincities.com/ci_21445585/minnesota-farm-drain-tiling-better-crops-but-at; Josephine Marcotty, "Who's Protecting Minnesota's Rural Rivers?," *Star Tribune*, April 28, 2014, http://www.startribune.com/who-s-protecting-minnesota-s-rural-rivers-from-cropland-runoff/256920531/; Elizabeth Dunbar, "Farmers Adapt to Big Rains but Send Trouble Downstream," *MPR News*, February 4, 2015, http://www.mprnews.org/story/2015/02/04/climate-change-farm; Tony Kennedy, "Green Scum and Fish Kills Have Albert Lea on Edge," *Star Tribune*, August 17, 2015, http://

www.startribune.com/green-scum-and-fish-kills-have-albert-lea-on-edge/
322010511/.

page 7   Eighteen thousand acres: Contemporary reports of the wetland's
size ranged from fifteen to thirty thousand acres. Researchers now estimate
the marsh at 18,279 acres. Nathan N. Boddy, *Implications of Change: A Study
of the Turtle Creek Watershed of Southeastern Minnesota*, MA thesis, University of Minnesota, 2004, 21.

page 11   Albert Lea Farms Company, *Hollandale the Wonderland*, 1926;
Georges Denzene and Beverly Jackson, *The Hollandale Story 1918–1950*
(Freeborn County Historical Society, 1989); Janel M. Curry-Roper and
Carol Veldman Rudie, "Hollandale: The Evolution of a Dutch Farming
Community," *Focus* 40.3 (Fall 1990).

page 12   Changes in Hollandale: Donald Draayer, *A Journey of Thanksgiving:
Lifetime Memories of Learning, Loving, Leading, and Looking Back*, photocopy, 2009, plus personal conversation with him and other Hollandale
natives.

page 12   Corn and soybeans reign: A few current efforts at innovation and
diversification are worthy of note: a locally owned hydroponic farm spe-
cializing in lettuce, a seed potato operation, and at least one organic farm.

Notes to "Freeborn County: Home, but No Biome"

page 17   Epigraph: Sue Leaf, "One Seed at a Time," *Minnesota Conservation
Volunteer* 66:387 (March-April 2003), 20.

page 17   Favorite country road: This section of Wedgewood Road and adjoining farmland have been replaced by the Wedgewood Cove Golf Club,
which includes a housing development. The developers were required to
conserve the wetlands on the property. I hope they will show the same
respect for the beautiful oak grove on the knoll above Pickerel Lake.

page 18   Oleomargarine signs: Minnesota's dairy industry had succeeded in
barring the sale of butter substitutes colored yellow like the real thing. Dave
Kenney, "Minnesota's Margarine Battles, 1885–1975," MNopedia, http://
www.mnopedia.org/thing/minnesota-s-margarine-battles-1885-1975.

page 18   Marshes, lakes, and sloughs: The various terms for wetlands are
often used interchangeably, but they do have distinct meanings. A bog is
spongy, acidic, and mossy and gets its water from precipitation. A slough
has water running through it. A marsh is characterized by reedy vegetation.
A swamp is dominated by woody plants.

page 19   I am indebted to the late naturalist and essayist Paul Gruchow for a guiding piece of writing advice: Remember that you live in an exotic landscape, and you need to make it vivid to people who can't imagine it. Yes, we all live in exotic landscapes.

Notes to "Looking for the Big Marsh"

page 20   Pelicans: Anne Brataas, *North Country Almanac: A Seasonal Guide to the Great Outdoors,* St. Paul Pioneer Press (Kansas City: Andrews and McNeel), 1996, 52; John R. Tester, *Minnesota's Natural Heritage: An Ecological Perspective* (Minneapolis: University of Minnesota Press, 1995), 176.

page 21   Carp: Brataas, *North Country Almanac,* 52.

page 21   Location of marsh: US General Land Office, Public Land Survey field notes and plats, Archives of the Secretary of State, MNHS; also the US Bureau of Land Management (BLM), http://www.glorecords.blm .gov/; Francis J. Marschner, *The Original Vegetation of Minnesota,* map, 1930, redrafted by Forest Service, US Department of Agriculture, 1974, MNHS.

page 21   1860 visitors: *FCS,* June 9, 1860.

page 22   P. D. McMillan: This McMillan family is not related to the MacMillan family associated with Cargill, Inc.

page 23   Fertile peat bed: Peat is a water-saturated soil type containing at least thirty percent dead and decaying plant material. It forms in the absence of oxygen and retains carbon so that when it is exposed to air, it releases CO_2 and becomes combustible. Peat develops very slowly and is not easily replaced once excavated or deprived of its water and vegetation cycle. International Peatland Society website, http://www.peatsociety.org/ peatlands-and-peat/what-peat. The Wikipedia entry on peat seems well researched and documented.

page 23   Source of Turtle Creek: A ditched outlet from Geneva Lake that follows the path of the original Geneva Creek, then turns south to connect with the ditch that Turtle Creek became, is now identified as Turtle Creek on Freeborn County plat maps. On the Freeborn County and Turtle Creek watershed maps published by Jones, Haugh & Smith, Inc., it is labeled "Main Open Ditch." Legally it is now known as Judicial Ditch 24.

page 23   Lea expedition: Albert Miller Lea, *Journal and Autobiography,* manuscript, MNHS, portions reprinted in *FCS,* March 13, 1879; Albert Miller Lea, *Notes on Wisconsin Territory* (Philadelphia: Henry S. Tanner, 1836);

Franklyn Curtiss-Wedge, ed., *History of Freeborn County Minnesota* (hereinafter 1911 FC History) (Chicago: H. C. Cooper, Jr. & Co., 1911), 40–45.

page 23 Kellar's estimate: 1911 FC History, 41.

page 24 "Mattras," etc.: Lea, *Journal and Autobiography*.

page 25 Wetland acreage: Benjamin Whipple Palmer, *Swamp Land Drainage with Special Reference to Minnesota* (Minneapolis: Bulletin of the University of Minnesota, 1915), 122.

page 25 Imagining a wetland: Tester, *Minnesota's Natural Heritage*, 167, with refinements suggested by an anonymous expert reviewer.

Notes to "No Empty Landscape"

page 29 Burial mounds: In the fall of 1963, excavation for a housing development opened the mounds southeast of Albert Lea Lake in section 19 of Hayward Township, word spread, and they were plundered for artifacts before archaeologists arrived to secure the site. There were thirteen mounds arranged in an arc. Carla L. Norquist, "Albert Lea Lake Salvage Project," *Minnesota Archaeological Newsletter* (Department of Anthropology, University of Minnesota) 12 (Fall 1967), "Indians" clipping file, FCHM.

page 29 Indians named: Albert Lea City Directory, 1955; *Tiger* (Albert Lea High School yearbook), various years.

page 30 Owen Johnson: The Owen Johnson Artifact Collection, donated to the DNR and catalogued by archaeologists of the Minnesota Historical Society, is housed at Myre–Big Island State Park. It is no longer on public display but open to researchers by appointment only. I toured it when it was open to the public, but for this work I consulted the description in Michael Bradley, "Environmental and Cultural Changes in the North Eastern Plains Over the Last 12,000 Years," copy supplied by the author; and Guy Gibbon and Scott F. Anfinson, *Minnesota Archaeology: The First 13,000 Years*, chapter 4, Publications in Anthropology 6, University of Minnesota, 2008.

page 30 Village site: E-mail correspondence with Michael Bradley, Eagle River, AK, April 15, 2002, August 20, 2012, and January 6, 2013.

page 30 Wahpekute: Alan Woolworth and Nancy Woolworth, "Eastern Dakota Settlement and Subsistence Patterns Prior to 1851" (The Second Council for Minnesota Archaeology Symposium, Spring 1977), 71–73; Samuel Pond, *Dakota Life in the Upper Midwest* (St. Paul: Minnesota Historical Society Press, 1986), 109; Gwen Westerman and Bruce White, *Mni*

Sota Makoce: The Land of the Dakota (St. Paul: Minnesota Historical Society Press, 2012), 85, 94, 108, 150; Helen Hornbeck Tanner, *Atlas of Great Lakes Indian History* (Norman: University of Oklahoma Press, 1987), 150; Paul Durand, *Where the Waters Gather and the Rivers Meet: An Atlas of the Eastern Sioux* (self-published, 1994), 98.

page 30 Other Dakota on Big Marsh: Westerman and White, *Mni Sota Makoce*, 94, 150, 197.

page 30 Wild rice harvest: Westerman and White, *Mni Sota Makoce*, 50; Pond, *Dakota Life in the Upper Midwest*, 29.

page 31 Edible marsh roots: Pond, *Dakota Life in the Upper Midwest*, 28.

page 31 Ice fishing: Pond, *Dakota Life in the Upper Midwest*, 30.

page 31 Maple sugar and muskrats: Westerman and White, *Mni Sota Makoce*, 98; Pond, *Dakota Life in the Upper Midwest*, 30.

page 31 Deer, elk, bison: Westerman and White, *Mni Sota Makoce*, 89–90, 94.

page 31 Areas of plentiful food as buffer zones: Westerman and White, *Mni Sota Makoce*, 94; Mary Wingerd, *North Country: The Making of Minnesota* (Minneapolis: University of Minnesota Press, 2010), 87, 107.

page 31 Shared hunting lands: Westerman and White, *Mni Sota Makoce*, 149.

page 32 Henry Rice: D. M. Pyle, *St. Paul Pioneer Press*, quoted in *FCS*, July 12, 1877.

page 32 Dakota presence in 1850s: 1911 FC History, 12; Westerman and White, *Mni Sota Makoce*, 197–98.

page 33 Pan of milk: Obituary of Joseph Rayman, *FCS*, January 3, 1929.

page 33 The words "woman" and, below, "wife" have been inserted to replace a deeply offensive word previously applied with impunity by white people to Native women.

page 33 "Mrs. Marrietta Whaley Came to Freeborn Co. In 1855; Writes Memoirs," *ET*, February 14, 1938.

page 33 Winnebago history: Patty Loew, *Indian Nations of Wisconsin* (Madison: Wisconsin Historical Society Press, 2001); Tanner, *Atlas of Great Lakes Indian History*, 143ff; Ho-Chunk Nation, History Timeline, http://www.ho-chunknation.com/media/9205/ho-chunkhistorytimeline.pdf; Winnebago Tribe of Nebraska, http://www.winnebagotribe.com/index.php/about-us/tribal-history.

page 34 Autonomous Winnebago: Wingerd, *North Country*, 137.

page 34 Winnebago in Geneva: 1911 FC History, 12.

page 34 Blue Earth Reservation: "Map of Winnebago Indian Reservation," MNHS; Wingerd, *North Country*, 223.

page 34 Competition with settlers: Wingerd, *North Country*, 137.

page 35 Winnebago at hanging: Wingerd, *North Country*, 335; Chuck Lewis, "Removing the Winnebago: A Tale of Frontier Journalism," *Minnesota's Heritage* 3 (January 2011): 64.

page 35 Faribault: Westerman and White, *Mni Sota Makoce*, 202; Wingerd, *North Country*, 338.

page 35 Ho-Chunk return: Newton H. Winchell, *The Aborigines of Minnesota* (St. Paul: Minnesota Historical Society, 1911), 574.

page 35 Inoffensive and harmless: *FCS*, December 9, 1903.

page 35 Flight to Omaha Reservation: The Winnebago Tribe of Nebraska website says they traveled by "nocturnal gravitation," whether navigating by the stars or under cover of darkness.

page 35 Winnebago Reservation in 1940: 1940 US Census, Winnebago, Nebraska. Winnebago who had fled back to Wisconsin during the various relocations formed the Ho-Chunk Nation near Black River Falls.

page 35 Return to Minnesota: Chuck Holmes, "Tribune's Tired Three," *Albert Lea Tribune*, 1961, "Indians" clipping file, FCHM; conversation with Betty McKee GreenCrow, Minneapolis.

Notes to "The Grid That Turned Land to a Commodity"

page 36 Sluggish stream: Land Survey field notes, box 295, Archives of the Minnesota Secretary of State, MNHS, available digitally at the BLM website, http://www.glorecords.blm.gov. Subsequent quotations about the survey in this chapter are from this same document.

page 36 Rubber waders: Inquiry to Thomas Shaw, clothing historian and owner, The Clothing Bureau; Ann Marie Somma, "Charles Goodyear and the Vulcanization of Rubber," Connecticut History website, http://connecticuthistory.org/charles-goodyear-and-the-vulcanization-of-rubber/.

page 37 George Washington: Andro Linklater, *Measuring America: How an Untamed Wilderness Shaped the United States and Fulfilled the Promise of Democracy* (New York: Walker, 2002), 44–45.

page 37 Township boundary: Land Survey field notes, book 2, 97.

page 41 Boustrophedonic: Linklater, *Measuring America*, 166.

page 41 Leavenworth: Letter to his aunt, August 21, 1856, Frederick Leavenworth Papers, MNHS.

page 41 Clerks made copies: Hildegard Binder Johnson, *Order Upon the Land: The US Rectangular Land Survey and the Upper Mississippi Country* (New York: Oxford University Press, 1976), 78.

page 42 Fitzpatrick in Wisconsin: US GenWeb, Wisconsin, Crawford, *History of Crawford and Richland Counties*, 871, http://content.wisconsinhistory.org/cdm/compoundobject/collection/wch/id/1815.

page 42 Gunter's chain: Linklater, *Measuring America*, 15–17, 77–78.

page 42 Horizontal plane: Johnson, *Order Upon the Land*, 76.

page 43 Iowa border survey: Johnson, *Order Upon the Land*, 123–24.

Notes to "Homing on the Marsh: The Speers"

page 48 Half-Indian Grandma Speer: Some recent but still inconclusive genealogical digging suggests that the family's Indian heritage, if any, traces to Robert's mother, Maria Johnson Speer, who was born on or near the Seneca Reservation in upstate New York.

page 49 Speer journey: "Reminiscences of Thomas R. Morgan," 1911 FC History, 498–502; *History of Freeborn County, Minnesota* (Minneapolis: Minnesota Historical Company, 1882), 1996 reprint (hereinafter 1882 FC History), 290; Whaley Memoirs.

page 50 Considerable blacksmithing: 1882 FC History, 495.

page 50 Botsford quotation: Whaley Memoirs. I have not found corroboration in the *Freeborn County Eagle*, but some microfilmed pages are blurred and indecipherable.

page 51 Speer's harvest and livestock: Agricultural Schedule, *US Census Office Nonpopulation Census Schedule: Minnesota*, 1860–80, microfilm, MNHS.

page 51 Hauling wheat: 1911 FC History, 196.

page 51 Resolution against mortgage foreclosures: Published in *FCS*, September 15, 1860. The story can be followed in successive editions of *FCS*, September and October 1860. It is also recounted in 1911 FC History, 195–96.

page 52 Skinner's return: *FCS*, October 27, 1860.

page 52 Speer data: Obituary for Mrs. Maria Speer, *Evansville Enterprise*, February 18, 1898; tombstone, Old Baptist Cemetery, Union, WI; genealogical materials, Janesville (WI) Public Library; *History of Washtenaw County, Michigan* (Chicago: Chas. C. Chapman & Co., 1881), 1275.

page 53 Town of Tyre: *History of Seneca County, New York* (Philadelphia: Lippincott, 1876), 124.

Notes to "The Trip from Otranto Revisited"

page 56 Old bridge: The bridge has been removed since the visit described here.

page 58 Cedar flooding: Cornelia F. Mutel, ed., *A Watershed Year: Anatomy of the Iowa Floods of 2008* (Iowa City: University of Iowa Press, 2010); Turtle Creek Watershed District website, flood data no longer posted.

Notes to "Claiming the High Ground: The Ostranders"

page 59 Bancroft farm: Land patent MW-0489–338, Chatfield Land Office, May 10, 1861, BLM website.

page 62 Ripon, Wisconsin: "D. P. Mapes' Account of Early Ripon, 1870," *The History of Fond du Lac County, Wisconsin* (Chicago: Western Historical Society, 1880), 355–56, http://www.wlhn.org/fond_du_lac/towns/ripon_mapes.htm.

page 62 Ostranders in New York: D. Hamilton Hurd, *History of Clinton and Franklin Counties, New York* (Philadelphia: J. W. Lewis & Co., 1880).

page 62 Muddy accident: *FCS*, May 20, 1875.

Notes to "What Counts as a Lake?"

page 67 Lures to Minnesota: Chicago, Milwaukee & St. Paul Railways, *Guide for Tourists, Business-men, Emigrants and Colonists*, 1871; and *Tourist's Manual to the Health and Pleasure Resorts of the Golden Northwest*, 1880, MNHS; Rev. H. Bushnell, DD, "Minnesota for Invalids," *FCS*, November 28, 1860.

page 67 Gem Lake: 1911 FC History, 257, 358; *FCS*, May 21, August 27, and October 8, 1884; *FCT*, April 17, 1896. Gem Lake is now known as Morin Lake, but some call it simply Alden Lake.

page 69 Township reports: *FCS*, November 23 and January 26, 1887, May 21, 1902, and April 15, 1903. The names of the township reporters to the various local newspapers were rarely published. I know from her obituary (*ET*, November 24, 1930; *FCS*, November 27, 1930) that Orra Dearmin was the Moscow and Oakland correspondent for both *ET* and *FCS* in the early decades of the 1900s. A frequent contributor of Moscow and Oakland news around the turn of the century identified as "C. B." may have been Clarenden D. Belden, a minister who served both Baptist and Methodist congregations in the area. He also became the editor and publisher of the *Mower County Transcript* in 1893.

page 70 Owatonna party: *FCS*, October 12, 1887, reprinted from the *Owatonna Journal.*

page 71 Hunting numbers: *FCS*, October 7, 1885; October 3, 1872; August 31, 1892.

page 72 Scathing rebuke: Evadene Burris Swanson, *The Use and Conservation of Minnesota Wildlife, 1850–1900* (St. Paul: State of Minnesota, Department of Natural Resources, 2007), 129.

page 72 Lake health: Darby Nelson, *For Love of Lakes* (East Lansing: Michigan State University Press, 2012).

Notes to "The Evolution of the Drainage Ditch"

page 74 Willard: Thanks to Martha Vickery of the Minnesota DNR for sending me a copy of this paper, a critique of what Willard called a "drainage epidemic."

page 75 European drainage: Leonardo da Vinci studied the flow and behavior of water and considered how to drain swamps to create farmland. One of his proposals was to siphon off the water. Leonardo da Vinci, *Codex Leicester* (1510), on exhibit at the Minneapolis Institute of Art, June 21–August 30, 2015.

page 75 First law: An Act to regulate and encourage the Drainage of Lands, passed August 8, 1858, *The Public Statutes of the State of Minnesota, 1849–1858*, 843–46, online archive of the Minnesota Office of the Revisor of Statutes (www.revisor.mn.gov) and on Google Books.

page 76 1858 travelers: "A Trip to Dakota," no. 2, *The Winona Republican*, July 14, 1858, in Willoughby Babcock, "Newspaper Transcripts and Index," box 5, MNHS.

page 76 Swamp numbers: Minnesota State Archives, State Land Office, Swamp Land Records, MNHS.

page 76 Drainage legislation and SMRR land: Palmer, *Swamp Land Drainage*, 33, 38, 92–94.

page 77 Progressive landowners: Palmer, *Swamp Land Drainage*, 38.

page 77 Red River: Palmer, *Swamp Land Drainage*, 64.

page 77 Next important improvement: *FCS*, July 24, 1873.

Notes to "A Watershed Year: 1877"

page 80 Beecher: *AR*, February 22, 1877.

page 83 Tramp: *AR*, July 19, 1877.

page 83 Independent Guard: *ALE*, August 2, 1877; letter from attorney and militia captain Theo Tyrer, August 1, 1877, State Archives, MNHS.

page 83 Elbert H. Ostrander, "The Grasshopper Scourge of the 70's," *Community Magazine*, undated copy in my files. Both Ostrander quotations in this paragraph are from this article.

page 83 Manchester Grange: *FCS*, August 2, 1877.

page 84 Cargill: *FCS*, September 6, 1877; 1875 Minnesota Census; 1879 Freeborn County plat book; 1880 US Census; John L. Work, *Cargill Beginnings . . . an Account of Early Years* (Cargill, Inc., 1965), FCHM.

page 84 Wheat figures: *FCS*, July 19 and August 23, 1877.

page 85 Henry Ostrander: *FCS*, September 20, 1877.

page 85 Wheat sieve: *FCS*, October 25, 1877.

page 86 Cattle and whiskey: *ALE*, March 22, 1877.

page 86 Dead horses: *FCS*, August 23, 1877.

Notes to "A New Home on the Prairie: A Speculation"

page 88 Running away to school: Lee Ostrander, Cahokia, IL, to Cheri Register and Nancy Wangen, July 9, 1977, my files.

page 88 Storm King: Elbert H. Ostrander, "The Prairies: A Narrative," loose printed page, no publication data, my files.

page 88 Mettie: Armetta Ostrander, Albert Lea, MN, to Elbert H. Ostrander, December 11, 1882, my files; obituary of Armetta E. Ostrander, *FCS*, March 15, 1883.

page 89 Cottonwoods: Ostrander, "The Prairies."

page 89 "S'rink" and "clowzet": My dad acquired these and other speech habits from his mother.

page 91 This imaginative exercise also draws on family research on Ancestry.com, family stories handed down orally, mentions of the Ostranders in *AA* and county newspapers, and Elbert Ostrander's other writings.

Notes to "Fire on the Marsh"

page 93 Such a calamity: *FCS*, September 12 and 26 and October 3, 1889.

page 93 Johnsrud's visit: *FCS*, October 17, 1889.

page 94   Peat as fuel: *FCS*, April 17, 1890.

page 94   Five-mile fire: *FCS*, April 3, 1895.

Notes to "The Alleged Conniver: Putnam Dana McMillan"

page 97   Burned area: P. D. McMillan, "History of Drainage of Riceland Marsh," manuscript, February 1915, Hollandale box, FCHM.

page 97   Visit to Holland: "Ricelawn/A Visit to One of the Largest Farms in Southern Minnesota," *MCT*, August 7, 1895.

page 99   Lunquist's name is often printed as Lundquist, the usual Swedish American spelling, in newspaper references and in some public documents, but Lunquist is most frequent. (It could be an Anglicized version of Lönnkvist.) His wife is identified alternately as Louise, Louisa, or Lovisa, the Swedish variant.

page 99   Emily McMillan: Kay Spangler, *Survey of Serial Fine Arts Exhibitions in Minnesota, 1900–1970*, 2:542, MNHS; Art Inventories Catalog, Smithsonian American Art Museum, online at the Smithsonian Collections Search Center, http://collections.si.edu/search/results.htm?q=McMillan+Emily+Dana.

page 99   McMillan's appearance: William W. Folwell, "An Obituary of First Lieutenant Putnam Dana McMillan Read Before the Military Order of the Loyal Legion," May 14, 1918, MNHS; Emily McMillan, *Portrait of Putnam Dana McMillan*, painting, image reproduced online, MNHS; passport application of May 11, 1897, Ancestry.com.

page 99   Social life: *Historic Minneapolis Tribune*, 1880s–1910s, formerly online at the Hennepin County Library Database website, now available on the Minnesota Digital Newspaper Hub, MNHS.

page 100   1897 profile: Marion Daniel Shutter and J. S. McLain, *Progressive Men of Minnesota* (Minneapolis: Minneapolis Journal, 1897), 344.

page 101   Other biographical sources consulted: *St. Paul Globe*, January 29, 1889; US Census, 1870–1910; Minnesota Census, 1875–1905; American Civil War Soldiers and Civil War Pension Index, Ancestry.com; Minnesota Death Certificate 1918–023458, MNHS; obituary in *Minneapolis Journal*, April 8, 1918; Minneapolis City Directory, 1889–1900; Christopher Webber Hall, *The University of Minnesota: A Historical Sketch* (Minneapolis, 1896), 19; McMillan family genealogy on Rootsweb; R. I. Holcombe and William H. Bingham, *History of Minneapolis and Hennepin County, Compendium of History and Biography* (Chicago: H. Taylor & Co., 1914); Horace B. Hudson, ed., *A Half Century of Minneapolis* (Minneapolis: The Hudson Publishing Co., 1908).

Notes to "The First Drainage"

page 102 First drainage: *ALE*, August 11, 1893.

page 102 Van Norman purchase: Deed index, FCHM.

page 102 Ditch plows: 1882 FC History, 370; *FCS*, January 6, 1881; *Freeborn County Directory*, 1902. Edwards Manufacturing Company is still in business in Albert Lea.

page 103 Spring Lake: *ALE*, February 23 and April 7, 1893.

page 103 How tiles work: Tiles were later made of concrete. Drainage systems now use perforated polyethylene tubing. See University of Minnesota Extension Service, http://www.extension.umn.edu.

page 103 Tile works: *FCS*, July 17, 1895.

page 103 Dredging advice: C. W. Lunquist to W. A. Morin, July 2, 1894, referencing dredging contractor "Mr. W. E. Dran of Minpls," Morin Family Papers, MNHS.

page 105 Temperance: A *Total Afholds Forening* (Total Abstinence Union) was organized, *FCS*, November 30, 1892; subsequent issues show the proliferation of both Scandinavian and English-speaking chapters.

page 105 Geneva snakes: Stories of monstrous snakes in Geneva Lake and elsewhere on the marsh appear in the *FCS* township news from 1883 to 1893. Most sound fantastic, but some are corroborated by sober witness accounts. As tempting as it was, I didn't pursue this theme, but it might make an interesting study of marsh lore, akin to the will o' the wisp in European folklore. It may also be inside humor specific to Geneva since several stories reference the Holmes family.

page 105 McMillan livestock: *FCS*, May 13, 1891; *ALE*, August 11, 1893.

page 105 Sailing: *FCS*, September 20, 1893.

page 105 Desired road to Albert Lea: Albert Lea's centrality for road travel was borne out when the Jefferson Highway came through after 1915, and again when Interstates 90 and 35 intersected there. The early overland route to Minneapolis also went through Geneva.

page 106 Road efforts (citations for this and the following paragraphs): *FCS*, July 12 and 19, 1893, and January 10 and September 5, 1894; *MCT*, July 19, 1983; P. D. McMillan and A. W. Hastings to William A. Morin, February 10, 1894, Morin Family Papers; Morin to McMillan and Hastings, letterpress,

58:501, 592, 601, February 16, April 27, and May 1, 1894, Morin Family Papers; Commissioners Record 3:389, Freeborn County Recorder's Office, County Courthouse, Albert Lea. The other commissioners in addition to Axel Brundin were E. W. Gleason, Carl Hendrickson, Ole Opdahl, N. T. Sandburg, and John C. Ross, who resigned in October 1895 and was replaced by T. W. Wilson.

page 107 Foolish prejudice: Morin to McMillan, August 21, 1897, letterpress, P63:115, Morin Family Papers.

page 107 Correspondence about draining Rice Lake: McMillan and Hastings to Morin, September 8, 1894; Morin to McMillan and Hastings, letterpress, 58:639, Morin Family Papers.

page 108 C. U. Christensen: 1911 FC History, 515; Curry-Roper and Rudie, "Hollandale."

Notes to "The Middle Man: William A. Morin"

page 109 Half the city: 1911 FC History, 754; Freeborn County plat maps, FCIIM.

page 111 The William Morin and Family Papers, MNHS, comprise thirty-five boxes. Another four boxes, one containing the third generation's family correspondence, remain uncatalogued at FCHM. William A. Morin's part of the collection is strikingly impersonal, consisting almost entirely of business matters, including orders and receipts. Researchers must look for subtexts or conclude that the man was "all business."

page 111 Maria Sanford: Correspondence, 1889–94, Morin Family Papers.

page 111 Swampland purchase: FCS, September 25, 1901.

page 112 Dan Hord: Correspondence, April 1911, Morin Family Papers.

page 112 Net worth: Online inflation calculators extrapolate from the consumer price index and other historical data, but the earliest year available is 1913.

page 112 Illinois Central: W. A. Morin to J. F. Wallace, September 31, 1899; telegram from Wallace to Morin, October 3, 1899, Morin Family Papers.

page 113 Yacht: W. A. Morin to prospective buyer S. R. Merrell, January 1910. He told Merrell, "I am not anxious for the cash." The boat had been for sale long enough that he had offered to trade it for a high-class touring car or farmland. Correspondence pertaining to the yacht *Albert Lea* is found throughout box 20, Morin Family Papers.

page 113   Morin servants: US Census, 1900, 1910; Minnesota State Census, 1895, 1905.

page 113   Chloe and W. H. Butler: Chloe was brought to Minnesota Territory as a slave by Samuel L. Hays, whom President Buchanan appointed to run the Sauk Rapids land office. Except for one daughter, her children were left behind on Hays's property in Virginia. General Sylvanus Lowry, the first mayor of St. Cloud, brought his slave William to serve as his butler. Their stories are told in Christopher Lehman, *Slavery in the Upper Mississippi Valley, 1787–1865* (Jefferson, NC: McFarland, 2011).

page 113   Albert Ratliff: The 1880 US census shows the Butler family living next door to William Morin on College Street, but Ratliff is not yet among them. The 1870 census shows Albert Ratliff living as a farm laborer with a white family in Virginia from whom he presumably took his surname. In 1880, he has a wife, Zilk, and is living independently in Gilmer County, West Virginia, where Samuel Hays had owned land and slaves. He continues to be counted as married in subsequent censuses, although his wife is no longer with him.

page 113   Colored man: *FCS*, January 20, 1892.

page 113   Ratliff obituaries: *FCS* and *T-E*, May 3, 1911.

Notes to "Robert Speer Travels through Time"

page 115   Alma mater: Words by Edwin H. Lewis, tune borrowed. The University of Chicago seems to have removed the text of the alma mater from its website since I confirmed the lyrics.

page 116   Woolly mammoth: Both mammoth specimens at the Science Museum of Minnesota came from eastern Freeborn County. The Hollandale Mammoth, a skeleton displayed since 1962, was found in the Rice Lake–Big Marsh area. The Lyle Mammoth is a skull found on the Lyle family farm in Oakland Township in 1996.

page 116   Railroad fares: *MCT*, September 6, 1893; *ALE*, April 13, 1893.

page 116   Belden's report: *MCT*, October 4 and 18, 1893.

page 117   My favorite published source on the Columbian Exposition is Erik Larson, *The Devil in the White City* (New York: Random House, 2003). For a video "tour" of the World's Fair, see http://www.wbez.org/series/curious-city/your-ticket-white-city-108994. The Field Museum in Chicago, built as the repository for the exposition's artifacts, had some of them on display in 2014. Sadly, illness prevented me from making the trip.

Notes to "Eighteen Yoke of Oxen"

page 118   Because I suspected that the number eighteen was an error, I posted
a query on Rural Heritage Front Porch, www.ruralheritage.com/message
board/frontporch/13041.htm, on April 1, 2010. I am grateful for the responses I received. Not only did I learn that hitching together all those
oxen was indeed possible, but I was told how it would work and what
equipment was required. Some respondents proudly sent me photos of
their own oxen. I also found much useful information on the website of the
Prairie Ox Drovers, www.prairieoxdrovers.com. A visit to the Oliver H.
Kelley Farm in Elk River, Minnesota, an MNHS historic site, enhanced my
respect for these mighty working animals.

page 119   Speer oxen: Agricultural Schedule, 1860–70.

page 119   Wilkinson profile: *FCS*, July 4, 1906.

page 120   Large dairy: *ALE*, February 2, 1893.

page 120   Flax machine: *FCS*, August 15, 1894.

page 121   Unemployed: *FCS*, July 18, 1894.

Notes to "The Great Ricelawn Ranch"

page 124   The visitors are not identified by name, but the banker was likely
Thorvald V. Knatvold of the Albert Lea National Bank, a member of
the Minnesota State Senate from 1895 to 1902. See "Legislators Past and
Present" on the website of the Minnesota Legislative Reference Library.
Harwood G. Day, editor of the *Standard*, would no doubt have taken this
excursion himself rather than assign a representative in his place. The professor may have been someone on the faculty of the Albert Lea College for
Women, if not a friend of McMillan's from the University of Minnesota.
The miller could be any of several local men. I can't say whose wives
attended or who the other two ladies were. Mrs. Henrietta Olberg of Albert
Lea, "an authority on the flax and linen industry," spoke at a convention of
the Minnesota Federation of Women's Clubs six years later. An account of
her speech was printed in the *Minneapolis Journal*, October 18, 1901. I'd like
to imagine her visiting Ricelawn Ranch.

page 125   Entirely dry: Turtle Creek had not been drained once and for all.
The bed may have appeared dry for the moment at that site in a dry summer season, or the claim may be hyperbole. Or else "it" may refer to the
adjacent land, the main subject of the paragraph.

page 126 Roads: The excursion and this account of it may have been timed to influence the county board of commissioners in its deliberations. The board did agree to a north–south connecting segment three months later, in October 1895.

page 126 Divide and sell: *FCS* mentioned this plan on at least one other occasion, but I have found no other evidence that McMillan and Hastings intended to do so. Everything points to their (or McMillan's) keeping the farm as a large experimental, industrial operation. Faculty members from the University of Minnesota's School of Agriculture were brought in on that plan early on.

Notes to "A Change of Hands Bodes a Change of Lands"

page 128 Parker: *MCT*, October 13 and November 10, 1897; *FCS*, January 30, 1898, and May 2, 1900.

page 128 McMillan buildings: *Minneapolis Tribune*, January 2, 1898.

page 129 Black barley: *FCS*, August 31, 1898.

page 129 Van Norman sale to Wilkinson: *FCS*, December 25, 1895.

page 129 Barber family: *The Biographical Record of Ogle County, Illinois* (Chicago: S. J. Clarke Publishing Company, 1899), 479–80; US Census, 1880, 1900, 1910.

page 129 Land sales: *MCT*, November 9, 1898; *FCS*, November 9, 1898.

page 131 Large commission: *Minneapolis Tribune*, November 13, 1898.

page 131 MacRae's land: Riceland, section 25, Freeborn County plat map, 1901, FCHM.

page 131 Professor Shaw: *ADH*, June 7, 1899.

Notes to "What's Black and White and Grazes All Over?"

page 132 Epigraph: 1911 FC History, 457–58.

page 132 Cows and people: *FCS*, August 6, 1902; *Population of Counties by Decennial Census*, compiled and edited by Richard L. Forstall, Population Division, US Bureau of the Census, Washington, DC, March 27, 1995, http://www.census.gov/population/www/censusdata/cencounts/files/mn190090.txt.

page 133 Cream separator: Biography of Gustaf de Laval, http://www.tekniskamuseet.se/1/1915.html.

page 133 Co-op origins: 1911 FC History, 454–79; A. W. Trow article in the *St. Paul Farmer*, summarized in *FCS*, December 18, 1907; Steven J. Keillor,

Cooperative Commonwealth: Co-ops in Rural Minnesota, 1859–1939 (St. Paul: Minnesota Historical Society Press, 2000), 112–17.

page 134 Diversified farming: 1911 FC History, 456.

Notes to "The Second Try"

page 135 Text of petition: Auditor's Notice of Pendency of Petition, State of Minnesota–County of Freeborn, *FCS*, October 2, 1901.

page 136 Supreme Court: Lien v. Board of County Commissioners, 80 Minnesota 58, 1900, summarized in *Studies in the Social Sciences* (Minneapolis: University of Minnesota, 1915), 52.

page 136 Chapter 258: *General Laws of Minnesota, 1901*, MNHS.

page 136 McMillan to Van Sant, April 15, 1901, Governor's Records, Van Sant, Correspondence, File No. 644, State Archives, MNHS.

page 137 Morin's purchase: *FCS*, September 25, 1901.

page 137 Editorial response: *FCS*, October 2, 1901.

page 138 Germans from Illinois: *Minneapolis Journal*, October 18, 1901, 17.

page 138 Fanning and Dappert: *FCS*, October 30, November 14, and December 4, 1901.

page 139 Immense drain: John F. D. Meighen to Thomas V. Meighen, November 3, 1901, correspondence, Meighen Family Papers, MNHS.

page 139 Estimates: *ADH*, November 13, 1901; *FCS*, December 4, 1901.

Notes to "New Man About Town: John Felix Dryden Meighen"

page 140 Large collection: John F. D. Meighen and Family Papers, 1852–1960, 40 boxes, MNHS. Meighen's desk, some photos, and other items are at FCHM.

page 142 Brother: John's relationship with Tommy, sometimes more avuncular than brotherly, would be an interesting study in itself. John was precocious and well spoken; Thomas, naive and boyish, even for his age. Sadly, Thomas died in France in October 1918, two weeks after being wounded in battle. Letters and telegrams from the Red Cross and from an army chaplain differ in their details. The collection also includes their mother's pleas for information.

page 143 Morgan away: Meighen to his parents, November 25, 1902.

page 143 Whirlwind trip: Meighen's diary, April 16–18, 1903.

page 146 One vast lake: Meighen to his parents, May 26, 1902.

page 146 Client's interests: Meighen to his parents, January 22, 1902.

Notes to "The People Protest"

page 148 Populist sheet: Meighen to his parents, January 22, 1902.

page 148 Remonstrations and comments: *MCT*, January 22, 1902; *FCS*, January 15 and 22, 1902.

page 148 Technicality: The commissioners serving at this time were A. G. Brundin, E. W. Gleason, O. A. Hammer, J. C. Johnson, and L. P. Wohlhuter.

page 149 Landowners' protest: The *ALE* published the text but not the names of the signatories on February 12, 1902. A report on the letter but not the text appeared in the *AR* on February 14 and on the front page of the *FCS* on February 19.

page 149 Townships: The twelve identified were Albert Lea Township, Alden, Bancroft, Carlston, Freeman, Hartland, Hayward, London, Manchester, Mansfield, Pickerel Lake, and Shell Rock. A communication from citizens in Geneva Township was read at the county board meeting. I have no information about actions taken in Bath, Freeborn, and Nunda.

page 150 The "Hollandale box," which also contains McMillan's handwritten account of the drainage, a photo of him standing in a drained field, and other items, was brought to a predecessor of the Freeborn County Historical Museum by Claude Hormel, the last manager of the McMillan Land Company. The packet of petitions looks like something J. F. D. Meighen would have asked his stenographer to prepare.

page 151 On file: Freeborn County Recorder Kelly Callahan believes the township statements may be among the many uncatalogued boxes in the basement of the 1882 section of the courthouse. Given respiratory problems, I didn't ask to look there. All county board minutes of that era were published in the year's newspaper of record, usually *FCS*. The handwritten original minutes are available in bound volumes in the recorder's office.

page 151 L. O. Greene: Either Greene identified himself as a capitalist or the term was supplied by the census taker, Will Ostrander, Elbert's younger brother.

page 151 Dead against it: P. D. McMillan to W. A. Morin, April 4, 1902, Morin Family Papers.

Notes to "How to Read a Flying Bundle of Twine"

page 152 Epigraph: Sterling Evans, *Bound in Twine* (College Station: Texas A & M University Press, 2007), 126.

page 152 Ostrander case: *FCS*, October 21, 1903; *AA*, October 29, 1903; Meighen diary, February 4 and 5, 1904.

page 153 Grundlach letter: *FCS*, January 7, 1903; *AA*, February 5, 1903.

page 154 Stillwater twine: The prison manufactured several varieties of twine, beginning with industrial hemp from Kentucky, then moving on to Yucatan sisal and Philippine manila. Evans, *Bound in Twine*, 126.

page 154 Twine sales: Article from the *Hutchinson Independent* reprinted in *AA*, April 30, 1903.

page 154 Twine and drainage committees: *AA*, January 15, 1903.

page 154 Injury: Well after I had composed this flight of fancy, I ran across this item in *FCT*, August 14, 1903: "E. H. Ostrander, who was recently injured by the careless handling of freight at the depot in this place, was obliged to go to Albert Lea Tuesday where Drs. Wedge and Burton placed a plaster cast over his right shoulder."

page 155 Parolees and peppermints: Lee Ostrander letter, July 9, 1977.

Notes to "A Lone Voice for the Environment: Fred McCall"

page 156 Morgan at meeting: *AA*, February 13, 1902.

page 156 Bird sanctuary: History of Pelican Island, "Pelican Island National Wildlife Refuge," US Fish and Wildlife Service, http://www.fws.gov/peli canisland/history.html. Five national parks were added during Roosevelt's presidency, and the Grand Canyon was declared a national monument.

page 156 National Audubon Society, www.audubon.org.

page 157 McCall letter: *FCS*, January 15, 1902.

page 158 Taylor statement: *FCS*, January 22, 1902. An earlier warning about "water shrinkage" and drought from Walter C. Brower of the state forestry association was published in *Farm, Stock and Home* in 1896 and summarized in *FCS*, February 5, 1896.

page 158 Arid desert: *FCS*, January 30, 1895.

page 158 McCall poem: *FCS*, November 21, 1901.

Notes to "Counterarguments"

page 160 Ice supply: *AA*, February 20, 1902.

page 160 Survey work and costs: *FCS*, January 22, 1902; *AA*, April 3, 1902; *FCT*, January 30, 1903.

page 160 Dappert and Meighen: Meighen diary, January 19 and 20, 1902.

page 160 Dappert's experience: Letter from Axel Brundin, *FCS*, August 27, 1902; Newton Bateman, et al., *Historical Encyclopedia of Illinois and History of Ogle County* (Chicago: Munsell Publishing Co., 1909), 2:874.

page 161 Educational campaign: Meighen diary, April 3, 1902.

page 161 Dappert's letter: The letter is dated April 7, 1902. *ALE*, April 23, 1902; *AA*, April 24, 1902.

page 162 Mayland's opinion: *FCS*, May 7, 1902.

page 163 Agin' us: Meighen diary, July 24, 1902.

page 163 Frogs go to and fro: *MCT*, April 23, 1902.

page 163 Heavy rain: *FCS*, May 7, 1902.

page 163 Opdahl statement: *AA*, May 22, 1902; *FCS*, May 28, 1902.

page 163 Morgan statement: *FCS*, September 10, 1902.

page 164 Brundin statement: Meighen diary, August 11–13, 1902; *FCS*, August 27, 1902.

page 164 Supreme Court: "State Ex Rel. Utick et al. v. Board of Com'rs of Polk County," *The Northwestern Reporter* 92, 216–21; summarized in *FCS*, November 12, 1902.

page 165 Fountain Lake: *FCS*, December 17, 1902.

Notes to "The Moscow Farm Prospers"

page 166 Frisbie carries Speer's body: Funeral card for Robert G. Speer, my files.

page 167 Speer estate: Freeborn County Probate Court, Final Decrees of Distribution, MNHS.

page 168 Register farm data: *FCS*, June 29, 1892, and February 7, 1894; *MCT*, January 24, 1900; March 27, May 15, and October 23, 1901; August 26, 1903.

page 168 Finest in vicinity: *ADH*, April 8, 1902.

page 168 Move into house: *ADH*, February 3, 1904; *MCT*, February 10, 1904.

page 168 Silver wedding: *MCT*, June 1, 1904.

page 169 Property tax: *FCS*, January 15, 1902, and January 27, 1909.

page 169 The Albert Lea College for Women, founded as a Presbyterian sister school to Macalester College in St. Paul, flourished from 1884 to 1916. Some records are at FCHM.

page 169 Mayo surgery: *MCT*, November 28, 1906; January 16 and 23, 1907; *ADH*, December 12, 1906.

page 169 Dog incident: *FCS*, February 25, 1903; *FCT*, February 27, 1903.

page 169 Emancipation notice: *FCS*, August 18, 1903.

page 169 Bert in Kansas City: *ADH*, May 19, 1908.

page 170 I remember Bert Register as a boyish old man living with his thrice-widowed sister Hattie on a farm near Austin. He enjoyed showing us around and taking us to a natural spring in the pasture when we visited. I am sorry that I don't remember his death, which occurred at Rochester State Hospital one month before I graduated from high school.

Notes to "Meighen in Court and Courting"

page 171 Viewers are agin' us: Meighen diary, February 26, 1903.

page 171 Majority report: *FCT*, March 6, 1903; *FCS*, March 11, 1903.

page 171 Minority report: *FCT*, March 27, 1903; *FCS*, April 1, 1903.

page 172 Barber letter: Mary J. Barber and Bryant H. Barber to Board of County Commissioners of Freeborn County Minnesota, March 28, 1903, Hollandale box, FCHM.

page 172 Official report of county board meeting: *FCT*, April 10, 1903; handwritten minutes, Freeborn County Recorder's Office.

page 173 Tired from dancing: Meighen diary, April 24–26, 1903.

page 173 Petitioners' appeals: *FCS*, April 29, 1903.

page 173 Ghosts: *FCT*, May 1, 1903; Meighen diary, May 4, 1903.

page 173 Rainy weather: *FCS*, May 13 and 20, 1903.

page 174 Engagement: *FCS*, September 16, 1903; Meighen diary, September 2, 1903.

page 174 Fragrant as a summer garden: From a song in *Dolly Varden*, a 1901 comic opera by Julian Edwards and Stanislaus Stangé that toured the country in succeeding years.

page 174 Barber's bill: Meighen diary, January 13 and 23, 1904.

page 174 Financial agreement with Morgan: Meighen diary, November 24, 1903.

page 175 Letter about Sybil: Meighen to his parents, February 14, 1904.

page 175 Dissolved a contract: Meighen diary, March 29, 1904.

page 176 Socialist meetings: *MCT*, March 16, April 20, and November 4, 1904.

page 176 Conjecture about US Supreme Court: *Minneapolis Journal*, June 23, 1904.

page 176 Friends will talk: Meighen diary, July 21, 1904.

page 176 Minnesota Supreme Court ruling: *FCS*, July 20, 1904.

page 176 Hate the delay: McMillan to Morin, July 19, 1904, Morin Family Papers.

page 177 McMillan's new forces: *FCS*, January 18, 1905.

page 177 Marie Southwick: Meighen diary, June 8, 1905, and passim.

page 177 Money going out: Meighen diary, February 3, 1905.

page 177 Anna Svanberg: *FCS*, November 14, 1906.

Notes to "The Winning Strategy"

page 178 Ostrander consumes time: Meighen diary, February 1 and April 8, 1905.

page 178 Lightning: *AA*, September 29, 1904.

page 178 Activities on marsh: Ads for trapping rights in *FCS*, October 17, 1906, and on; hunting lodge in *ADH*, October 13, 1906; picnic in *MCT*, August 16, 1905.

page 179 Public utility and muskrats: McMillan to Morin, February 3, 1905, Morin Family Papers.

page 179 Smaller ditch: Meighen diary, January 25 and April 29, 1905.

page 179 Standing in way of progress: McMillan, "History of Drainage of Riceland Marsh."

page 180 Chapter 230 drainage law: *Minnesota Senate Journal 1905*, scattered references from February 17 (221) to April 18 (1211), MNHS.

page 180 Refusal to pay: *FCS*, March 7, 1906; correspondence between Morin and B. H. Barber, April and May 1906. McMillan and Morin finally settled with the county board for $2,662.23, with Meighen and County Attorney Norman Peterson negotiating. Meighen diary, April 25, 1907; *FCS*, May 1, 1907.

page 180 Content of new law: Chapter 230, 1905 statutes, website of the Minnesota Revisor of Statutes, https://www.revisor.mn.gov.

page 181 Signatories: Census data, Ancestry.com; Freeborn County plat maps, 1901 and 1913, FCHM.

page 181 Meighen identified Lewis Brown as a druggist in his diary; the US Census identifies him as a dentist. The Freeborn County Directory of 1906 lists both Browns in the business section as real estate agents.

page 182 Dappert wandering: Meighen diary, December 30, 1907.

page 183 Excites the people: *FCS*, January 31, 1906.

page 184 Full and final drainage plan: James W. Dappert, "Report of Engineer in Judicial Ditch Proceedings, Counties of Freeborn and Mower, State of Minnesota," August 11, 1906, on file at the engineering firm of Jones, Haugh & Smith, Albert Lea, MN.

page 184 Formal objections: File #6310, Judicial Ditch No. 1, Freeborn County Auditor's Office.

page 185 Two navigable lakes: One was, of course, Rice Lake. It is not clear whether mention of a second refers to Mud Lake, a much smaller lake in Geneva Township, or to fears that Geneva Lake would be inadvertently drained.

page 185 Scene in court: *ET*, January 23, 1907; John Register's presence: *MCT*, January 30, 1907.

page 186 Cedar's water supply: *T-E*, February 20, 1907.

page 186 Registers' withdrawal: *ET*, February 18, 1907; Minnesota Death Certificate 1907–57–962, MNHS; *T-E*, February 27, 1907.

page 186 *Tribune's* summary: *ET*, February 18, 1907.

page 187 Construction bids and notoriety: *FCS*, November 20, 1907; Meighen diary, November 23, 1907; Meighen to his parents, February 27, 1908.

page 187 McMillan's office: *Minneapolis Tribune*, October 27, 1907.

page 187 Purchase of Sharp land: Meighen diary, Meighen to his parents, May 6, 1907.

page 187 Proficient hands: Diary of Arra C. Jeffries, filed with Meighen's diaries, Meighen Family Papers.

page 187 Barber and Trumbauer in England: Passenger lists, Ancestry.com.

Notes to "Rice Lake and the Big Marsh Go Down the Drain"

page 189 Assembling dredges: *MCT*, September 25, 1907; *FCS*, August 28, 1907.

page 190 *Swamp Angel: FCS*, October 23, 1907.

page 190 Goodnature's delivery: *FCS*, October 30, 1907.

page 190 The launching: The report didn't appear in *FCS* until October 23. This explanation appeared on October 16: "Greatly to our regret, our reporter's extended and interesting report of the launching of the big dredge boat on the Moscow-Riceland ditch, and facts and incidents of the important event, has to be deferred. The Standard is rarely compelled to be delinquent in this way, but unexpected difficulties of other work render it unavoidable. However, the delay will be more than made good in the far better report we will give them next week."

page 191 Longfellow's poem reads:

She starts,—she moves,—she seems to feel

The thrill of life along her keel,

And, spurning with her foot the ground,

With one exulting, joyous bound,

She leaps into the ocean's arms!

page 191 *Herald*'s coverage of launching: *ADH*, October 9, 1907.

page 192 Ditch's dimensions and pace: *FCS*, January 29, 1908.

page 192 How the dredge worked: *ADH*, November 14, 1908.

page 193 Living arrangements: *ADH*, October 9, 1907.

page 193 Cogdal's resignation: *FCS*, April 28, 1909.

page 193 Mechanical breakdowns: *FCS*, May 12 and 19, June 2, and August 18, 1909; *ADH*, May 11 and 27, 1909.

page 193 Baseball team: *FCS*, May 5, 1909.

page 193 Local labor: *FCS*, December 16, 1908; *ADH*, August 10 and November 6, 1909.

page 193 Cogswell: *ADH*, August 19, 1908. *ADH* routinely called him Cogswell. His name was, in fact, Cogdal; the Freeborn County folks weren't just hearing it as Norwegian. Name confirmed by US Census, 1910 and 1940, Texas Death Index, and US World War I Draft Registration Card, Ancestry.com.

page 194 Visits to dredge: *ADH*, July 13, 1909; *FCS*, July 21, 1909.

page 194 Game birds: *FCS*, March 10, April 28, September 1 and 22, 1909. Louis Kroessin, who bought pelts from trappers, sold fifty pairs of pheasants to the Game Protective Association out of an even larger supply.

page 194 Anderson's prediction: *ADH*, November 6, 1909.

page 194 Meighen's land: Riceland Township plat map, *Farmers' Atlas of Freeborn County*, 1913; J. F. D. Meighen to Thomas V. Meighen, September 22, 1910.

Notes to "The *Swamp Angel* Plays Cupid"

page 197 Visit to Alden: *ADH*, May 19, 1909.

page 197 Friendship with Lida: *MCT*, October 14, 1908; *ADH*, November 3 and December 1, 1908.

page 198 Courtship: *MCT*, December 16, 1908; *ADH*, February 16 and March 17, 1909.

page 198 Wedding announcement: *MCT*, September 1, 1909; *AA*, September 9, 1909.

page 200 Farm prices: Blackwell's *Dictionary of American History* online reports, "Farm income dropped from 15 percent of national output in 1920 to 9 percent in 1928; 454,866 owner-managed farms disappeared in the 1920s, and the farm population decreased by 3,000,000." http://www.black wellreference.com/public/tocnode?id=g9781577180999_chunk_g978157 718099920_ss1–26.

page 200 Loss of farm: Leslie sold the indebted farm to Edward and Oscar Olson in 1922 but lived there a few more months. John bought it back in 1929 when it went through foreclosure and was listed at a sheriff's sale. He offered it in 1932 to his son Roy, who had become the Moscow Creamery's buttermaker, creating a rift in the family that mostly remained unspoken. Roy's widow, Isabel, sold it to the Greibrok family in 1948, seven years short of a century after the Speers' preemption claim. I am grateful to Roger and Jackie Jacobson, inhabitants of the house and fourteen acres, for letting me visit and look at the title papers. The Jacobsons moved in after losing their family homestead near Clarks Grove in the 1980s recession. The rest of the Speer/Register land is now owned by a trust in the Twin Cities. Property map accessible via the website of the Freeborn County recorder.

Notes to "The New Model Farmer"

page 202 Change of business: Marion Daniel Shutter, *History of Minneapolis: Gateway to the Northwest* (Chicago: S. J. Clarke Publishing Company, 1923), 175; *Poor's Manual of Industrials: Manufacturing, Mining and Miscellaneous Companies* (New York: 1913), 256.

page 202 Railroad spur: *Fortieth Biennial Report of the Railroad and Warehouse Commission of the State of Minnesota* (1927), 128, MNHS.

page 202 Tiling test: *MCT*, November 2, 1910.

page 203 Bungalow: *ADH*, March 29 and April 5, 1910; *MCT*, August 24, 1910.

page 203 Dana's hiring: Press release on the occasion of Putnam D. McMillan's golden anniversary at General Mills, Inc., October 22, 1953, General Mills Archives.

page 203 Work under way at ranch: *MCT*, May 10 and 17, 1911; *FCS*, May 17, 1911.

page 203 Gushing article: *FCS*, July 19, 1911; reprinted in *MCT*, August 2, 1911.

page 204 Still no road: *FCS*, September 6, 1911; reprinted in *ADH*, September 7, 1911.

page 205 Thank-you note: McMillan to Meighen, January 3, 1914, Meighen Family Papers.

page 205 McMillan's death: Minnesota Death Certificate 1918–023458, MNHS; *Minneapolis Journal*, April 8, 1918; *FCS*, April 8, 1918; *ET*, April 8, 1918; *ADH*, April 8, 1918.

page 206 Dana at General Mills: Harry A. Bullis to P. D. McMillan, October 14, 1953; *Eventually News*, October 5, 1921; press release on golden anniversary; other biographical documents, General Mills Archives.

page 206 Agricultural policy: Putnam D. McMillan, "Helping the American Wheat Farmer or Who Killed Cock Robin?" pamphlet, originally published in the *Minneapolis Journal*, November 31, 1931; "Marginal Land and Marginal Thinking," review of a Putnam Dana McMillan article in the *Saturday Evening Post*, *Minneapolis Journal*, June 1, 1935, General Mills Archives.

page 206 Profitable ranch: This quotation and the information in the following paragraph, P. D. McMillan to C. W. Plattes, December 15, 1949, General Mills Archives.

page 206 Dana's death: "Putnam D. McMillan, Milling Pioneer, Dies," *Minneapolis Tribune*, April 8, 1961, General Mills Archives.

Notes to "The Victor's History"

page 210 Fisk case: "Former County Official Dies," *FCS*, October 22, 1917; Rochester State Hospital Patient Records, File No. 216, MNHS; "Frank Fisk Insane," *FCS*, October 20, 1915. I have not been able to locate the county probate court's insanity files for 1915. They were allegedly sent from the county courthouse to MNHS some time ago, but they do not appear on any lists of MNHS holdings.

page 211 Moral code: I learned one of my earliest and most indelible moral lessons, my work ethic, from Grace Ostrander Register. On Sunday afternoons at her house, I could best avoid my boisterous male cousins by holing up in a corner with a book. The Little Golden Book edition of *The Little Red Hen* always lay out where I would find it.

page 212 Yankees and Yorkers: June D. Holmquist, ed., *They Chose Minnesota* (St. Paul: Minnesota Historical Society Press, 1981), 61, shows Freeborn

County with three times as many Yorkers and Midland migrants as Yankees by 1880, when the first generation of white settlement was complete.

page 212 Flowing downhill: Conversation with Steve Penkava, drainage engineer, Jones, Haugh & Smith Inc., Albert Lea, MN, July 18, 2014.

Notes to "The Mysterious Fall of Bryant Barber and Other Endings"

page 213 Barber houses: Henry's is NRHP #74000770, added March 28, 1974; Bryant's is NHRP # 92001849, February 10, 1993.

page 213 Barber bio data: *Tri-County Press*, November 22, 1917, Polo Historical Society.

page 213 Barber's death: Rev. John Heckman, et al., *Voice of the Prairie: A Brief History of Polo, Illinois* (1957), excerpt posted on a Polo High School history website, no longer available. The site, found on a Google search for Bryant H. Barber, was where I first learned how he had died.

page 214 News account: *Tri-County Press*, November 22, 1917, Polo Historical Society.

page 214 Insolvency and suit: *Tri-County Press*, November 29, 1917, Polo Historical Society.

page 215 Waning commitment: Milton Trumbauer to W. A. Morin, April 12, 1906; Barber to Morin, April 21; Morin to Barber, April 23; Barber to Morin, May 7, Morin Family Papers.

page 215 Condition of drained land: Merlin H. Dappert, "Minnesota Swamp Land Reclaimed for Farm Use," *Engineering News-Record* 87.14 (October 6, 1921): 552–54.

page 216 Morin obituary: *FCS*, May 22, 1912; *T-E*, May 22 and 29, 1912. The mayor asked all places of business in the city to close for Morin's funeral from 1:30 to 3:00 on May 23.

page 216 Prest for money: Meighen diary, November 5, 1909.

page 216 Psychic moment: Meighen diary, July 30, 1915.

page 216 Too friendly with a widow: Meighen diary, September 11, 1915.

page 216 Mother is more sane: Meighen diary, May 14, 1916.

page 217 A day of datum planes: J. F. D. Meighen to Katherine Morin, July 1, 1916.

page 219 Hollandale ditch contention: Minnesota Conservation Department, Waters Division, Files on County Ditches, Judicial Ditch 24 (old #1), MNHS.

page 219 J. F. D. Meighen obituary: *ET*, April 18, 1957.

page 219 Sybil Koontz obituary: *ET*, September 3, 1974.

page 219 Katherine Meighen obituary: *ET*, November 25, 1968.

page 219 "Passing of Bear Lake," *Community Magazine* 13.1 (January 1931): 6, 7.

page 220 Farm always indebted: Lee Ostrander letter.

page 221 Last poem: Elbert H. Ostrander, "The Marching Men," published with his obituary, *AA*, April 22, 1937; obituary, *Freeborn Patriot*, April 23, 1937.

Notes to "From Booty to Beauty"

page 225 Splendidly turgid: Anthony M. Clark, "The Putnam Dana McMillan Collection," *The Minneapolis Institute of Arts Bulletin* 50.4 (December 1961): 8, Minneapolis Institute of Art Library.

page 226 Profile of Dana McMillan: Carl J. Weinhardt, Jr., "Introduction," in Clark, "The Putnam Dana McMillan Collection."

page 226 McMillan and Davis: Jeffrey A. Hess, *Their Splendid Legacy: The First 100 Years of the Minneapolis Society of Fine Arts* (Minneapolis: The Society, 1985), 59–60, MIA Library.

page 226 It is hard to give: Clark, "The Putnam Dana McMillan Collection," 6.

page 227 Picasso: Clark, "The Putnam Dana McMillan Collection," 6.

page 227 Monet quotation: Gallery label at MIA, online at www.artsconnec ted.org/resource/671/the-japanese-bridge.

page 227 Works bequeathed: The artists represented are Beckmann, Bonnard, Braque, Chagall, Degas, Derain, Ensor, Feininger, Fromentin, Kirchner, Kokoschka (the MIA later bought Oskar Kokoschka's *Portrait of Putnam D. McMillan*), Léger, Luce, Matisse, Modigliani, Monet, Morandi, Picasso, Signac, Toulouse-Lautrec, Vlaminck, and Vuillard. Catalogue, "The Putnam Dana McMillan Collection," 56.

page 227 McMillan's will: "Institutions to Share McMillan Estate," *Minneapolis Star*, April 19, 1961; "Former Milling Official Willed Stock to 3 Men," *Minneapolis Tribune*, April 20, 1961, General Mills Archives.

page 227 Emily as director: Hess, *Their Splendid Legacy*, 59.

page 227 Emily's excitement: Weinhardt, "Introduction."

page 228 Margaret's donations to MIA: search at https://collections.artsmia .org/index.php?page=search#query=%22Margaret+McMillan+Webber %22.

page 228 Persian art collection: Given in memory of her mother, Katherine Kittredge McMillan, it comprises thirty-three paintings, ten examples of illumination and calligraphy, and three drawings. "The Margaret McMillan Webber Bequest of Persian Paintings," *Bulletin of the Minneapolis Institute of Arts* 40.27 (November 3, 1951): 134, MIA Library. The article describes the art but says little about Margaret or the story of her gift.

Notes to "Wo Wacintanka"

page 230 Bachelor farmer: Alvin Nordean Christianson, birth and census records show, was born in 1911 to Henry J. and Nettie C. Christianson, both children of Norwegian immigrant parents. He died in 1994. The spinster sister was Nina, five years older than Alvin. She died two years after the sale of the farm.

page 231 Reinvest in Minnesota program of the Minnesota Board of Water and Soil Resources, http://www.bwsr.state.mn.us/easements/index.html.

page 231 Other government programs: Freeborn County Soil and Water Conservation District, http://www.freebornswcd.org/programs.htm.

page 231 How to restore a wetland: Conversation with Steve Penkava. See also US Department of Agriculture Conservation Easement Program, http://www.nrcs.usda.gov/wps/portal/nrcs/detail/national/programs/easements/acep/?cid=stelprdb1242695.

page 232 Bill Bryson's efforts: William H. Bryson, "The Battle of Bryson Marsh," *Minnesota Conservation Volunteer* (July–August 1979): 17 23; Mark Herwig, "A Maverick for Wetlands," *Minnesota Conservation Volunteer* (March–April 2010): 32–39; "County of Freeborn by Tuveson v. Bryson, 243 N.W.2d 316 (1976)," in *Justia US Law*, http://law.justia.com/cases/minnesota/supreme-court/1976/45601-2-0.html.

Note to "For the Birds"

page 236 True home in Minnesota: Elbert H. Ostrander, "The Flight," *Community Magazine* 13.12 (December 1931): 6. Also published in *Fins, Feathers and Fur*, undated photocopy in my files.

Image Credits

Unless noted below, all images are courtesy of the author.

pages 8, 38–39, 50
Cartographic print production by Matt Kania/Map Hero

pages 10, 38–39, 50, 100, 104, 141, 144
Minnesota Historical Society collections

page 22
Photo by Gayla Marty

page 61
Bidney Bergie Collection, box 9, Freeborn County Historical Museum

pages 110, 204
Freeborn County Historical Museum

page 130
Polo, Illinois, Historical Society

Big Marsh is set in the Arno typeface family.

Book design and typesetting by BNTypographics West Ltd., Victoria, B.C. Canada

Printed by Versa Press, East Peoria, Illinois